MEMORIES OF
MARGARET

Also by Don Bailey

MEMORIES OF
MARGARET

My friendship with Margaret Laurence

by Don Bailey

Prentice-Hall Canada, Inc., Scarborough, Ontario

Canadian Cataloguing in Publication Data

Bailey, Don
    Memories of Margaret

ISBN 0-13-574393-1

1. Bailey, Don.   2. Laurence, Margaret, 1926–1987 —
Friends and associates.   3. Authors, Canadian
(English) — 20th century — Biography.*
I. Title.

PS8553.A54Z53 1989   C813'.54   C89-093794-X
PR9199.3.B344Z53 1989

Prentice-Hall Inc., Englewood Cliffs, New Jersey
Prentice-Hall International, Inc., London
Prentice-Hall of Australia, Pty., Sydney
Prentice-Hall of India Pvt., Ltd., New Delhi
Prentice-Hall of Japan, Inc., Tokyo
Prentice-Hall of Southeast Asia (Pte.) Ltd., Singapore
Editora Prentice-Hall do Brasil Ltda., Rio de Janeiro
Prentice-Hall Hispanoamericana, S.A., Mexico

ISBN 0-13-574393-1

Excerpts from *A Jest of God* by Margaret Laurence, copyright 1966, 1974 by Margaret Laurence, reprinted by permission of the Canadian Publishers, McClelland
and Stewart, Toronto, and the Margaret Laurence estate.

Interior Design: Monica Kompter
Cover Design: Kinetics Design & Illustration
Cover Photography: Zinger Photographics Inc.
Manufacturing Buyer: Luca Di Nicola
Composition: Lithocomp Ltd.

1 2 3 4 5 G 93 92 91 90 89

Printed and bound in Canada by Gagné Printing Ltd.

Dedication

This book is for ordinary people, the "nobodies" whom Margaret
Laurence celebrated in her work and loved in her life.

Contents

Author's Note

The pages that follow are based on my memory of Margaret. Margaret said to me many times: "We remember the way we want to.... What we want to.... We make a choice about how we will remember."

I agree. While working as a parish minister I encountered many men who lived on skid row. They approached me for money and were prepared to trade their tragic tales for cash. Their way of remembering was slanted toward despair. They were skilled at recounting the sad, depressing memories that had become their livelihood. They rarely mentioned a happy memory. Their lives were joyless.

I have met other people who choose to ignore any memory that is even vaguely negative. They skip over those memories that could cause them pain. They demand of themselves to remember only pleasant things. Unfortunately, pain and joy are often found in the same memory. When the memories that contain pain are blocked out, the joy is also lost. This kind of editing diminishes a person.

I have tried to remember and recreate the Margaret I knew in a truthful way. The truth, of course, is subjective. It is also, as Margaret said many times, risky. The Margaret who speaks and acts in these pages is the Margaret I experienced. I loved her. I respected her. We engaged in each other's lives and I have struggled to recount those moments as accurately as I could. My goal in committing these memories to the page is an attempt to give some small sense of who Margaret Laurence, the human being, was. To me at least.

Prologue

In the months since I committed myself to writing a book about Margaret Laurence I've found myself afflicted with great reluctance to proceed. So powerful has the resistance been that I've actually ventured out on to the roads of Winnipeg behind the wheel of a car.

Margaret hated cars. She never owned one. She never learned to drive. As a passenger she refused to sit in the front seat. She could, and did, give clear instructions from the back seat. No one ever drove slowly enough for Margaret. Cab drivers who didn't heed her advice found themselves glared at in their rear view mirrors. If that didn't work, she'd lean her elbows against the back of their seats in a tense, vaguely threatening fashion, as though she might vault into the front seat and do serious harm to their cassette players. Margaret would not tolerate music or news reports to distract the driver from her commands.

Over a drink or two one night I asked Margaret her view on sex in a car. She didn't hesitate.

"I'm for it," she said. "It's about the safest thing you can do in a car. At least you're parked."

I guess she influenced me. I don't own a car anymore. I'm still capable of making it to the 7-Eleven on foot. If driving is absolutely called for I borrow my wife's car. I insist on driving. My need to be in control is even stronger than Margaret's.

Back in May, my oldest daughter visited me, with her two daughters. I figured a couple of hours at the zoo was in order. Kids love animals, don't they? I don't have a lot of contact with my grandchildren or my oldest daughter. I wanted to find an activity that would make us all happy and divert us from the issue of how strange we seemed to each other. Nothing like a polar bear to distract you.

I've got to digress here to explain that I'm in my

fourth term of matrimony. I have participated in the procreation of children in all these unions except the present one. I have no excuses for my various failures in relationships except to say I have been unintentionally careless. The result is that I live with a passionate need to compensate those I feel I've short-changed in the love department. Margaret understood this better than anyone I've ever known. In fact I believe it may have been the foundation of our friendship. Guilt bonded us.

Anyway, there I was, driving cautiously along Grant Avenue, heading for the zoo. Sitting beside me was Estelle, the grownup woman who somehow managed to survive the wreckage of my second marriage. In the back seat, smearing sticky substances all over the upholstery of my wife's new car, were my two lovely granddaughters, Rachel and Megan.

I'm more than a bit uneasy with Megan, who is six, because she asks me awkward questions. And she has the eye. You know, that piercing, laser device that goes right to the control room of your bullshit centre. Margaret had the eye, too. Always demanding the truth. God, I hate that look. My kindergarten teacher had it. A social worker who tried to reform me when I was nine had it. Margaret. And now a granddaughter.

Megan wanted to know why we call our dog Megan. I avoided the question and explained that when this really good friend, Margaret Laurence, got sick and died, my wife wanted to do something to overcome how badly we all felt. So she went out and bought a dog.

"Who named her?" my granddaughter asked.

"Me," I confessed.

Rachel, her eight-year-old sister, laughed loudly and pounded the seat with plump fists. Her reaction was out of proportion. She was deriving far too much delight from this minor coincidence of names.

"I wish you hadn't given her my name," Megan said.

Her sister was hysterical. Her mother glared at her in the rear view mirror. It had no effect.

"Megan's a lovely name," I said. "She was such a lovely pup. The name just came to me."

Megan took a deep breath. I cringed in anticipation as I felt the heat of a cosmic truth hurtling toward my soul.

"The trouble is," my granddaughter said, "she's stupid."

This was an inarguable point. Megan the dog has been run over by cars twice, side-swiped by trucks, bicycles and postmen, right in front of our house. She has been pinned together so many times that when she dies I plan to sell her as scrap metal.

So I said nothing, an acidic stew of guilt simmering in my stomach.

I reached the intersection of Roblin and Grant. The light was red, so I stopped. When it turned green I waited. I've lived in Winnipeg long enough to know that some drivers are profoundly affected by the weather. In the winter they navigate their cars through a sheen of snow blindness. In the summer they hallucinate with sunstroke. Better safe than sorry. I'll wait.

But traffic was moving forward. The guy behind me honked. I accelerated and then out of the corner of my eye I saw a shiny, wine-coloured van racing into the intersection from the south. I was heading west. The driver of the van was oblivious to the traffic signals. He manoeuvred around the oncoming traffic with the determined skill of a kamikaze pilot. At least three collisions should have taken place but he managed to avoid them. But then he cranked the wheel around to miss another car and headed straight at me. I braked. He swerved. The side of his van smashed into the driver's side of my car. He was going so fast that he bounced off us and carried away our bumper.

Everyone in the car was screaming, except me. Being the mature adult on the scene I confined my comments to a whimper. My foot hurt as I hobbled out of the car. My daughter and grandchildren seemed okay. Just frightened. Then I approached the other driver. He was furious. But we exchanged driver's license numbers and got the names of various witnesses, some of whom were rocking the man's van. I got out of there as quickly as I could.

The car still ran and I made it to the zoo with no further mishaps. I speculated about whether or not heaven has bars, or at least liquor commissions, because I could hear Margaret rattling the ice in her glass of scotch and laughing, her laughter hanging above me, like thunder in the clouds.

The day after the accident I found walking difficult. My whole right side seemed out of whack. My shoulder had a sharp pain that even a good shot of rye didn't cure. My neck throbbed as if I had slept standing on my head. So I stayed in bed, watched game shows on television and dosed myself with large helpings of medicinal spirits. The next day my condition was worse. I tried to ignore it, thinking perhaps the pain was the result of a substantial intake of whisky. But the pain was persistent. By the end of the day I made the unpleasant decision that medical attention was unavoidable. I called a doctor and made an appointment for the next day.

Margaret said there were two kinds of doctors, the real kind that poked and prodded with efficient competence, and the school of AMWAY medical graduates. Real doctors are dangerous because they often locate ailments that call upon you to give up things like cigarettes, whisky and fatty foods. They encourage you to exercise and take responsible care of yourself. The AMWAY types recognize your need to be reassured that whatever is bothering you will pass quickly. They are usually blatantly cheerful and it's difficult to be genuinely sick in their presence. They won't stand for it. But if you insist on remaining morose they'll give you a prescription for valium.

For some reason I know a lot of doctors. Most of them are painfully real. So I avoided them and went to a local fellow with my aches and pains. Within moments he announced I was having muscle spasms. He then gave me a prescription for pain killers that succeeded in blocking all conscious thought and feeling for a week.

But I wasn't cured. I decided a change of scene was what we all needed. So I hauled my computer to a rustic fishing camp near Kenora. The summer was unfolding bright and warm. My wife Daile and my son Daniel took long walks and swam while I stared at the blank screen of my MAC and popped codeine pills as if they were jelly beans.

I tried to locate a path that would lead me to Margaret, but she eluded me. I realised I had felt no grief when she died. Was I now being punished by the Old Testament God she so abhorred? Must I atone in some way, rend my garments, pile ashes on my head? I thought the car accident was bad enough.

So I moped. One day, Daniel, who is twelve, couldn't stand it any more. He insisted I take him fishing.

I rented a boat and we journeyed north on the majestic Winnipeg river, keeping our eyes open for rocks that lay just below the surface, and pointing at the flocks of pelicans that bobbed on the waves. The sight of grey herons gliding through a grove of dead trees made me nostalgic for my cabin on the Otonabee river back in Peterborough, Daniel's birthplace. He had been baptised in the Otonabee, while Margaret laughed with satisfied glee as the minister dunked him in the fast flowing waters, Margaret with her shoes off standing in the river, her face solemn as she vows to be the child's godmother.

We arrived at a reed bed that Daniel has named Manhattan. I don't know why, he just likes to give names to places. We've caught a lot of northerns here in the past and we like to think of it as our secret spot.

We cast for a while but the fish weren't biting. I put my rod down and opened a can of beer, lit a cigarette and watched the kid. His eyes squinted against the bright sun, his expression determined. He's a good fisherman, flicking his line out in a smooth motion and reeling back in slowly. He has great patience for someone his age. As I watched him I felt a tingle of gratitude for his presence in my life. I guess I smiled because he grinned back at me, put down his rod and opened a Coke.

"Having trouble with the Margaret book, eh?"

I nodded.

"How come you want to write about her?" he asked.

I hate that kind of direct question so I stalled by lighting another smoke. I looked toward shore and saw an astonishing sight. Circling over the forest was a huge bird, one I had only seen in photographs. I pointed and his eyes followed the arc of my finger.

"An eagle!"

I was so excited I stood up, but my ankle crumpled and I almost fell out of the boat. Daniel thrust out his hand and steadied me. We started to laugh. It was a wonderful sound, a joyous feeling.

"That was something," I finally said. "An eagle. I thought they were almost extinct. I never thought I'd see one around here."

He sat, waiting.

"Margaret was fascinated with birds. She had this little gadget somebody gave her. It was made of two pieces of clay that you rubbed together and it gave off a sort of twittering sound."

He nodded his head, waiting for the punchline.

"I guess you were too young to remember. She'd sit under the big spruce on her front lawn and twiddle with this thing for hours. The chirping it made drove the starlings nuts. They'd leave their nests under the eave of her cabin and gather in small flocks out over the water and then every so often swoop back toward the house as if they were going to attack her. And she'd laugh like crazy."

"I don't remember her laughing much," Daniel said.

"What do you remember?"

His expression turned inward as though he could see the past. He smiled.

"She was my mother's best friend," he said. "I remember them sitting on the dock. Talking all the time. And the fence. You told me about that. About how when I started walking Margaret came over and said you had to put a fence around both your places so I wouldn't fall in the river. She offered to pay for it. But when I was...how old was I?"

"Two."

"Yeah." He grinned proudly at the memory. "I climbed it one morning when you were making breakfast and fell off Margaret's dock."

"But by then you could dog-paddle."

"You were mad, though."

"It was a good thing Margaret wasn't around. She would have bitten my head off."

"Why?" he asked.

"She loved you. And Margaret loved like a bear. Protective. Ready to fight off anything that might hurt you."

He thought about that for a moment. Then he shook his head in the affirmative.

"She was like that with my mother, wasn't she?"

"Yes."

"That bird call thing sounds neat," he said. "Did she ever let me use it?"

"Lots of times," I said. "One day it attracted a cardinal."

"The red bird that looks like a jay!" he said excitedly. "I remember that!"

"You were pretty proud of yourself."

"Why don't I remember more?"

"You will."

He shook his head: no. Then he looked away from me, far out over the water.

"Sometimes I think of mommy. I think of something nice, like being in the tube floating down the river together. I even see Margaret sometimes on the shore waving, smiling at us. One time she started dancing around like a cheerleader.... And then they're dead. Both dead."

He picked up his rod and cast toward the reeds. His line snagged and he jerked it loose with much more force than was needed.

The next day we packed up and left. My computer disc was still empty. Back in the city I went to a real doctor. X-rays revealed that my ankle was broken and the ligament has been torn from the muscle. My shoulder had a hair line crack that unfortunately had now healed. It will ache until my heart stops. Internal pictures of my neck showed two crushed vertebrae. No wonder I was feeling lousy.

I was sent off to an orthopedic surgeon who decided to operate right away. While I was on the table another doctor noticed a mole on my back that looked funny. After a couple of weeks in bed recovering from the ankle surgery I went to a dermatologist who declared that I have skin cancer. More surgery. The mole was cut out. My ankle incision infected. Back to bed. God, this is boring, but distracting. I haven't been at my computer for weeks.

The surgeon who cut out my mole called me in and told me he removed a malignant melanoma and that traces of the tumour are evident in the edges of the incision. More surgery is necessary. A week after the second surgery he removed the stitches and told me the margins were clear. By then I had an inkling that my body may be trying to communicate something. What I wasn't sure. So I asked the cutter if I was cured. He's a serious guy and told me this kind of cancer travels around, sort of like a gypsy looking for the perfect campsite. But I'm not to worry, when it shows up again he'll just cut it out!

That night I allowed myself to entertain a little terror. I knew all this medical stuff had been stressful for Daile so I reached over to her side of the bed with the intention of cuddling. I thought the gesture would comfort us both but as I moved my arm I felt a tearing sensation in my back at the incision site. Within seconds the sheets were soaked with blood. Daile moved like a bullet. She tore off the bloody dressing and slapped on a pressure bandage. She wanted me to go to the hospital but I was too busy laughing. It's Friday night. The emergency rooms would be a zoo and I teach a class in the morning. I have to be there. This four-hour class is the only real work I've done for months.

With spare dressings in my pocket I made it to the college the next day. I was fine until the third hour, when I started dripping. Two students volunteer first aid. They're thrilled. This is a creative writing course but wow, how often do you get an instructor who brings live drama into the classroom, complete with blood.

The wound infected and spread to my ankle. Antibiotics exclude the use of home spirits. Another bad mole was found on my back. This could become depressing.

A federal election was called and I decided I've had enough of sickness. I left my bed to attend Wonderful Wednesday, a gathering of local card-carrying Liberals. When I first met Margaret she told me I had to learn to be more political. She said you never knew when a politician in the pocket might come in handy. I have memberships in all three parties but in my fence-sitting position I lean toward the Liberals because the membership consists of people who live at their credit limit. Just like me.

I don't like social gatherings of more than five people. That was another thing Margaret and I had in common. She used to talk about feeling cannibalized. Of course a lot of that had to do with her fame. I don't have that problem but I still leave crowds with a sense of being gnawed on.

I got myself a glass of Niagara Nectar and lurked in a corner. I like to watch and listen to people at these gatherings as they put huge amounts of energy into conversations about snow tires and the use of fertilizer to melt the ice on your sidewalks instead of salt. I feel like a spy. Then I was spotted. A young woman named Doris bustled over, dragging another woman with her. The introductions revealed that the new person was called Nancy and she was studying Canadian literature at the University of Manitoba. Doris drifted away toward two other uncoupled people.

"I'm studying Margaret Laurence," Nancy said, her eyes bright with the intensity of the experience. "God, she's hard to read. I mean it's like swallowing carpet tacks sometimes."

"You don't like her stuff?" I asked.

"Oh, I love it! But the pain and misery. It gets to be unbearable. Have you read her?"

"Yes," I replied.

"I'm just finishing *A Jest of God*," she said. "It's wonderful but horrible too. You know what I mean."

"I think so."

"I think she was addicted to pain," Nancy said. "I'm writing a major paper on it called 'Manawaka, the Birthplace of Pain'."

I laughed. I knew I shouldn't but I couldn't help myself. Nancy was not a kid. She was close to forty so she didn't have the resilience of youth. I had hurt her unintentionally.

"Sorry," I said. "I was imagining Margaret's reaction. That's all."

"You knew her?"

"Yes, we were neighbours and friends for a long time."

Her face lit up.

"I'd love to pick your brain," she said.

I put my glass of untasted wine down carefully. This was my signal to leave. I smiled at Nancy, hoping for a graceful exit.

"Sure," I lied, "but I've got to get home right now."

She had a pen out. She scribbled her name and number on the torn cover of a cigarette package and handed it to me.

"I'll be busy reading and researching for the next week," she said, "but after that give me a call."

"Okay," I said, and turned to leave.

I knew I should have left well enough alone, but a mad compulsion made me turn back to her.

"If reading Margaret is so painful, just think what it must have been like to write those books," I said.

"My point exactly!" she replied. "She must have flourished on it, like some kind of emotional masochist."

I got out the door as quickly as I could and discarded the number in a snowbank.

Now it is late at night, early morning really. I sit here staring at the lighted screen, the words to locate Margaret slipping in and out of my mind but never quite right. Am I afraid of something? Will the act of revealing the Margaret I love be a betrayal?

My computer screen becomes a mirror in which I see reflected the photograph of Margaret that is framed and hanging on the wall behind me. It feels like she's giving me the eye, willing me to drive slowly, carefully, but for Gawd's sake, get on with it!

I laugh, inside. I don't want to wake Daile and Daniel who are sleeping, dreaming their dreams. I laugh silently because when I look in the screen and see Margaret's reflection, right beside it is my own. The image of myself in this story is what has frightened me. Scared of my own shadow all along.

So I begin... .

The Road to Margaret's Door

In the fall of 1968 I was doing time in Warkworth penitentiary. It's a modern institution laid out like a college campus from an architect's nightmare. Whoever won the contract for the concrete made a fortune. The place was a cement maze. The living compound was made up of six slab buildings that each contained forty cells. A round glass-enclosed control room was erected in a central, elevated area so the guards could see any activity that was taking place along the four corridors. One guard locked in his bullet-proof bubble could control the whole place. The cells had electronic locks and if you wanted out, you pushed the red button over your desk and the guard might buzz the steel door open, or he might ignore you. Often it depended on his mood.

But Warkworth is a modern prison with a multitude of programmes and work situations, so you don't spend much time in your cell. It was a place you went to sleep, and you had to return there after breakfast, after lunch and after dinner so you could be counted. Guards spend a lot of time counting their charges. Unfortunately they're not very good at it and often they ended up with too many inmates or too few. So they counted again, sometimes three or four times, until the total corresponded with the official count that was written on a chalk board in the keeper's office.

When you leave the cell compound to go to the administration building for your mandatory counselling, or to the school where daydreaming was the main activity, you walk through an open air corridor that has cement pillars placed four inches apart. An unusual and creative idea since you can see the great outdoors, the beautiful grounds tended by inmates with low risk security status, and you sort of feel part of the larger environment. But you aren't. You're locked up. I must have walked that corridor five thousand times. It leads to the cafeteria, the gym where you go to lift weights or play basketball.

The slotted corridor continues on to the laundry where you pick up fresh clothes once a week. This ventilated tunnel of despair ends at the chapels. There are two, one Catholic and the other Protestant. A lot of us attended church in a ritualistic attempt to maintain hope. The problem was that the priest had a more intimate relationship with his communion wine than with us, and the Protestant chaplain gave psychology lectures rather than sermons.

On a particular Sunday one of the guys took exception to his little speech and ran up to the front, pulled the chaplain from his pulpit and began to beat him with the bible that was lying open at the day's lesson on the dais. Four guards came running from the back and pounded the inmate into unconsciousness with their truncheons in about ten seconds. The chaplain had a bleeding nose, and some of it dripped and spotted his white robe. The service was declared over. I often wondered what the biblical lesson for the day had been. It was near Easter and could have been about the blood of the Lamb. The chaplain often chose passages that spoke of forgiveness, turning the other cheek. One of his favourites was do unto others as you would have them do unto you. Through the grapevine I heard that the chaplain demanded his attacker receive ten strokes of the strap. He also insisted that the inmate be shipped back to maximum security at Kingston. I don't know what happened but the inmate disappeared and the chaplain toned down his lectures slightly. Perhaps he remembered that he was just an employed civil servant, the same as the guards, teachers and administrators. He may have worn a minister's collar, but in his heart he was just another self-righteous bureaucrat.

I didn't agree with the chaplain's opinion that inmates are irresponsible louts. I'd been in jails and institutions almost all my life and most of the inmates I encountered were emotional refugees. They were people who wanted to be normal but didn't know how to achieve it. The real cripples were often the staff who ran the places. I felt sorry for both groups. They lacked vision. One group put a spit polish on their boots so the other group could inspect them.

I considered myself an exception. Not better or smarter. But I was a thief. Prison didn't bother me much. I knew why I was there. I robbed banks and this was the price I had to pay for getting caught. I felt better off than many of the guards whom I overheard speaking to each other about how in a month or two their father-in-law's car business was going to pick up and they were going to be taken on as a salesman. It never happened. They were stuck there for life. I was only doing twelve and a half years.

What I liked about Warkworth was that there were no steel bars on the cell windows. Again they used cement pillars set four inches apart. My window faced west so I could see the sun set. Some nights I stood on my bed and looked at the stars. It's easier to pretend you're not in jail when you look out a window with cement bars. The porous material absorbs the warmth of your hands more easily than steel.

Warkworth was my third prison. I'd spent three years in Kingston penitentiary because I was considered a security risk. In my first year I was asked to be the recipient of a series of twelve shock treatments to curb my violent nature. I agreed to it. I thought it would look good on my file. I was a cooperative guy. However, the treatment didn't accomplish much for me at all. My memory was messed up for a while and I developed a distaste for anything rubber. I still have an aversion to paying my hydro bill.

In Kingston I got lucky. I was put on the paint gang. There were forty of us with enough work to keep two guys busy. We passed the time playing cards or pacing the floor with a buddy. Telling each other stories, most of them lies. But there was one guy who stayed off by himself. He grew plants in old tobacco tins. He got the dirt from the exercise yard and planted grapefruit seeds, radish and carrot tops. Sometimes he got someone in the kitchen to give him white beans and pieces of raw potatoes. He had hundreds of plants growing and when he wasn't pacing, he'd be watering the plants or feeding them a compost he made from old scraps of food that he kept in a covered garbage pail. Everyone stayed away from him. He was short, skinny and balding, probably in his early forties, but there was a menacing energy about him. I approached him one day and asked about his plants.

"How come you waste your time trying to grow plants? They never flower."

He looked at me with contempt and spat on the floor about an inch from my boot. The other inmates had stopped talking. No one was pacing. Everyone waited. I shifted my weight, ready to lash out with a swift kick. I'm small but I'd been in lots of fights. Fights were an everyday occurrence in prison.

"You the kid that put the Indian in the hospital?" he asked, his voice thick with a French accent.

I nodded yes. My first week in Kingston I'd been assigned to the Buller gang. I was teamed up with a big native guy. Our job was to clear the debris from a cell block that was being renovated. We took turns shovelling the chunks of broken stone and cement into a wheelbarrow and then pushing it outside and dumping it into a pile where another group moved it somewhere else. Most of the time the native guy worked the wheelbarrow. A guard stood nearby making sure we didn't stall. The first morning passed fine but early in the afternoon, the guard went off for a smoke. I was bending over to fill my shovel when suddenly I felt a hand on my behind, squeezing hard.

"You got a nice tender ass there," the native guy said. "You and me go down to the washroom on break and I'll show you what it's for."

I guess he was pretty sure of himself but I'd been in jail before. You don't let anyone get away with fondling your ass. You lose your dignity and you're dead. So I swung the edge of the shovel at his knee. It made a satisfying crunch. He went down hard, smacking his head on the floor and screaming in pain. Before he could get up I used the flat of the shovel to smash his face. Pretty soon the grey dirt and dust was mixed with his blood.

Three guards came running and grabbed me. They whacked me a couple of times with their batons but they weren't particularly vicious about it. I was sent to the hole for ten days and I lost thirty days off my good conduct time. When I was released back into the main population no one came near me.

Except now, this prisoner who grew plants and faced me with a challenging look.

"That was me," I said.

And then he laughed.

"I hate Indians," he said. "I hate niggers too!" he shouted as he glared at several blacks in the shop who were watching. Everyone laughed nervously and then went back to their own activities.

"Anybody else?" I asked.

He laughed.

"Just a fish and already you're a smart ass."

"I've been in plenty of jails," I said.

"Oh, so you're a tough guy? How old are you?"

"Nineteen," I said. And I wanted to explain to him that no, I didn't feel like a tough guy. I stood five feet, two inches and weighed a little over a hundred pounds. I thought of myself as a survivor. There was something about this guy that made me want to explain myself. I had a feeling that I could learn things from him. I didn't know what but I wanted him to think well of me so he'd let me in on his secrets. He looked like a man with a lot of secrets.

"You read?" he asked.

"Sure."

"What, comic books?" He walked away from me but I trailed after him.

"I read a lot," I said. "I just finished Truman Capote's book, *Other Voices, Other Rooms*."

He stopped and looked at me and then slowly began to shake his head. The expression on his face softened for a second and then he spit contemptuously on the floor again.

"American crap," he said. "They can't write. They pee their pants, put it in a book and call it a novel."

He began to pace up and down again, walking quickly, his face set in an expression of tense concentration. Then he stopped, came over and poked me in the chest.

"You wanna learn about real books?"

"Yes," I said. I wasn't sure what he meant but I didn't want to make him mad.

That night when the tapper came around to our cells with his bucket of hot water for those of us who wanted to shave, he slipped a thick hardcover book through the open bars of my cell door.

"Ernie said I should give you this," he said. "You know he's crazy, don't you? He taught at some fancy French school in France. Thinks he's smarter than everybody else. But he's just crazy."

I took the book and began to read. It was by Honoré de Balzac. I stayed up all night reading by the light of the twenty-five watt bulb that dangled outside our cells so the guards could see if we'd strung ourselves up, slashed our wrists, or found some other means of escape.

The next day I paced the paint shop floor with Ernie, discussing the book. He ridiculed my perceptions of the characters. He explained belligerently that the plot was secondary to the characters. That night another Balzac novel arrived. Over the next few months I read all of the Balzac novels that made up "La Comédie Humaine."

Then he started me on Maupassant. I raved about the simplicity of the stories and Ernie put me on the dummy for the rest of the morning. After lunch he approached me.

"I'm wasting my time," he said. "You read but you don't understand."

A few nights later, the tapper brought me a novel called *The Castle* by Franz Kafka. It took me two days to read it. I avoided Ernie until it was finished. When I closed the book I felt deflated. Ernie was right. I was stupid.

I went up to him in the paint shop and confessed the book had me baffled. He smiled—a rare occurrence.

"Good," he said. "We're making progress."

We sat down on a couple of paint cans. His pant legs were pulled up and I noticed he wasn't wearing any socks. It was the middle of winter and we had to walk through the snow to get to the shop.

"Don't your feet freeze in the snow?" I asked.

"It's not snow," he said. "Every morning I walk over the white, warm sands of the Riviera."

I must have looked puzzled.

"I'm doing twenty years," he said. "They'll deport me back to France in seven. In the meantime they can lock up my body, but not my mind. Not my imagination. The books help. Read the books. Maybe you'll find out something worthwhile."

As the months passed I became his pupil. He introduced me to Nabokov, Proust, Tolstoy. Much of what I read I didn't understand but Ernie forced me to voice my opinion. I began to learn that a lot of writers had deep, dark places within themselves. Hideouts. Places they had fun, did crazy things, expressed their rage, their sorrow. As I did. It made me feel less alone.

Secretly I began to write my own stories. This wasn't a new thing for me. As a child living in different neighbourhoods in Toronto as I moved from foster home to foster home I learned to be afraid to declare myself out loud. I might say something that would offend my new parents. So I made up stories of the life I would like to have. Often they were happy stories, simple and carefree. Other times they were tragic, peopled by figures I could only imagine: my father who was killed in the war, a dimly remembered mother who dumped my brother and me with our grandmother. My brother Teddy. He and I had been placed in several foster homes when we were four and five.

Sometimes foster parents thought it was cute to have a matched set. But he never fit in as well as I did. He wet his bed all the time and cried for our mother. It gave our foster mothers migraines so he was always sent back to the orphanage.

When he was seven Teddy hung himself in the orphanage washroom. He stood on top of the toilet cubicle, tied a piece of clothesline around a pipe and then made a slip knot that he put around his neck. Then he jumped. I guess it was lucky he was so light or else the pipe might have broken.

But all these stories were kept locked in my head. I did badly in school and almost all my report cards remarked that I daydreamed too much. But in grade six an event occurred that gave me a release.

I was living with a couple by the name of Fox. They lived in a comfortable house in an area of north Toronto called Forest Hill. He owned a printing business and she spent her days shopping, buying expensive oriental rugs to put over the wall-to-wall carpeting. This was 1953 and television was a brand-new, expensive novelty product, but they had three of them. Every bit of floor space in the house was taken up with occasional tables and corner display cupboards that were jammed with Dresden china figures. The house was an obstacle course of fragile, breakable objects. Fortunately I had a room in the basement and I spent most of my time there. Out of harm's way.

The Foxes were nice people. She had a tipped womb and couldn't bear children. So they had taken me in as a foster child. I figured they had me on loan, in the way people borrow a car while their own is in the shop getting repaired. They rarely talked to me. Mr. Fox rose at six every morning, ate breakfast alone and had left for work before I was up. Mrs. Fox often slept in so I ate alone, made my lunch and went off to school.

But then the storm came. Hurricane Hazel. The basement of their house flooded. The rain was relentless. It rained for twenty hours straight. The streets became rivers and school was cancelled. Volunteers built sandbank walls around the rivers and creeks that were flooding the streets.

What I remember most was sitting at the top of the basement stairs sandwiched between the Foxes as we watched the water slowly creep up from the basement, stair by stair. It smelled awful, like sewage. And Mrs. Fox, who never raised her voice, and hardly ever smiled, began to cry.

"It's all ruined," she said. "Everything we worked for."

Mr. Fox, who was not a demonstrative man, put his arm around her shoulders.

"The insurance will cover it," he said.

"We're being punished, Tommy," she said. "God is punishing us. He wouldn't let us have a baby and now this."

"It's just a bit of bad luck," he said.

"All our dreams being washed away," she said.

"No," he said. "It's just a little set-back. In a few days it'll be over and we'll clean up and start over."

She stopped crying and looked at him with a strange smile.

"We stopped dreaming, Tommy. And this is our punishment."

He hugged her tightly and muttered over and over, "No. No."

They clung to each other like people I'd seen in the movies who really love each other. I realized that I'd always thought of them as being silly, stiff as kids in a play pretending to be grownups. He kissed her eyelids and it was the most tender thing I'd ever seen. They didn't talk much but I knew as the water crept up the stairs something important in their lives was changing. I felt happy for them but it was like I wasn't there. But I was and I felt like crying. I wanted to be part of the comforting somehow but I didn't know how. And I knew there must be something wrong with me.

The hurricane ended the next day. When school opened again our teacher asked us to write a story about the storm. I wrote about the Foxes, about how for the first time I saw them as real people. People with feelings, sorrows, and dreams. I think it might have been a story about love. I was too young to know but the teacher liked it so much she sent it to a magazine and they published it. They sent her a copy and she read it aloud to the class. It was my proudest academic achievement.

Six months later Mrs. Fox got pregnant. I lived with them until their son was born. They invited me to join them in their joy but I withdrew. I began to get into fights at school. My grades, which had always been bad, got worse. I asked to be returned to the orphanage. My social worker at the time told me I was stupid, that I was giving up the chance of a lifetime. He claimed the Foxes loved me like their own son. Maybe they did. But I never stayed to find out.

From the ages of eleven to fifteen I lived in at least twenty more foster homes. I was a restless kid. My new foster parents always wanted me to do weird things like take ballet lessons, tap dance lessons, or learn how to play the piano. One family strapped an accordion on me the minute I got through the door. Every new home was like a giant furnace where they wanted to melt me down and then pour me into a mold where I'd be reshaped to fit their fantasies. I rebelled, became mean-spirited and often ran away. But the cops always found me wandering the streets and I was returned to the orphanage. That was my real home.

There was an older girl at the orphanage named Louise. She was fifteen, but with makeup, high heels and a skirt that fit like a banana peel, she could easily pass for eighteen. One day when I was heading out the door for school with my lunch she asked me if I wanted to go downtown with her. I was thrilled. She taught me how to panhandle money on Yonge Street, playing the sad-eyed kid who'd lost his car fare. On a good day I could make seven, eight bucks in an hour. She'd take most of the money but leave me enough to buy a ticket into an all-day movie house. I'd watch four or five movies and meet her in front of the Brown Derby bar at the corner of Yonge and Dundas and we'd take the bus home together. While I'd be watching movies she spent the day in the bar meeting guys. Sometimes she was a bit drunk but she sucked Sen Sens on the bus trip to cover up the liquor smell on her breath.

Louise was my hero. We became a team. One night she crept into the office of Mrs. St. Jean, who ran the orphanage, and using the embossed letterhead, typed a letter to my school informing them that I was being transferred to a foster home out of province and that my new school would contact them for my school records.

I delivered the letter to the principal's office the next day and he shook my hand and wished me good luck. I'm sure he was glad to get rid of me. For the next month Louise and I went downtown every day. I did my panhandle trick and got enough cash to get me into the movies. The rest of the money I gave to Louise, who needed it to buy the first drink when she went into a bar. After that there were always guys who competed to keep her glass filled. She told me sometimes they took her back to their hotel rooms and ordered in room service. And sometimes they gave her tips because she was so young and pretty.

At thirteen I knew about sex. Sort of. I worried that Louise was going to turn out to be a prostitute but I never said anything. She never mentioned sex. Sometimes when a guy gave her a big tip, she'd pay for a taxi to drive us back to the orphanage and I'd hold her hand, although we never did that on the bus. We always got out of the cab a block away from the orphanage. It was all right to be a rebel but there was no point in flaunting it.

One day we were in a cab heading back and all the Sen Sens in the world couldn't cover up the smell of booze. We were sitting in the back seat and she put her arm around me and pulled me close to her breasts.

"I wish you were older," she said. "We could just keep driving."

I watched the meter, as the total kept rising.

"Maybe we should get out and walk the rest of the way," I said.

I was afraid the staff were going to see how drunk she was.

"I went with three guys today," she said, and pulled a wad of bills out of her purse. "We could get our own place."

I made the driver stop, took some of Louise's money and paid him off. It was still a long walk and Louise staggered so much I had to hold her up.

"They all told me they loved me," she said.

Then she laughed.

"It's all bullshit, isn't it!" she said.

"I love you, Louise," I said, and meant it, within the limited bounds of understanding I had on the subject.

She stopped and embraced me. Then she started to cry. It must have been a funny sight for the passing motorists because she was at least six inches taller than me in her high heels.

"I know you do," she said. "I just wish you could be like you are now, but older."

By the time we got to the orphanage she'd sobered up enough that none of the staff noticed she'd been drinking. Because she was the oldest resident she had her own room and once we arrived, she headed straight there to hide out.

I went outside to the playground. A buddy of mine, Ray Peets, who was another foster home refugee, grabbed me and pointed toward the swings.

"Cute eh?" he said.

I looked and saw a thin, sandy-haired girl swaying listlessly on the swing.

"She just came in today," Ray said. "Margaret Little. She comes from Owen Sound. Mom died and her old man started... ."

He made a circle with his thumb and index finger and then poked the index finger of his other hand through the hole.

"She won't talk to anybody," Ray said. "But she's cute. I wouldn't mind... ."

Ray was fourteen. He bragged about all the girls he'd banged but I figured it was all talk. The orphanage was co-ed and you might figure with a bunch of boys and girls together there would be all kinds of sexual activity. But there wasn't. Sometimes a boy might sneak into the girls' dormitory but it was usually to play tricks on them, steal their shoes, or sometimes their underwear. But no real sex. We were too scared. Sex was being close. Too close.

I walked over to the swings and sat on the one next to Margaret Little. Her head was bowed and I couldn't see her face very well.

"My name's Don," I said.

"So!" she said.

"Just trying to be friends," I said.

"Everybody knows about me," she said fiercely.

"People are always telling stories around here," I said. "Most of them are lies."

She looked up at me with eyes like blue, flaming arrows.

"I'm going to the movies tomorrow," I said. "You wanna come?"

"I have to go to school," she said. "They already registered me today."

"You like school?" I asked.

"I hate it!" she said. "All the other kids know. The boys grab me."

"Owen Sound's a long way from here. No one will know anything about you."

"Somebody always tells them," she said, and her face became sad and defeated. For a second I thought of my brother Teddy. Sometimes he'd looked that way.

"Come to the movies with me," I said.

"I don't want to get into any trouble," she said.

"You won't," I promised. "The staff around here haven't got a clue what's going on."

She giggled but then got serious again.

"You better not try anything with me," she said.

"I won't," I said.

The next day Louise was hung over and not in the best of humour. But I convinced her to write a note for Margaret explaining she needed some medical tests and wouldn't be in attendance for several days. Not only did Louise write it but she delivered it to the vice principal's office posing as a staff member of the orphanage, while Margaret and I hid behind a tree across the street from the school. After that victory Louise's mood changed and she seemed amused to have the two of us tagging along.

I had to work especially hard that day at my panhandling. I developed a new approach—I told people that I'd lost my lunch money. Most people were sympathetic and one guy even gave me a dollar. Before long we had enough money to go our separate ways: Louise to the Brown Derby, and Margaret and I to the local theatre.

It's funny what you remember. There were four movies playing that day but I only remember one. It was called *Pony Express* and starred Guy Madison and Andy Devine. During the first three films Margaret sat stiffly beside me, her body never coming in contact with mine. I didn't care. I was just glad for the company. But during the climax of *Pony Express* it appeared that Guy Madison might be killed. He was being chased by Indians who didn't want the mail delivered. I guess they thought the mail provided a link between the white men who were taking over their country. The scene was tense with danger. Suddenly Margaret put her head against my shoulder and then her hand reached out and took one of mine. She squeezed my hand until the crisis in the film passed. Then she held it gently and even stroked my fingers. It was the nicest feeling in the world.

All that week, Louise, Margaret and I headed out to school with our bagged lunches but we always ended up downtown. Margaret and I went to the movies and both of us cried a lot through films like *Lassie Come Home, Love is a Many Splendored Thing,* and *A Farewell to Arms*, especially when the woman died at the end. We held hands and laughed at the Three Stooges, Red Skelton, and Laurel and Hardy. Poor Ollie, always getting smacked on the head for something he didn't do. One day we saw *High Noon* and Margaret buried her face against my chest so she wouldn't see Gary Cooper get killed in the final shootout. But of course he didn't. When we left the theatre to meet Louise at four, as we did every day, the two of us were singing the theme song: Do not forsake me oh my darling, on this our wedding day... .

We were truants, living in our own make-believe world. But we were happy. Although school counsellors, social workers and the orphanage staff were always warning us about a future filled with failure, we didn't care. Now was what counted.

Louise used to say, "If ya spot a little happiness, grab it and swallow it whole!"

On the Friday of Margaret's first week at the orphanage whatever fool's paradise we were living in came to an abrupt halt.

We arrived home to find Margaret's father sitting in his truck in the driveway. He threw open the door as soon as he saw us. Margaret ran but he chased her across the grounds and tackled her. He was big and once she was subdued, he back-handed her across the face twice and pointed toward the truck. Louise and I stood there watching, not knowing what to do. Then Mrs. St. Jean came out of the building and walked up to Margaret's father.

"This is not proper," she said. "You have no authority to take her."

"She's my daughter! I can do anything with her I like. She's just lazy. That's why she runs away. Just because she has to do a little extra work since my wife died. She's got a brother and sister to look after. Don't you worry about her... . She won't run away again."

I didn't like Mrs. St. Jean much. She was the director of the orphanage and acted as judge and jury. She sentenced me to peel more potatoes than I imagine they harvest in a peak year in P.E.I. A couple of times several of the young male staff members had beaten Ray Peets and me with coat hangers to show us who was in charge. Mrs. St. Jean knew about those incidents and others in which kids were banged around. But she never did anything. In that moment I prayed, I actually muttered pleading words to a God I didn't believe existed, for her to step forward and stop this guy from taking Margaret. But she didn't. She stepped aside as he got into his truck, and called after him.

"I'll see to it the social worker gets a report on this!"

What a joke.

The amazing thing was that no one had discovered we were skipping school. The orphanage staff were suspicious. They used to walk around hunched over, their eyes darting everywhere, seeking out trouble as if it was all hidden like lint under the chesterfield. But they rarely saw anything that took place before their eyes. For instance, the staff was paranoid about us stealing food from the kitchen. I don't know why but we were always hungry. After dinner each evening, which took place in a large hall in the basement, six of us had to do the dishes, and six more of us were put on the sandwich-making detail. There were always about forty kids living at the orphanage, and we were each allowed two sandwiches for our lunches. Two staff members would prowl the kitchen while we worked. But then they'd get bored. Or if they were a man and a woman, they might start flirting. Sometimes they even disappeared into the locked pantry where supplies were kept. The second they were out of sight we'd take the extra twenty or thirty sandwiches that we'd made right in front of them and quickly load them into the dumb waiter. Then one of us would give the rope pulley a yank and the other kids would haul our booty up to the third floor. We never went to bed hungry.

After lights out on the night Margaret Little was kidnapped by her father, Ray Peets and I sneaked down to the second floor where the girls slept and had a whispered conference with Louise.

"You gotta do something," she said. "You know what that bastard's gonna do to her? You think he wants her just to cook and clean the house?"

She was furious, but crying. I'd never seen Louise cry. She was the toughest person I knew.

"But they live in Owen Sound," Ray said, always ready with the practical obstacles.

"So?" Louise said.

"How're we supposed to get there? And anyway what can we do?"

Louise looked at me. Her eyes glinted with the same fierce confidence that she used to hypnotize me into believing that if I asked strangers for money, they'd give it to me.

"We'll kidnap her back," I said.

Ray was skeptical but I needed him to come along. He was a year older and weighed about a hundred and sixty pounds. A fair bit of that was fat, but he wasn't an easy guy to push around.

"How?" he asked.

Louise glared at him.

"You want some old man doin' it to your sister?" she hissed.

"I ain't got no sister," he said.

She let a second or two go by. Her voice lost its harshness. She sounded like she might weep again.

"What am I, your mother? Who takes care of us here? Who? Us!"

Ray looked sheepish.

"I just mean, it's none of our business, it'll just make more trouble."

"Then don't do anything," she said quietly.

The next day Ray and I told the staff we were going to a movie downtown and wouldn't be back until after supper. It was Saturday. They didn't care. Weekends were lax.

We took a bus to the end of the line and began to hitchhike. Owen Sound is only about a hundred and fifty miles from Toronto but it took us ten hours to get there. We looked in the phone book and found four Littles in town. The first two were the wrong houses but at the third place we tried, the door was opened by Margaret herself. She started to cry when she saw us.

"You shouldna come!" she said. She had a broom in her hand as though we'd interrupted her sweeping the floor. Suddenly her father appeared in the hallway.

"What the hell do you punks want? Get outta here!"

He pushed Ray out of the doorway with one hand and pulled Margaret back inside. But I grabbed her broom. It had a thick wooden handle and I charged at the guy, using it like a spear. I caught him by surprise and he slipped backwards. Ray had regained his footing and the two of us started to kick at her father, focusing all the rage of our young years. But he was a powerful man and scrambled to his feet. He punched Ray in the stomach, oblivious to me thumping his leg with the broomstick. Ray threw up, then fell. Margaret's father kicked him in the face. Before he could hit me, I kicked him as hard as I could in the balls. He bellowed in pain and bent double, clutching himself. I hauled Ray out the door and forced him to his feet. We began to run.

The cops picked us up before we got two blocks. They drove us to a wooded area and made us lean over the trunk of their car. Then they smashed us a couple of times in the kidneys with their billy clubs. They left us to make our own way back to the highway. We got lucky and were picked up by a transport truck. The driver gave us a lift all the way to Toronto, but he had to stop a few times for Ray and I to puke.

Life is strange. The two cops that banged us around decided to go back to Margaret's house. Probably they needed more information to fill out their report. They found Margaret lying on her father's bed, beaten and naked. Her father wasn't arrested but Margaret was bundled up and late Sunday she was back at the orphanage.

I saw her in the playground sitting on a swing, not moving. I approached her and sat down beside her.

"I'm sorry," I said. "We wanted to help and we just made more trouble."

She turned her bruised face toward me and I think she smiled.

"I know why you did it," she said.

I nodded as though I knew what she was talking about.

"My mother told me that when a boy loves you, he'll do anything for you," she said.

I nodded again but I didn't say anything. She got up and walked inside. I didn't see her at supper that night. In fact, I never saw her again. During the night she sneaked out of bed and locked herself in the tub room. She ran a warm bath. She must have been very quiet because the two staff people on duty that night claimed they heard nothing. When the tub was filled, Margaret took off her nightgown and lowered herself into the warm, soothing water. She had a razor blade. She knew enough to make the cuts vertical as well as horizontal. I guess she just fell asleep as her life flowed from her. I hope she drifted into dream and found her mother, who I think must have really loved her.

It was Louise who broke down the door and found her. An ambulance was called and the body was taken away. I don't know who cleaned up the mess. Mrs. St. Jean came down to the dining room and gave a little speech.

"Life is full of trials," she said. "For everyone. We must be strong and brave and not give into the temptation to quit. It is a sin to give up and God will not forgive us... ."

"Bull shit" yelled Louise, leaping up and running for the door. I was right behind her. We took the bus downtown and I panhandled that morning with belligerence. I stepped in front of people, wouldn't let them pass until I had money in my hand. I insulted women who tried to sneak by me. That day I ended up with more bills in my hand than silver. It gave me a certain satisfaction but inside my stomach was seething.

"Listen," Louise said. "Why don't you come with me today. Screw the movies. There's this guy I want you to meet."

"I can't get into a bar," I said. "I'm too young."

"It's okay, I know the waiter. I'll tell him I gotta babysit for a while. He'll put us in a back booth."

I wasn't really in the mood to go to the movies by myself so I agreed.

The bar was dark and noisy. The air was thick with smoke. Louise had a whispered conversation with a waiter who smiled knowingly and then whisked us to a booth at the rear of the place. Louise ordered a whisky sour and I asked for a coke. Before our drinks came, a couple of musicians wandered on to the stage, a narrow platform set in the middle of the circular bar area. The musicians began to tune their instruments. Our drinks arrived and I watched Louise get more and more excited. I couldn't understand why. Then suddenly the drummer did an extended roll, a spotlight was turned on and a young man wearing a white sports jacket with a pink flower pinned to his lapel strolled up to the microphone.

"That's him!" Louise exclaimed, squeezing my leg.

The band began to play, the singer crooned into the microphone in a seductive voice.

"A white sports coat and a pink carnation.... I'm all dressed up for the dance...."

I was stunned. He sounded just like....

He sang about six songs, bowed to the applause and came directly over to our booth.

Up close I saw he wore thick makeup to mask a serious case of acne. He lit a cigarette and stared at me sourly.

"What's he doing here?"

"I told you Marty, he's just like my brother."

The guy snorted.

"You kidding! I'm taking a chance with you. I get caught on the road with some underage kid the cops'll throw me in the slammer. Besides, there's only room in the trailer for the two of us."

"You sound just like Marty Robbins," I said.

"What makes you think I'm not?" he snarled, then laughed. The sound made me think of a Hollywood muffler, sort of a throaty growl. "I do a pretty good imitation. They book me in as Marty Rubbins and a lot of the local yokels don't know the difference. My own stuff hasn't caught on yet... but it will. I've just been filling in for a few days but tonight, we're gonna hit the road."

"Two weeks in North Bay." he smirked. "They love us there."

"He's taking me with him," Louise said.

"Then we got three weeks lined up in Sudbury. I like playing in the smaller centres. Gives me a chance to try out my own stuff. By the time we head back to T.O. I'll have enough material to make my own album."

"Great," I said, although I suspected that once Marty Robbins's big hit was off the chart this guy would be lucky to find a job washing dishes in Timmins.

"Is Louise really eighteen?" he asked me suddenly.

I wasn't fourteen yet but I knew in that second that this guy was a phony. Worst of all, a coward. He'd ditch Louise in a second if he thought she'd cause him any trouble.

"Marty," she said, "I told you a million times... ."

He slapped her. Not hard, but it wasn't a playful tap either. I wanted to take my glass of coke and jam it down his throat, but it was Louise's life. She wouldn't thank me for messing it up for her.

"How many times I gotta tell ya," he said. "Off stage you call me by my real name. Chuck. Remember. Chuck!"

She put her hand to the cheek he'd slapped, her fingers smoothing away the pain.

"Chuck Berry I presume," I piped up.

He slid out of the booth and pointed a shaking finger at me.

"I gotta get ready for the next set. This midget motormouth better be gone when I get back or you ain't going anywhere with me."

Louise and I sat in silence, she sipping her whisky sour, me my coke.

"You don't like him, do you?" she said.

"He's a creep," I said.

She smiled and snuggled close to me.

"Remember that time I said I wished you were older and the two of us could take off?"

"Yes," I said.

"It's still true. But life's not like that. I gotta get away and this guy's my ticket."

I drained my coke and started to get up. She grabbed my hand and pressed five dollars into it.

"For the movies," she said, and then suddenly her voice changed. The bright cheerfulness was gone.

"You never took me to the movies," she said.

"I didn't think you wanted to go. You never asked."

"I wanted you to ask me," she said.

"Sorry," I said.

"I used to wonder what you did when you went off by yourself like that. I figured when you took Margaret, you probably sat there necking all day."

"No," I said. "Sometimes we held hands."

"Come here," she said.

I leaned back into the booth and she put her arms around my neck and kissed me, full on the mouth. Her lips were soft and opened gently so my own rigidity melted. For a second her tongue darted into my mouth. It tickled and made me smile. Our mouths separated. It was my first grownup kiss and I felt excited, elated, but also afraid. It was a kiss of farewell.

"Don't forget me," she said.

"I won't," I said and walked away, just as Chuck, or Marty, was taking the stage again.

I should have returned to the orphanage but without Louise and Margaret, I decided that part of my life was finished. I walked along Dundas for a couple of blocks and took a seat in the bus terminal. I had about eight bucks and I checked at the counter to see how far that would take me. Not very far. And what would I do when I got there? I sat in a chair and watched the passengers coming and going, imagining their destinations, speculating on how their lives would change when their journeys ended.

In one of the foster homes where I stayed briefly, they made me go to Sunday school. I remembered the story about the prodigal son. This young guy wanted to leave home and his father gave him a pile of loot to get him started, but the guy blew it all on wine, women, and song. He was flat broke and had to face the humiliation of going home and facing his father. Now you'd think his old man would take him behind the shed and kick his ass, but no. When his father heard that he was heading home he actually walked along the road to meet him. When he spotted him, he ran toward the son and hugged him. That night the father had a big feast to celebrate his son's homecoming. It was a story about forgiveness. I never really understood it but I liked it. Sometimes I wished there was someone around who'd forgive me.

It was starting to get dark so I went into the snack bar and had a hot dog. Then I bought a paperback novel, *Martin Eden* by Jack London. I loved to read, which in a way was peculiar because the foster mother who taught me how had a strange method.

Her name was Eleanor and she was a bustling woman. The kind of person who couldn't wait for you to finish eating your bowl of cornflakes so she could get her hands on the dish and wash it up. She liked to brag that you could eat off her kitchen floor. I lived with her when I was four. She and her husband had no other kids so I got her full attention. At night she'd read to me, which I enjoyed. Then after a couple of months she woke me up one morning, handed a book to me and asked me to read the first page. I couldn't. Besides, I had to go to the bathroom.

"No pee pee until you read," she said.

I was a stubborn kid and refused even to look at the page. So she marched me down the hallway and locked me in the hall closet. It was dark and the tiny room smelled of moth balls. After about half an hour my bladder exploded and I stood there in my drenched pyjamas.

I spent many hours in that hall closet, stinking of urine. Every hour or so she'd check on me and see if I was ready to read. It didn't take long to break me down. She was a good teacher and by the time I started kindergarten I could read better than any kid in the class. The trouble was that I got addicted to it. I'd rather read than listen to the lessons being taught. Books became a way to escape the world around me. Books often made more sense to me than the world I lived in.

Anyway I was deep into *Martin Eden*. Suddenly there was an older man in a suit sitting beside me.

"Hi," he said.

A cop, I thought.

He put his hand on my knee.

"No place to go?" he asked.

A gearbox. Living in an orphanage you learn pretty early that certain guys prefer guys to girls.

"I'm just waiting for someone," I said.

He smiled. His teeth were small and white. I looked him over. His clothes looked expensive. Maybe he's the good samaritan.

"I've been watching you for quite a while," he said. "It looks like whoever you're waiting for isn't going to show up."

I marked the page of my book and closed it but didn't say anything.

"I don't live far away," he said. "You could stay at my place tonight and maybe tomorrow...the people you're waiting for will show up."

I figured it was better to be blunt.

"I'm not queer," I said.

He chuckled.

"You can sleep on the couch," he said, "It's okay. You'll be safe."

It's funny how you make choices. The guy suddenly reached over and took my book.

"Jack London," he remarked. "I think I've read everything he's ever written. I've got a lot of his books at my place."

"Okay," I said. "Just for tonight, but no funny stuff."

He handed me back the book and I followed him out into the night, feeling tough but scared too. I wondered for a moment about Louise. Was she on the road yet? Would I ever see her again?

For three years while I was in Kingston penitentiary Ernie Caron tutored me. I read my way through Europe, Russia, avoided England altogether and just before I was transferred, started on South America.

I never knew if Ernie harboured any affection for me but the day I was packing up for my move to Collins Bay prison, he got a pass to leave the paint shop and came to my cell.

"You keep reading," he said, standing at the bars. He seemed nervous. "Maybe someday you'll even write something worth reading."

We both laughed. I'd let Ernie read two of my stories and he'd thrown both of them on the floor of the paint shop and spit on them. But in a strange way, he'd nurtured me. Just like his plants. We parted that day with no handshake, no real goodbyes. I've never seen him since.

The first two years in Collins Bay were barren. But I read, looking for something. I was hungry for food I'd never tasted. Nostalgic for places I'd never been. Lonely for people I'd never met.

Then I discovered that a professor from Queen's University was offering an informal literature course. I enrolled and met David Helwig. The first night ten inmates shuffled into the prison school room, and a rope-thin, bearded man with glasses handed out mimeographed copies of the lyrics to the Beatles' song, "Lucy in the Sky With Diamonds." He claimed it was a poem and then stunned us all by singing the words in a rich baritone voice.

We laughed. He smiled. We were hooked. For the next year he appeared one night a week and we discussed the book he had assigned us the week before. One evening he made the foolish mistake of asking if any of us wrote. I hauled in a cardboard box of stories the next week but he wasn't fazed. It took him a month to get through the stuff and he picked out one story.

"This is pretty good," he said. "But why don't you write in your own voice?"

"What do you mean?" I asked.

"In class you tell stories," he said. "They just flow naturally. Why don't you try writing that way?"

What a simple idea.

But then I was moved to Warkworth, a brand new prison a hundred miles away. I was assigned to work as a clerk in the stores area where all the incoming building and maintenance material was inventoried and stored. I had taught myself to type with one finger so this qualified me to be the inmate clerk.

I wrote to David Helwig and sent him the poems I had begun to write. He was always generous with his responses. He passed on several of the poems to *Quarry* magazine and the editor agreed to publish them. I decided to take a correspondence course in creative writing offered by the provincial government.

The prison authorities tried to discourage me, suggesting I upgrade my formal education to at least grade ten. But I insisted on the writing course.

My clerical job only took an hour a day so I had plenty of time to write stories for the course. The first one was called "Bread and Jam." The marker gave me a B+ and raved about the story. My next assignment was to do a "personal experience story," but in fictional form.

I decided to follow David Helwig's advice and write the story as though I was telling it to a friend over a cup of coffee. I called it, "If You Hum Me a Few Bars I Might Remember The Tune."

The response I received was scathing. Under the title was a large zero with a line drawn through it. This was followed by a sarcastic note from the marker saying that no one would read a story with a title like that. Titles had to be short and snappy. But he had read the story and frankly…it was about a part of life that he, and most other people, would prefer to know nothing about. The story, he suggested, was obscene.

All prison mail in those days was censored. Even correspondence lessons. I was called in to see the warden who told me that my writing must cease. I argued that writing was my hobby. Inmates were allowed to do petit point, make leather belts and handbags. Some men painted or did line drawings.

"No!" the warden declared. He held up a photocopy of the marker's letter and smiled.

So I wrote the solicitor general's office in protest. I sent a copy of the offending story and asked for official permission to pursue my hobby of writing. The guy in charge of the department was Pierre Trudeau. I never heard from him directly but one of the bureaucrats replied that I had permission as long as I didn't write about prison life. Or crime. He suggested I write about pleasant topics.

David Helwig suggested in his letters that I try reading some Canadian literature. I didn't know there was any. So I went to the prison library. The librarian was Mr. Julian, a peculiar Englishman with a moustache that danced when he talked. He was delighted. His library was rarely used and he appreciated my business. He found me a copy of Timothy Findley's *The Last of The Crazy People*. A wonderful book. Thank God it was my introduction to Canadian writing, because the next novel he gave me was by Frederick Phillip Grove. I thought I'd die before I'd trudged my way through its pages. Then Sinclair Ross. Adele Wiseman's *The Sacrifice*. Good stuff but tough and hard to digest, sort of like the boiled meat they served in the cafeteria.

I had stopped writing stories. Sure, I'd won a battle with the prison administration, but between them and my correspondence course marker, whatever flicker of confidence I had in my ability was snuffed out. I still wrote poems and sent them to David. The voice in his letters was warm and encouraging but it was a long way off.

Then one day as I entered the library, Mr. Julian ran up to me with a hardcover book in his hand.

"Just came in," he said. "She lives in England but she's Canadian. Some critics are saying she's the best we've got."

The book was called *A Jest of God*. It was by Margaret Laurence. I started to read it after supper that evening. Within pages I felt like I had fallen into a volcano of my own festering dreams. The voice of Rachel Cameron was so real to me, it was as though the writer had entered my soul with a tape recorder and listened in as I battled to get through another day, pretending to be sane. But this was a story about a woman. An unfulfilled spinster who worried and fretted over buying herself new underwear. I was a bank robber, doing twelve and a half years. People got in my way, I shot them. In the joint I was perceived as tough. Solid. A loner.

But something inside me melted as I turned the pages and followed Rachel's tentative, uneasy voice along the path of her life. I wept when, moments after making love with Nick, she learns he is married and has children. But she accepts the situation. As though her life is controlled by fate.

"In my bedroom, I undress in darkness. I lie down quietly, and place my hands on my thighs, and now I don't remember and won't remember anything except how it was tonight. All I will ever remember is that he arched over me like the sun. I won't remember anything else. Nothing.

It does not make any difference, his being married. It isn't as though I ever thought it would come to anything. The idea hardly crossed my mind. Everything is just the same as it was. I still would have done the same, even if I'd known. I'm not so stupid as to imagine these chance encounters ever lead to anything permanent.

Except that all my life seems a chance encounter, and everything that happens to me is permanent. That isn't a clever way to be."

No, I thought as I read, no Rachel Cameron, it is not a clever way to be. I asked myself, am I like that too? Is that why the voice inhabits me so strongly?

Too soon it ended.

"I will be different. I will remain the same. I will still go parchment-faced with embarrassment, and clench my pencil between fingers like pencils. I will quite frequently push the doors marked *Pull* and pull the ones marked *Push*. I will be lonely, almost certainly. I will get annoyed at my sister. Her children will call me Aunt Rachel, and I will resent it and find then that I've grown attached to them after all. I will walk by myself on the shore of the sea and look at the freegulls flying. I will grow too orderly, plumping up the chesterfield cushions just-so before I go to bed. I will rage in my insomnia like a prophetess. I will take care to remember a vitamin pill each morning with my breakfast. I will be afraid. Sometimes I will feel light-hearted, sometimes light-headed. I may sing aloud, even in the dark. I will ask myself if I am going mad, but if I do, I won't know it.

God's mercy on reluctant jesters. God's grace on fools. God's pity on God."

I have never felt more alone, more vulnerable and yet somehow more brave than I did when I finished reading the last line. The voice inside of me, the voice that had comforted me, cajoled, and tempted me all these years, beckoned me to sing.

I took up pad and pencil and began to write furiously. I wrote all night and as dawn broke, I stood on my bed and looked out the cement slats of my prison window watching the starlings, daydreaming of some day meeting this writer named Margaret Laurence. This writer I had spent the night imitating. I laughed aloud and felt both joy and fear. The story I had written was about Louise. Not the teenage girl I knew in the orphanage but the person I now imagined her to be. It didn't matter if it was a good story. Margaret Laurence had led me to my own history, nudged me into risking the declaration of a love that had always embarrassed me.

I typed my story, "Ring Around A Rosie," the next day, sent it off to a contest sponsored by the Prison Arts Foundation and forgot about it. Several months later I was called up to the Protestant chaplain's office.

"You've been paroled," he beamed.

"I didn't apply," I said.

"I did, on your behalf," he said.

"Where will I go?" I hadn't meant to say that out loud.

"I called your wife this morning," he said. "She's expecting you."

My wife? Sure, I was married. But I was just a kid. I'd only seen her once in all my years inside. She had brought my daughters to visit. One still an infant in her arms and the other a toddler. They didn't know me, I didn't know them. What would we do, or say?

"Don," the chaplain said, "I've put a lot of trust in you. There's one thing I'd ask of you...you can do it as a sort of thank you."

Thank him! For what?

"Sure," I said.

"Once you're settled in a couple of weeks or so.... I want you to run an ad in the paper...an ad to find your father, Don. I don't believe he's dead. And your mother. Look for them both. I promise you if you can find either one, or both, you'll never see the inside of these walls again. Resolve the past and the future will take care of itself."

I wanted to laugh but I realized he was solemn and sincere. One snicker and it was goodbye parole. I nodded, shook his hand, and left.

Two days later I was on the bus to Toronto.

Every ex-con has his own release fantasy. I jumped in a cab and had the driver take me to Shopsy's Deli on Spadina Avenue. I ordered six lean pastrami sandwiches. Then I picked up a bottle of champagne and a quart of rye. One last stop at a florist for some flowers and I headed home.

Home.

Meeting Margaret

On July 20, 1969, Neil Armstrong walked on the moon. On that night Nathan Phillips Square, in front of Toronto's City Hall, was jammed with cheering, screaming people, celebrating and embracing. It was as though each of them believed that the faltering steps of the astronaut on another planet meant that they too could do anything. It was a hopeful gathering. Hundreds of transistor radios were tuned to Armstrong's crackling voice as he spoke with concise awe: "It's beautiful!"

The crowd roared with optimistic energy. Some threshold had been crossed. I doubt that anyone could explain why they were excited but it was like New Year's Eve, when the old garments of sin and error are shed and in new, clean cloaks, we reclaim our innocence.

I was there too. It was my third night out of prison. My wife and I had run out of things to say. While I'd been away, another man had served as husband and father. He was anxious to return to his family, his home.

Suddenly the radios in the square began to blast out music. By some strange psychic agreement everyone tuned into the same station. The dancing began. A woman grabbed me around the neck and waist and propelled me into the dance. Old men raised grandchildren into their arms and waltzed around the square to the Rolling Stones' wailing of "I Can't Get No Satisfaction." One middle-aged male couple tangoed. Five women in their thirties formed a circle and jitterbugged, the choreography learned in their recreation rooms fifteen years before now recalled flawlessly. Couples of all ages clung to each other, arms draped over shoulders, mouths molded together.

From somewhere cases of beer appeared and bottles of wine. All of it was passed around and shared generously. I felt happy enough to weep. I missed the prison community. It had been like the orphanage.

Terrible places with rigid rules that conspired to control your every move, but at least you belonged. You knew who you were.

But that warm July night in Nathan Phillips Square I felt entitled to be among the crowd. I felt a part of the mass human affection and sensed that if I had the will, I could become a real person. I'd never walk on the moon but I had dreams. All I needed to do was put them into action.

I stayed until four in the morning. When I got back to the apartment, my wife Stella was furious.

"You haven't changed at all," she said angrily. "I've been worried sick. What if your parole officer had called? You're supposed to be in by twelve. And you've been drinking. They could revoke your parole for that."

She was right.

"One more day," I said. "Just one day. I've got a few things to do and then I'll leave."

I walked out to the balcony and looked out over the brightly lit city. I wasn't drunk. I just felt good to be alive. Free and full of ideas. Scared that I would fail in those ideas. But excited too. Stella followed me out. I lit a cigarette and leaned against the railing.

"We had some good times," she said, taking my hand.

"Yes," I said. "And I'm sorry for all the grief I've brought you too."

She laughed in the dark.

"I remember when they sent me back to Smiths Falls from the girls' residence. When I got pregnant. Remember?"

"Sure."

"And you took a train up there and demanded to see the director of the hospital."

"They made me wait two days."

"But you waited. Twice a day you came back. Everyone knew. Even the nurses were talking about it. Who was this kid...you were just seventeen...who was he to think he could see the director?"

"But you should never have been there in the first place. It was a hospital for retarded people. It was just bureaucratic bungling that got you there. They had no right to keep you. You were over twenty-one. They just didn't want to admit their screw-up."

"Then finally he saw us both. He had my file on his desk, all spread out and was shaking his head at what it said."

"Yeah, he turned out to be okay. What I remember most about him was how he said he was sorry. It wasn't even his fault. He was new in the job. He took your file and tossed it in the wastepaper basket. He shook our hands, wished us luck and we left."

She laughed. It was a gentle but hurried sound, like the gurgle of a river flowing to some far-off destination.

"He gave us fifty dollars," she said. "Remember. To help us on our way."

"Yeah, he did."

We were quiet for a moment or two.

"On the television, it said there was dancing at City Hall," she said. "You were there, weren't you?"

"Yes."

"I knew it. Did you dance?"

"Yeah, but I don't know who with."

"I wish I'd been there. I'll never forget the night we met. Somebody got the bright idea that the guys at the boys' residence where you lived should invite us girls to a Halloween party."

"They served Freshie, and had Cheez Whiz on Ritz crackers."

"But the minute I saw you," she recalled, "I knew you'd ask me to dance."

"I've always had a thing for older women."

She punched my shoulder with her fist, playfully. And laughed again, as she reminisced.

"We won the jive contest. Two free passes to a movie."

"And the rest, as they say, is history."

Her nostalgia reminded me of guys in prison. Always talking about the past but making it over. Leaving out the bad parts.

"What will you do," she asked, "when you leave here?"

"If you'll let me, I'll take the typewriter you bought, get myself a room and write."

She laughed again, loudly, and nervously.

"I only paid five dollars for that thing at a church basement sale. I kept asking the guy if it was a real typewriter because it seemed so cheap. Have you tried it yet? I mean, maybe it doesn't even work."

"It works fine, Stella. I cleaned the keys yesterday. The ribbon's a bit old but I'll get a new one. It was good of you to get it for me. When I walked in the door and saw it, I felt like... I don't know. Like you had faith in me. It lifted my spirits. But you've always done that."

"I'm glad," she said. "I do have faith in you... ."

Suddenly I realized we were saying goodbye. We might see each other again. I was the girls' father. I would come and visit them and Stella and I would be polite. We would be pleasant with each other, but whatever intimacy we had shared was disappearing into the air like the smoke from my cigarette.

"You've been a good wife," I said.

"I wouldn't recommend you as husband material," she replied.

We both laughed. Then she yawned.

"I owe it to the kids to give them a stable life," she said. "Carmello's a good father to them. If it was just me... ."

"I understand."

Her hand squeezed mine in the dark.

"You wanna come to bed?" she asked.

I pulled my hand away and got out another cigarette.

"No," I said. "I think I'll wait and watch the sun come up."

"Yes," she said. "I understand. That sounds like a nice thing to do."

She went inside and I stood there for another hour, smoking cigarettes while waiting for the first glow of light, afraid of what I was losing, knowing if I dug in and fought, I might win my family back. But I also knew that my yearning to write would get buried in the debris of battle. I made a selfish decision. I had to write. It was the only thing that made me feel worthy of being alive. When I wrote I was real. Even if only for a moment.

At ten o'clock the next day I phoned the offices of *Saturday Night* magazine. A woman answered.

"I'd like to speak to the editor," I said. "Robert Fulford."

"Who are you?" she asked.

"A writer," I said.

"Oh." The cheerfulness in her voice dropped with a weary sag. "I'll see if he'll talk with you."

The line buzzed for a few seconds and then a nasal voice spoke.

"Bob Fulford here. Who am I speaking to?"

"Don Bailey," I said. "You don't know me but a couple of months ago you ran a prison article by Juan Butler."

"Yes," he said, "Nice piece. Well received."

"It was awful," I declared. "The guy didn't have a clue what he was writing about. Prison's not like that."

"I don't recognize your name," Fulford said. "Who do you write for?"

"You, if you let me," I said. "I just got out of prison a couple of days ago...I'd like to write about how it really is."

"And how's that?" he asked.

"Prison's about nostalgia," I said.

He laughed. It sounded skeptical.

"What about the gang rapes, the stabbings, all the corruption?" he demanded.

"Those things happen," I admitted, "but prisons are places of memories. Everyone adds his own threads until this fabric of nostalgia gets woven and it's like a shroud you'd put over somebody who's dead. But it's like a blanket, too, that you huddle under on those cold lonely nights."

There was silence on the line for a few seconds. Then I heard him clear his throat.

"Interesting," he said. "If you ever write it, I'd like to look at it."

He hung up. But I was elated. It was in the bag. I ran down to the drug store and bought a new typewriter ribbon, some carbon paper and the heaviest bond paper they had in stock. I rushed back to the apartment and began to work in the livingroom. I banged at the keys for hours and only stopped when the mail arrived. There were four letters for me.

The first was from David Helwig, welcoming me back to the land of freedom. He sent his phone number and told me to get in touch. The second letter was from the Prison Arts Foundation. I was afraid to open it. I had sent "Ring Around A Rosie" to their short story contest. It was probably a form letter thanking me for submitting. Or it might be a scathing criticism of the story. I left it and opened the letter postmarked Warkworth penitentiary. It was a two-line letter from Ed Laboucane, the joint gambler, hustler, and drug dealer, but somehow also my best friend. The letter read: "We haven't forgotten you. Don't forget us."

But I had forgotten. Already.

A group of us would sit around at night in the cell block, or over at the gym, and talk about getting out. Without admitting it out loud it was acknowledged that we were afraid of the world out there. We knew we needed something more than parole supervision to make it. All of us had seen the same guys return to the institution over and over again. Some didn't last a week outside. We had talked about forming an organization made up of ex-cons who would help each other. There were eight of us in the group and I was the first one out. It was up to me to get something started. The note made me angry. What was I supposed to do? Tomorrow I wouldn't even have a place to live. All that prison talk, it had just been a way to pass the time. Daydreaming out loud. I tossed the note aside and opened the letter from the Prison Arts Foundation.

As I pulled the letter from the envelope a cheque fell out. Fifty dollars. I'd won! Not second or third prize, but first. I was so stunned that I opened the next letter without reading the return address. It was from Jane Rule. She had been one of the judges in the contest, and in the warmest of phrasing she told me I was a writer, whether I knew it or not. She lived in Vancouver and offered to put me up if I needed a place to stay. She also suggested that I contact Robert Weaver at CBC radio, as he bought stories to be read on the air.

I was so excited I couldn't work. I didn't tell Stella my good news. Her decision had been made and I didn't want her to think I was trying to sway her my way. I left the house and walked the few blocks to the Riverdale zoo. I wandered among the cages marvelling at my good fortune but then feeling terrified that it was all a fluke. I wasn't really a writer. And what about Ed and the guys inside? The promises I'd made?

Weary from thinking and the carouselling of my emotions, I sat on a park bench for a smoke. I had to get back to the apartment and finish the article. For the moment, though, I lacked the will. The sun was too warm. My dreams were too vivid, too powerful to be smudged with reality. Then I noticed a guy sitting at the other end of the bench looking at me. At first glance he looked like a skid row resident. His black hair was long and bushy, and his beard was so thick it threatened to swallow his face. He was wearing heavy woolen pants too long for him and rolled at the cuffs, worn work boots, a T-shirt, and a suit jacket at least two sizes too large. He had an open book that he suddenly snapped shut.

"It's too beautiful a day to read theology, don't you think?" he said. "A day to smell the roses."

"I haven't read much theology," I said. "Just Martin Buber."

"*I and Thou*," he said, standing and putting out his hand. "Nourishment for the soul.... My name's Barry Morris."

I took his hand awkwardly. I didn't feel up to a wacko, even one who smiled so pleasantly and had eyes that could roast chestnuts.

"Don Bailey," I said.

"You live around here?" he asked.

I laughed. He waited patiently for me to explain.

"After tonight, I don't know where I'm living."

"Maybe I can help you out," he suggested. "You looking for a room?"

I hadn't thought about it. I didn't need much.

"Sure, just big enough for me to work in."

"Then I guess it depends on what you do.... I mean, if you train dancing elephants... ."

I laughed. This weird guy was funny.

"I write," I said.

"Well now, isn't that something...a writer. Maybe we can help each other."

He took out a small notebook and wrote his name and an address on a page, tore it off and handed it to me.

"Meet me here tomorrow," he said. "About eleven. Bring your stuff. I think I've got just the room for you."

He started to take off across the lawn at a brisk pace. I ran after him.

"What is this place? This address where I'm meeting you."

"297 Carlton Street," he said. "Just an old house a few blocks from here. The official name is the Toronto Christian Resource Centre, but there's no sign or anything."

"You mean it's a church?" I asked.

"They pay for it," he said. "All kinds of things happen there but I think what'll interest you the most is that we have writing workshops every Wednesday night."

He took off again.

"Are you a writer too?" I called after him.

"No," he yelled back. "Just a student."

"What kind?"

He stopped and walked back toward me, then spoke quietly.

"Theology," he said. "But I haven't decided if I want to be ordained. See you tomorrow."

This time he took off on the run.

I walked back to Stella's place and sat down at the old

Underwood. I discovered that journalism is different from fiction. I couldn't digress as much. I had to make certain points. It looked easy when I was being critical of someone else, but I learned the structure was different. Journalism was hard. It had to be credible in a different way. Several times during the night I gave up and went out to the balcony, smoked cigarettes and stared at the moon. I was convinced I'd never get it right. What did it matter anyway? This Fulford guy never expected me to show up. Maybe I should just stick to fiction. Why make a fool of myself? Winning the contest was probably insignificant. Half the guys in the joint were illiterate. I must have written a thousand letters for different guys to their girlfriends and wives, pretending I was them, and that they could write.

But my stubbornness kept me pecking at the keys. I went through all my carbon paper and over two hundred sheets of bond, but by the time the kids were heading off to school, I was finished. I put the clean copy of the article into a manila envelope, packed up my stuff, called a cab and waited.

"Did you say goodbye to the kids?" Stella asked.

"I figured I'd leave that to you," I said. "I mean I hardly even said hello to them. I imagine Carmello will be back with you tonight. They'll forget all about me in a day or two."

She looked worried.

"I wonder if that's true," she said.

"What, that they'll forget me...that Carmello will be back? What?"

"I just want to do the right thing for them," she insisted. "I'd like for us to get a divorce right away."

"No problem," I said. "They've got the new law now so that if you don't live together for a couple of years, you can get a divorce almost automatically."

"Except we slept together. That first night when you got home."

"Well, I'm not going to tell anybody. Consider it an act of charity. I mean it really wasn't lovemaking, or even sex. It was like you were defusing a bomb."

She laughed.

We were standing on the balcony watching the parking lot for the cab. When it arrived I grabbed my stuff and started to leave but Stella grabbed me.

"You'll let me know where you are...so I can tell the lawyer?"

"Sure," I said.

She pulled me closer and kissed me.

"Good luck," I called as I rushed out the door, wondering if the Underwood I was lugging would give me a hernia.

I had the taxi take me directly to the offices of *Saturday Night*. The receptionist was very cool. She saw a short skinny guy, huffing and puffing, holding a typewriter and an overnight bag, standing in front of her.

"You have an appointment with someone?" she asked.

"Robert Fulford," I wheezed, handing her the manila envelope.

"He's expecting you?" Her eyebrows danced in disbelief.

"I spoke to him yesterday about this article. Said I'd be bringing it in."

"Well, leave it with me and I'll see that he gets it."

Was she crazy? I was loopy from lack of sleep, but not stupid. No way was I leaving without seeing the man. In prison, lower echelon bureaucrats were always trying to give a guy the fast shuffle. Take his request, promise to deliver it and get him out the door. Then into the wastepaper basket with the request. Cut down on the paper work. But this was the real world. Same system but institutional indignation wasn't going to win me anything. I figured dumb innocence might be the winning bingo number.

"It's okay," I said. "I'll just sit over there and wait."

"For what?" she asked.

"For him to read it," I replied, settling myself on the edge of a couch.

She wasn't happy with my move but she got up and stomped down the hallway with the envelope. In a few seconds I heard familiar nasal laughter coming from one of the offices. The receptionist returned and offered me coffee. I smiled and said no. One more cup of coffee and I'd throw up on the expensive rug. Instead I smoked another cigarette and sweated.

Suddenly he appeared behind the receptionist. A tall guy, going bald, with a bit of a paunch. He had his suit jacket off and the sleeves of his white shirt were rolled up, his collar was open and his tie loosened. He adjusted his dark glasses with one finger and then, giving me a dimpled grin, signaled with the same finger for me to follow.

In his office he held out his hand. The grip was limp and fleeting.

"Bob Fulford.... So you're Don Bailey...."

"Yes, sir."

He picked up the article and tapped the edges of the paper together so they were even.

"Charming piece," he said. "We'll run it. Like the title too. 'Nostalgia Just Isn't What it Used To Be.' Very nice."

I wanted to shout. This was big-time stuff. I had no idea what the circulation of the magazine was but they had to sell thousands of copies. Thousands and thousands. All those people would read what I'd written.

"That's great," I said. "How much...?"

"Ah, remuneration. Yes, well we pay two hundred for a piece like this. On publication. Let's see...."

He looked at a calendar chart on the wall.

"I'm going to schedule this for January."

January! That was almost six months away. I guess the disappointment was evident in my expression.

"Tell you what, though...did you really just get out of prison? What is it now, a week?"

"Five days," I said.

"And you just wrote this article after talking to me yesterday?"

I nodded and he leaned back in his chair and let loose his high-pitched laugh.

"I don't know if I should encourage you or call the guys with the white coats...."

"Encourage me," I said.

He smiled and nodded, and then there was a peculiar kind of sadness in his expression. Just for a second then it was gone. I thought of guys in the joint, how it was almost impossible to tell how they really felt about things. Except sometimes when I was sitting in a cell with one of them, writing a letter to the guy's wife that was a response to her Dear John letter. Sometimes the guy would be trying to find the words to tell his woman he loved her and the words wouldn't come. I'd suggest something. Maybe just a phrase, and the guy would start to cry. Big guys sobbing because of some words that maybe gave a shape to their feelings. Then the guy might get up and pound his fists against the walls, sometimes until the knuckles bled. To stop the flow of tears. One pain replacing another.

Strange. And for a second there Fulford reminded me of those guys. It didn't make any sense.

He picked up the phone.

"I'll call Madelaine. Her office is at the end of the hall. See her and she'll give you an advance of a hundred dollars. Give her an address so we know where to send the rest."

"Thanks," I said, standing up. "This means a lot to me. I mean, not just the money... ."

He waved me out the door, then called after me.

"You get any more ideas like this, you call me."

"Yes, sir."

An hour later I was sitting in the vestibule of 297 Carlton Street, waiting for Barry Morris. I'd been to the bank, opened an account and even though they were reluctant to give it to me, I had seventy-five bucks, cash in my pocket. Rich.

The place was weird, a huge old house, oak panelling on the walls, oak floors, even oak bannisters. Three stories high and on every level, something seemed to be happening. People were everywhere, most of them looking like refugees from skid row, nut houses, and various other kinds of institutions. So me, my overnight bag and the Underwood fit right in.

I was a bit shy at first and didn't venture beyond the front room where I asked for Barry. An old fellow in a long, heavy overcoat, wearing a bandanna around his head to keep his long hair out of his face, scowled at me and said:

"We're all waitin' on him."

I took an empty chair, put my stuff down and pulled out my smokes. Immediately everyone in the room came to life. It was worse than the joint. Within seconds an almost full pack had been reduced to two cigarettes. The guy beside me puffed away at the cigarette, sucking at it like he was drawing nutrition from it. Then halfway through he tossed it on the floor, leaped to his feet and stomped on it. He walked over to the radiator, genuflected toward it, and brought his forehead crashing down on the thing. No one seemed to take notice. Is this what the real world's come to, I wondered. Prison was full of wackos, oh yes, but they had some self-control, some had style, there were even those who had intelligence.

The old guy miraculously hadn't made his head bleed, but now he had his ear against the radiator and was speaking in a low whisper.

After a moment or two he came back and sat down again. He leaned over and began to speak at me, his voice quiet but urgent, his breath so rank, I'm sure it could have melted synthetic material.

"The spirits move through the water system," he said. "They demand homage. It pisses them off when we ignore them. They do all our dirty work, see?"

I nodded. He was big, and I didn't want to tangle with him. If he wanted to believe that rubber duckies floating in a bath tub formed a religious pageant, I was ready to be supportive.

Just then a tall, lantern-jawed guy entered the room with a broom. He walked over to the guy beside me, leaned down and spoke in a hoarse whisper. Then the thin Boris Karloff lookalike turned his attention to me.

"You here about the job?" he asked.

"Yes," I said, desperate to escape.

He pointed with his broom toward a hallway.

"Go down and talk to Anne," he instructed.

I went to pick up my stuff but he poked my arm with the broom.

"I'll keep an eye on it. Don't worry."

So I hustled down the hall which opened into two large rooms. The first was the office and reception area, and beyond it, I could see a kitchen. There was a young blond woman pounding on an Underwood, very similar to one I used in the joint when I was a clerk. I stopped in front of her and gave her my best smile. She ignored me.

"You Anne?" I asked.

"Yeah," she said, not looking at me, as if her life depended on getting that letter typed.

"My name's Don Bailey...." Nothing. "The guy with the broom said I should speak to you about the job."

"Gene?"

"I don't know his name. Tall, skinny, looks like he could work in monster movies."

Still typing. Can't catch her eye.

"That's Gene. He's the caretaker.... You a community worker?"

I didn't know what a community worker was. Maybe a burglar of some kind, who sticks to one neighbourhood. Working the same territory over and over again. Getting all the alarm clocks, transistor radios, maybe the odd colour T.V. A neighbourhood like this, the pickings would be slim. But that wasn't what she was talking about.

Why did I always think like a criminal? Simple. I'd never been much else.

"Actually, I'm a writer," I said. "I met this guy Barry Morris yesterday and he said I should meet him here."

She stopped and for the first time looked at me. She had one of those sharp-featured faces, high cheekbones, thin crooked nose, a mouth with the lips pulled against the teeth so it's impossible to know if she's going to kiss you or spit in your eye. And great eyes. Blue like mine but a lighter shade and seething with energy, battery-charged rage. My kind of woman, because I knew she was mad at men. And that was me. I knew all that in a second. I felt like someone was rubbing two sticks together inside me, trying to start a fire.

She stopped working.

"One of Barry's lost souls... ."

She stood up. Trim figure, taller than me by two or three inches.

"You want coffee?"

"Sure," I said, and followed her into the kitchen where she pointed to a pot of coffee and handed me a dirty cup. She poured herself one and then hiked one leg up on a chair, raising her skirt and giving me a view almost to the top of her thigh.

I felt hungry, more than horny. Like how I imagine a pitcher plant must feel in the middle of winter when there are no flies to catch and the thing is starving, ready to snap at the air. That's how this woman made me feel. It terrified me.

"So what makes you think you're a writer?" she asked.

"Well, I've published some stuff... ."

"Books!" Belligerent, challenging tone.

"No, but I just sold a piece to *Saturday Night* this morning."

"Really. What on?"

"Prison," I said, getting a little pushy myself.

"You some kind of expert?"

"I just got out a few days ago... . Did almost nine years solid." I was desperate to impress her but I could see my presentation was having no impact. She began to look beyond me toward the typewriter. Then Gene lurched into the room with his broom. His face was contorted into a grotesque shape and his tongue was hanging from his mouth. He stood twitching for a few seconds and then fell to the floor in convulsions.

"Get a spoon!" Anne yelled. She was already on the floor beside him holding down one of his thrashing arms. I grabbed the spoon and knelt beside her.

"Get it in his mouth! So he won't bite his tongue... ."

I did what she told me.

"Get his other arm!" she shouted. Just then Barry came running into the room. He plunked himself down on the big man's legs, reached over with his hand, grinned, and said:

"Hi Don, welcome to the Toronto Christian Resource Centre."

The epileptic seizure was over in just a few moments. The big man got to his feet slowly. Anne and Barry helped him to a chair.

"Gene, I've told you a million times, you've got to take your medication," Anne said sharply.

I stood there watching, feeling stunned. Nothing seemed to shake these people. They were like lifers in the joint who have twenty years in; they've seen it all. But it hadn't made them hard like it did the lifers. Somehow they'd managed to hang on to caring for all this human debris.

I had the horrifying realization that I was no more than human garbage. Sure I'd won a rinky-dink fiction contest, sold a story to a magazine. So what? I was still an ex-con with a million miles to go before I could claim membership in the straight world.

"You ready to go?" Barry asked.

"Sure, my stuff's in the front room."

The room was on Sackville Street, just two blocks from the Centre. On the way I told Barry I wanted to start some kind of organization to help other guys coming out of prison.

"Write down your ideas," he said. "I'll bring it up at a staff meeting and if people like it, maybe we can help you."

The room was on the third floor of a Victorian house. An Asian family lived there and only the teenage daughter spoke English. It cost eight bucks a week. I took it without even looking at it.

Barry helped me lug my stuff up the stairs. The room was large but because the peak of the roof dictated the shape of the walls, there wasn't a lot of walk-around room. But it did have a tiny little balcony that looked out on the street and for some reason that thrilled me.

There was a bed, a beat-up desk where I put my typewriter, a makeshift bookshelf that held a few pots and pans, even a couple of plates and cups. There was a hot plate to cook on but I had to go to the second floor washroom for water.

On the wall next to the bed someone had nailed up a foot-high picket fence. A crude drawing of a face was just above the fence, and the thickly scrawled words: Don't Fence Me In. On another wall was a painting of a man who looked like he was dancing, his arms open but empty. Music notes had been painted to give the impression of a band playing. There was a caption that read: To Know Me Is To Love Me.

Barry saw me looking at the crude art work. The back wall had a flock of birds in flight and just the word: Free.

"The person who lived here before you was a sailor. Polish. Jumped ship and asked for political asylum."

"Where's he now?"

"Couldn't take the strain, waiting," Barry said. "Government was taking forever to give him landed immigrant status. One night, he took off all his clothes and headed for the street. Cops picked him up and he's been locked up at Queen Street ever since. He got asylum."

"Springboard," I said.

"What?"

"That's what I want to call this ex-con thing. It's what you need before you get out, a springboard back into society."

"Catchy name," he said. "See you Wednesday night?"

"For what?"

"The writer's group. They meet at the house at seven. Anne runs it but she sure could use some help."

"I'll be there," I said.

Alone at last. Or again. Time to think. To dream. And write.

I filled pages with my ideas on Springboard. Wrote letters to David Helwig, Jane Rule and Ed in the joint. Finally I worked up the nerve to walk over to the CBC radio building and ask for Robert Weaver. To my surprise, the receptionist on the front desk said he'd see me immediately. She directed me to the third floor where I found him in a little cubbyhole of an office, surrounded by manuscripts.

He was in his late forties I'd guess, losing his hair, wore clear-rimmed glasses that he played with a lot, and had one of the kindest faces I've ever encountered, open, eager, like a child anticipating some new and wonderful gift.

"I read the 'Hum Me a Few Bars' story in *Quarry*," he said by way of greeting. "I'd be pleased to buy it. And to look at any more you have."

This was before I'd even sat down.

"Let's go across the street for coffee," he said, grabbing his pipe and pouch of tobacco.

I followed in a daze. CBC would pay two hundred and fifty dollars to broadcast my story. And I had two more with me. I would be elated if he only liked one of them. Both of them had been written in the joint. One was called "The Parking Lot Attendant." I thought it was a bit weak. But the other was called "The Brew." It was about a guy I'd met who was doing life for the murder of a cab driver in North Bay in the late fifties. He had been sentenced to hang but since he was only sixteen, the government commuted the sentence to life. When I'd met him he had served twelve years. His nickname was the Brewmaster because he spent every waking hour setting down home brews around the joint. More often than not he got caught, but what could the authorities do to him? Life is life. They couldn't give him any more time.

Near the end of my joint time I'd been sent to Smithfield, the government experimental farm where they tried to grow square tomatoes. Wayne, the brewmaster, had been there too. He laid down a massive brew in two large plastic garbage pails off in the woods. Fruit cocktail, cherry preserves, any kind of fruit he could find. And a batch of baker's yeast mixed in with pounds and pounds of sugar. He let it cook for a week and then we were all invited to partake.

We sneaked out of our trailers late one night and made our way through the forest to his stash with one flashlight. We brought along some dixie cups to drink the stuff. The first swallow made me gag. It was putrid. Awful. Fizzy, yeasty-tasting fruit juice. But we drank it. Quarts of it. And we raved about how good it was. Not because we were a bunch of drunks who'd drink anything. The guy was doing life and he hadn't caved into the system. Making the brew was his way of keeping his dignity. We had to go along with that.

I remember that as we made our way back to the trailers that night, all of us feeling more queasy than high, we stopped at the swimming hole, shed our clothes and dived in. We pretended we were drunk and did fancy dives from the makeshift springboard we'd made out of an old plank and a couple of truck springs. It was a night of peculiar joy.

Weaver was well known in the coffee shop. Within seconds the waitress had slid cups in front of us and was filling them.

"Helwig put me on to you," he said, filling his pipe. "He thinks you've really got something…and you have. Something…. Who else have you met?"

I found the question strange. Who was he talking about?

"Writers, I mean," he clarified.

"No one," I said. "I'd like to meet Margaret Laurence."

He laughed as he lit his pipe.

"She's a tough one to know. Brilliant writer. Keeps to herself though. Living in England. But I hear U of T has invited her to come as writer in residence…. Have you contacted a publisher?"

"No…. I don't have enough work."

"House of Anansi is looking for young writers, got Fetherling lined up. Should meet him. Very original. Doug Fetherling. And Cohen. Difficult personality. Good writer though. And of course Peggy. Dennis is editing her next book."

Who was he talking about?

I smiled as I realized that this tweedy-looking guy with everyone's favourite uncle smile was a gossip. It did not escape my attention that he himself wielded tremendous power in the literary world. He was executive producer of CBC's Anthology, a programme that broadcast short stories, poetry, essays and interviews with new and old important writers in the country. He was also editor of *Tamarack Review*, one of the most prestigious literary magazines in the country.

I told him my story of Fulford and *Saturday Night*. He loved it and roared with laughter.

"You and Garner would get along," he said. "That's his style. Just walk in and demand to see the top dog."

"Hugh Garner?" I asked.

"Yeah…he's started writing these damn mysteries. He's got to eat of course but I think I've got him talked into doing his biography. He's pretty much on the wagon these days."

He looked at his watch. He was a man filled with energy. Although fascinated, I was tired from just listening to him. He stood up and held out his hand.

"Call me in a week," he said. "I'll have the contract ready for the first story and we'll see about the others."

"I write poetry too," I said.

He cleared his throat and tapped his pipe into the ashtray.

"Actually David sent me a batch of your poems... . It's all a matter of taste, of course, but I prefer your fiction."

He patted me on the arm and was gone.

Wednesday night came and I attended the writing workshop at the Christian Resource Centre. I went because I wanted to see Anne again.

The gathering was bizarre. It took place on the second floor in a large room with a collection of old couches and chairs pushed together in a circle. There were ten of us, counting Anne. One white-haired old fellow, with a nicotine-stained beard, chain-smoked and read indignant letters he had written to the editors of newspapers, who had refused to publish them. A middle-aged, red-haired, freckled-faced carpenter read to us from a book he was writing on running and eating your way to good health. He was ten years ahead of his time. Ted Plantos was there, a poet who gave a reading of a poem that was a series of plaintive wails. It was powerful, and forlorn. It made me think of guys locked in their cells who finally crack when the burden of their sentence crushes them, and the future becomes a black hole.

Then someone about my age with long hair and a bushy moustache that turned down at the corners of his mouth, so that he appeared to be scowling, read a poem about the prairies. It was beautiful in a lonesome, longing kind of way that struck a chord of hunger, an appetite that you know can never be satisfied. His name was Dale Zieroth.

After the workshop a few of us went to the Winchester Hotel on Parliament Street to drink draft beer. I engineered it so I could sit next to Anne.

"So what did you think?" she asked.

"How come you didn't read anything?" I asked.

"I'm not really a writer... . I just go to facilitate."

"One thing you are," I said.

"What?"

"The woman of my dreams."

She gave me a terrified look, grabbed her coat and purse, and headed out the door.

"Whadja say to her?" Ted Plantos asked.

"A compliment, I thought."

He shook his shaggy head.

"You gotta go slow and easy if you want to make an impression there. She's from the suburbs. Different view of the world."

"Yeah, but she works in Cabbagetown."

"That's the key word, man. We is her work."

Barry came rushing up to the table, out of breath, behind schedule as usual. I pushed him over a draft beer and he downed half of it.

"I read your Springboard proposal," he said. "It'll be on the staff meeting agenda tomorrow. I think there's a good chance people will go for it."

What did that mean, I wondered. My eyes were on the doorway through which Anne had fled. Dale saw me looking, winked, raised his glass of beer and spoke with a mournful grin.

"Women and pain.... So tell us about Springboard."

So I told them my idea of recruiting nice middle-class people, probably more women than men, who would work as volunteers and help stabilize an inmate's family so he had a home to come to when he got out of prison. I talked about the volunteers providing a transportation service to the wives and girlfriends of men locked up, because getting to see a prisoner was one of the biggest problems. So many of the Ontario prisons were constructed as economic gifts to depressed areas that were often remote and hard to reach. No public transportation, and cab fare from the nearest centre was forty or fifty dollars.

The more I talked, the more possible, the more plausible my plan sounded. My own words convinced me that Springboard could become a reality. Full of pickled eggs and draft beer, I staggered home to my little room but instead of sleeping, I wrote what was to be the first in a series of St. Anne poems.

I kept writing the next day. Waited for Barry to show but he didn't. I had an appointment with my parole officer at the John Howard Society. I mentioned Springboard casually but couldn't sneak it past this guy. He suggested I get a job and then start the self help group. I agreed but then out on the street, I looked up the phone number of a guy Barry had mentioned: John Sewell. He was a lawyer who planned to run as alderman for the ward I lived in.

Sewell answered the phone himself and agreed to see me within the hour. Again I articulated the Springboard idea and it became clearer to me. Sewell said he'd serve on a board, do anything he could.

But I'd need money. Had I though of the Atkinson Foundation? What were they? Based at *The Toronto Star*. Okay, I'd get right on to them. In the meantime I'd work on Sewell's campaign. Knock on doors. Hand out campaign literature. I felt good when I left his office. Never once had he questioned my intentions or my sincerity.

I was learning something about how the system worked. You asked for something but you had to have something to trade, even if the other guy didn't ask for it. You offered it. Again, not a lot different than the joint. A favour for a favour.

I phoned Bob Weaver at the CBC and he told me he wanted to buy "The Brew." He wasn't too keen on the other story. Just what I thought. Still, another two hundred and fifty dollars. That would keep me going for a while.

I went to the writing group at the centre the following Wednesday. Anne left after I read my first St. Anne poem. Later in the hotel, both Ted and Dale tried to warn me off.

"She's going out with about four different guys," Ted said. "They're all doctors and lawyers."

"She's a tight ass," Dale said. "Find somebody who appreciates you."

They left early and I sat there by myself thinking about what Dale had said. He was right. Obviously I was attracted to a woman who did not want my attention. What kind of weird person was I to pursue someone I seemed to terrify?

Barry joined me at the table.

"Metson wants to see you," he said.

"Who?"

"Rev. John Metson. Director of the Christian Resource Centre. He's interested in Springboard. People have been calling, asking about you."

"People?"

"John Sewell, Dean of the Anglican Diocese, bunch of other clergy...you've been busy."

"I figured the more support I drummed up, the easier it'd be to get the thing off the ground."

"Good strategy, but you should see Metson. He's a political animal and could give you a lot of help. So tomorrow...at ten."

"Okay," I said.

Then he put his hand on my arm.

"Man to man, okay?"

"Sure," I said.

"This thing with Ann...let it go. She doesn't know what she wants. You're a guy fresh out of the joint. You'll just get hurt."

"Sure," I said.

John Metson showed up an hour and a half late for our meeting. I went into the kitchen several times and got myself coffee. Anne was typing away. On my third trip she stopped and glared at me.

"Was that poem you read last night supposed to be about me?"

"No," I answered honestly. "You were just the inspiration."

Then she started to cry. I began to apologize but had no idea what I done wrong.

"I'm sorry...."

She grabbed her purse and ran down the hall. I followed her and found myself facing a frowning, sharp-faced guy with glasses who was wearing a suit. His eyes followed Anne out the door.

"What happened?"

"I don't know. She asked about a poem I wrote. I answered her and she ran out the door."

"You're Bailey," he said.

"Yes."

"In here."

I followed him into his office. He closed the double sliding doors and sat behind his desk, studying me. I felt like a bacteria specimen being examined under a microscope. I wanted to squirm, get up and walk out.

"How serious are you about this Springboard thing?" he asked.

"Serious enough to have hung around here an hour and a half waiting for you," I said.

He smiled. He had a good smile. It warmed him up. Made him more human.

"Punctuality is one of my failings," he said.

"I noticed. Your time is valuable, but others', less so."

He didn't like that. I didn't care. We glared at each other. Then he smiled again.

"This is a big undertaking. My main concern is can you follow through."

"I don't start things unless I can finish them," I said.

There was a slight pause. More measuring. Then he got up from his desk, came around and took a chair next to me.

"Let's talk about what you need. But first...you'll be coming on as staff. Non-paid. But still staff. I have a cardinal rule. No fraternizing between staff. You understand?"

"Stay away from Anne?"

"Good."

So we talked. Laid out a plan. The guy was smart. Proposals had to be written, money raised. I'd be given a small office on the second floor. There was a typewriter I could use, and a phone. Volunteers had to be recruited and trained. The institutions would need to be contacted. If I wanted to have the organization directed by the inmates inside, I'd have to get permission to go in and hold meetings. He would open doors for me. I'd have to walk through them.

In my mail that day was a letter from Ed. I was glad he'd nudged me. Springboard was really going to happen. He'd be getting out in three months and I'd have someone to help me. My mail also included an invitation to something called "The Family Compact," a literary evening sponsored by John Robert Colombo. Doug Fetherling and Bill Howell were scheduled to read. It was free. I'd go. Why not? How did they get my name? I didn't have a clue.

There was a package from Jane Rule that I saved until last. In it was a signed copy of her book, *Desert of the Heart.* And a beautiful letter full of optimistic energy and sunny comfort. The letter ended with a P.S. that read: Margaret Laurence dropped me a note. Said she'd like to meet you. She's in Toronto. Contact her at either of these numbers.... .

It probably doesn't make sense but I was scared. Excited, sure, but afraid. Margaret Laurence was great! What could I say to her that wouldn't sound stunned? Dumb?

I went up the street to the Winchester. By now I'd discovered that besides the men's beverage room, the mixed beverage room and the lounge where you could dance to live country and western music on Thursday, Friday and Saturday nights, the hotel also had a little bar upstairs in the hotel called the Alpine Room. Great spot to hide out and think. It had a bar with cushioned stools. Nick, the Greek, with his slicked-down hair, poured and had a good intuitive sense when and when not to engage in conversation.

I sat there nursing a rye and water. Sort of laughing at myself. Here I was confident that I could somehow put together a self help group for inmates, hundreds, maybe even thousands of inmates, but I was terrified to phone a writer who said she wanted to meet me, in case I made a fool of myself.

As I pondered this madness, Anne suddenly appeared and slid on to the stool beside me. Nick came over and she waved him away.

"What do you want from me?" she asked.

"I don't know. Just to be with you. Find out who you are."

"Why?"

"Because a vision of you has taken root in my mind."

She frowned at me for a few seconds and then laughed.

"You even talk like a poet. What does that actually mean?"

I felt so relieved to hear her laugh that I joined in.

"It just means I can't shake you out of my head."

"I'm involved, you know. Almost engaged."

"I know. I'm not asking you to marry me. Just spend some time with me."

"You're dangerous," she said.

"What?"

"You are!"

I finished my drink and slid off the stool. Then I pulled out the Family Compact invitation and flashed it at her.

"I'm going home to clean up and then I'm going to this shindig. You act like you're interested in literary stuff. You're welcome to come...see if I bite. It's a large public gathering. Should be reasonably safe."

She took the invitation and studied it. Then handed it back to me.

"I'm working tonight. But thanks."

Before I could move she was off her stool and out the door. I sat down again.

"Pour me another, Nick," I said. "And explain to me about women. I'm stupid."

After another drink I went back to my room, had a bath in the mammoth tub on the second floor and changed my clothes. Waiting in front of the house, pacing up and down the sidewalk, was Anne.

"I've only been working at the centre for a couple of weeks," she told me on the streetcar. "I was in Europe for six weeks. In Paris I met a student painter from Hong Kong. It was so wonderful. We'd stay in bed all day drinking wine and making love...and at night he'd paint me. While I was asleep."

This woman is strange. No wonder everyone worries about her. She's kind of nuts.

"I didn't have a clue what I'd do when I got back. There was a guy in Germany. He wanted me to stay. Live with him. I almost did. He still writes me. My mother heard about this job...I didn't want to stay at home so I took it. But it's just temporary. I may go back to Europe."

"Where do you live?"

"On Winchester. Right across from the hotel. The big house next to Sam's Variety. I share a flat with another girl, Jenny Silcox. She's a community worker. I'd like to do that...or write. Maybe paint."

You better learn something about colour, I thought. She was wearing a green pleated skirt and an orange sweater. On top of the outfit she wore a white trench coat that was torn and stained. Even her lovely blonde hair was scraggly, needed a good shampoo, a trim and a lot of loving care from a brush. Is this the style with young people, the skid row, down-and-out look?

"My mother really wants me to get married," she said, "I'm going out with two lawyers. My family's known theirs for ages. Nice guys. One's already an assistant Crown prosecutor.... And there's this other guy from university.... He's in Ottawa now, working on his Master's. Political Science and computers.... I was going to go to Carleton, take my master's in Social Work, just so I could be close to him...but Brian, that's his name, he won't make a commitment.... Some guys, a lot of guys are like that...scared.... So I guess you can see, you're wasting your time."

The literary evening was held in a dark, smoky basement of a club down on Queen Street. The tall, thin man who took my invitation at the door introduced himself as Doug Fetherling. He was a very sweet, gentle man who stuttered a little when he got nervous. He took me around and introduced me to Dennis Lee, who invited me to submit some poetry to an anthology he was putting together for House of Anansi. I met Elizabeth Woods, Bill Howell, and even the great man himself, John Robert Colombo, a sly looking guy with a mischievous but cunning smile. He invited me to a party at his house that was taking place in several weeks. He explained that a celebrated Russian poet was to be the guest of honour and he was inviting the young, up-

and-coming poets of Toronto to come and meet this important writer.

Anne was impressed with all this. She spoke to Colombo as though they were old buddies.

"I just came back from Europe," she said. "I was doing some research for Doug Spettigue, tracking down some of Frederick Phillip Grove's papers."

Colombo beamed at her.

My mind began to drift, and I began to think about the rituals that took place when you arrived as a fish in the joint. The serious power freaks approached you like the three wise men bearing gifts. They promised to protect you, supply you with chocolate bars or chewing gum in return for the occasional blow job or anal sex. These guys needed sexual dominance to feel okay about themselves. They never perceived themselves as homosexual. In fact, they hated queers.

The queens, wearing grotesque makeup, made their pitches, licking their lips lasciviously. They twitched their hips and competed madly to have the largest entourage of young men in their stable. They were openly gay and the more suitors they had, I guess, the better they felt.

Then there were the solid guys. No sex for them. Just tough, close-mouthed, walk the yard for the rest of their lives kind of guys, but they were lonely for a partner. Someone who was in on a good beef, a bank robber or safe cracker, who, when he got pinched, took the fall himself. Didn't squeal on anyone even though everyone knew other people were involved. Solid. Someone you could talk a few years away with. Share some bullshit. Rationalize your life of crime and bestow their blessings on you. Make you feel okay about yourself even though sometimes you felt like a zero.

Lower down on the pecking order were the skinners, the walking wounded, the rounders, the junkies and the dealers. Everybody wanted something. I guess in the end what counted was that you had a visible position in the hierarchy. It was critical that you were somebody to somebody, that somebody cared who you were because they either feared you or they liked you.

My second day in Kingston a rounder I'd known in the Don Jail for a year approached me in the gym with six hard boiled eggs and a block of cheese. He told me to stash the stuff because there was going to be a riot later in the day. And he showed me how to wet my handkerchief and hold it over my nose and eyes when the tear gas came. His name was Pete. He only had one eye and most of the time he worked hotels in Europe, sneaking into rooms and stealing jewellery while the occupants were sunning themselves on the beaches. He was German. In Canada people left their valuables in hotel safes so he went into cheque writing. But his English wasn't the best. He looked a little strange with his glass eye. Wrong line of work. So he was doing five.

His gesture of kindness toward me was a signal. He knew I'd arrived with the newest batch of fish. He knew I was a loner. Like him. And loners have to stick together.

Anne and I listened to Gwendolyn MacEwen read her poetry and I looked around the room and wondered, what's the difference? Everybody here was jockeying for position. Just like the joint. Looking for allies. Some of them generous of spirit, others ready to skewer you out of the competition.

After an hour or so, Anne excused herself to make a phone call. She came back crying.

"John says he's going to fire me. I was supposed to be at a board meeting to take the minutes."

I dragged her out to the street and hailed a cab. In the back seat I put my arms around her and let her sob into my chest.

"Somebody'll have taken notes," I reassured her. "The meeting will still be going on and you'll stride in there, apologize for being late and take over from them. They'll be grateful. You'll be humble. This is the Christian Resource Centre. They'll forgive you."

"I'm such a screw up," she moaned.

"No," I said. "I'm the screw up. You're an amateur."

She stopped crying and smiled. I gave her my hanky to blow her nose and wipe her eyes. Hankies were a hangover from the joint but it did the job. She left the cab on the run.

I waited a week to call Margaret. I kept rehearsing the little speeches I'd make to her on the phone but they all sounded phony. So I just called her at the university. A secretary put me through.

"Hello," she said.

Shit. Should I call her Margaret? Mrs. Laurence? She was married, wasn't she? Or maybe Ms. Laurence. That was catching on.

"Ah...yeah, hi...ah...this is Don Bailey, Jane Rule...."

"How wonderful! You called me. I didn't think you were going to. Look, they've booked me wall-to-wall with people here every day.... Half of them are crazy and the rest are such delicate flowers. God, it's just exhausting."

"I guess," I said, although I didn't have an inkling of what it might be like to be writer-in-residence.

"So let's get together at my place. Supper. Tomorrow. Can you?"

"Well sure...I...."

"I'm sharing this house up in some God forsaken place. Lawrence and Eglinton. Lucky to get it, I suppose.... And a lovely young woman...she actually enjoys cooking. I don't mind. God knows I've cooked my share but I'm completely bushed when I leave here. She'll whip us up something you've never heard of. Something stuffed with something. But delicious.... Oh I'm so looking forward to meeting you.... Tomorrow then, at seven.... Did I give you the address?"

I spent the next day unable to work. I went to my office in the centre and made phone calls from lists of potential volunteers for Springboard. But I couldn't concentrate. I kept drifting off to daydream, imagining myself meeting Margaret and discovering that she thought I was someone else. I could see her shocked face clearly in my mind as she looked me up and down and railed at me: Imposter! Fraud! You're not the Don Bailey I was expecting!

I went down to the kitchen and poured myself coffee. Anne was working at her typewriter but I ignored her. I had enough problems. But she wandered into the kitchen and gave me a flirtatious grin. God, she could be...beguiling.

"You were right about the other night," she said. "All was forgiven."

"Good," I said.

"What's wrong?" she asked.

"Nothing."

She put her hand on my arm and fixed me with a look of concern. "Tell me," she said.

"I'm going to Margaret Laurence's house for supper tonight and I'm in a quandary about whether to take red or white wine...."

She chortled and sort of slapped me.

"I should be flattered but I keep telling you, you're wasting your time...John Kneale, he's one of the lawyers I told you about, is taking me to a reception of trade delegates tonight. And then a formal dinner at the Royal York. He's been accepted into the foreign service...."

For a second or two I had the urge to pitch her out the window. I was infatuated with a social snob. What an idiot I was.

"You think I'm making this up to impress you?" I demanded, dumping my coffee and preparing to leave. She was startled by my anger.

"Sure. I mean why would... ."

"Because I'm a writer. Just like her!"

"You probably badgered the poor woman. Just like you do me. You're hard to turn down... . I mean you push and push."

"I've barely spoken a word to you for a week. You made it clear I'd have to take a number and stand in line. I don't do that! I am drawn to you. Attracted to you, would like to weave you into the web of my dreams. Fondle your fair body. All those things, but no broad is going to turn me into an emotional swizzle stick!"

I said my little speech in a tightly controlled voice. I'd forgotten to breathe and found myself gasping for air at the end. Anne looked annoyed.

"I'm no broad!"

"That's right! Excuse me. You girls from the suburbs are a different breed. Don't fart or burp in public. Probably never shit either. In public or private."

I stomped out of the room and went back upstairs to my little office feeling like a jerk. My feelings for this woman were not healthy.

A few minutes later she poked her head through the door.

"Are you really going to Margaret Laurence's?" she asked.

"Yes," I said. "And she invited me."

"My major was English you know. I did a couple of Canadian literature courses and her novels were the only ones I really enjoyed."

"She's a wonderful writer," I said. "The best!"

"I'm not trying to start an argument with you," she said. "I agree. I'm impressed that she wants to meet you... . Take red and white. That way you can't go wrong."

"I will," I said stiffly.

"What time you going?" she asked.

"Seven," I said.

"Stop by my place at 5:30."

"Why?"

"I want to inspect," she said. "Make sure you look presentable. Check that you've got your fly up... ."

"I don't need a mother."

"There's usually a few beer around. Jenny, my roommate, knocks it back pretty good. I'm sure we can spare one."

The truth was I'd dropped into Frank's Haberdashery on Parliament Street earlier in the day and bought myself a new pair of cords, socks, underwear and a soft, yellow sweater to go over a light-blue shirt. I bathed carefully, shaved, played with my hair and finally left my room clutching an envelope holding the Rosie story.

I took Anne's advice and bought a bottle of German white wine and a bottle of French burgundy. Then I walked over to her place on Winchester. The door was answered by a slim, red-haired woman who hid her body under slacks and a sweater that were two sizes too large for her. But her eager, smiling face betrayed the energy of a curious, intelligent person. Her brown eyes beamed out the hopeful light of one seeking romance.

She held out her hand.

"I'm Jenny," she said. "You must be Don."

"Yeah."

"Welcome to the waiting room," she said, and headed up a flight of stairs. I followed.

"Anne's getting ready. Great trauma. John's due at 6:00 and she hasn't chosen what slip to wear yet."

We entered the second floor flat, and I found myself a chair among the Salvation Army furniture, while Jenny ducked into the kitchen. She returned with two beers, handed one to me and with the other, flopped herself on a mattress covered with a comforter.

"Anne says you're a writer."

"I write," I said, "but most of my time these days is taken up by trying to get this self help group started. It's for ex-cons...."

"Yeah, Barry told me about it, but just the bare bones.... What're you trying to do?"

I spent the next half hour explaining, enjoying the process because she seemed really interested and also because the more I spoke about it, the clearer the vision became. Time passed but Anne did not appear. She was heard from. Muttering, sometimes yelling, from the other room.

"Making oneself presentable for the opposite sex is a trying burden," Jenny remarked.

"Is that why you avoid it?" I asked and realized I'd said something stupid and insensitive.

But Jenny laughed.

"I'm a street worker. I'm working for John Sewell's organization TCUP. We're trying to stop the developers who want to build high rises south of Carlton Street. If they had their way, they'd block-bust every street, turn the single family homes into slum rooming houses, and then when the area is completely rundown, get permission to build another St. James Town."

I guess I looked clued out. I was.

"St. James Town," she said impatiently. "All those towers up on Wellesley. You know, over five thousand people live in that one square block. The highest density development in Canada."

"Is that bad?" I asked.

She laughed.

"You are a lamb, aren't you.... Yes, it's bad. Too many people all crowded together. They go nuts."

"Like prison," I said. "No space. No privacy. Always feeling like someone's sitting on your head."

"You got it," she said.

I could see into the kitchen. It was after six. I began to get restless.

"I better go," I said.

Jenny finished her beer and took my empty bottle. She smiled in delight.

"Anne!" she yelled. "Don's leaving... ."

Anne came running into the room in a bathrobe. Her hair was wrapped in a towel. She looked a long way from being ready but her expression was annoyed.

"I wanted to talk with you before you went," she said.

"Going to give me instructions on how to behave?" I said. "Or do you have an etiquette brochure?"

She pouted for a second and then smiled.

"You look nice," she said.

Suddenly the bell rang downstairs. Jenny started for the door.

"That'll be your date!" she yelled over her shoulder.

"Get him a beer and ask him to wait," Anne called after her.

Then for no reason I could fathom she grabbed me, hauled me to her, and for an instant her lips crushed against mine. Then she released me.

"Good luck," she whispered. She ducked back into the bedroom just as Jenny entered with a tall, trim, good-looking guy who held his hand out, smiled gracefully and announced: "I'm John Kneale. Jenny tells me you're working with ex-cons. Like to talk to you about it sometime... ."

"Sure," I said, flashed Jenny a smile of gratitude and got my buns out of there. I didn't understand these straight people at all. Was this guy stupid? He was a lawyer. He must have had some idea that I was interested in his woman friend. Didn't straight guys get jealous? Very confusing.

I took the subway up to Eglinton, and then a bus to Lawrence Avenue. It was just a short walk to the address Margaret had given me. The kiss from Anne had had a good effect. I was in a state of shock. It's corny to talk about how the touch of another person can make you tingle but I felt like a walking gong that had been struck by a mallet wielded by a giant.

I arrived at Margaret's door and rang the bell. It was answered by a beautiful young woman wearing a clinging silk dress that appeared to have taken dance lessons.

"I'm Eleanor," she whispered. "Margaret's in her study. Come with me."

I followed her up a set of stairs and watched the dress do the fandango. She stopped in front of an open door and made a sweeping gesture with her arm for me to enter. I did.

Margaret came to her feet instantly. She had been sitting at a desk piled high with manuscripts. She grabbed my hand and shook it. I mean pumped it up and down, so the procedure was aerobic. Then, still hanging on to my hand, she directed me, nudged me actually, into the chair next to her desk.

"Don Bailey! What a treat to meet you."

"I'm...honoured" I said. "I can't tell you... ."

"Can the honour bullshit... . We're just two writers, lucky to meet each other. All day I get these people who parade through my office. They want to be writers...bless their souls, the poor buggers. But they ain't. And I doubt that any of them'll even get close."

She was still standing. Still holding my hand. The smile that broadened her face was gone now, replaced by a fierce, intense look that scrunched up her facial features. She let go of my hand and picked up her glasses, dark-rimmed, thick-lensed glasses that made her look severe.

"Why not?" I asked. "I mean, they come to you. They must be serious."

She plopped herself into her swivel chair and gave a throaty laugh.

"There's a big difference between wanting to be a writer and being one... ."

"Sure," I said. "A lot of practice. Hell, I must have written two hundred stories before I wrote one that was any good. Most of it was drivel."

"Damn right," she said. "It's hard work, but more than that... ."

I waited for the rest but instead she opened a deep drawer in her desk and hauled out a bottle of scotch and a quart of rye.

"I hope you're a rye drinker," she said. "The scotch is for me."

I nodded dumbly as she took a Kleenex to a glass on her desk, wiped it and handed it to me. She poured herself a hefty drink into the other glass and added a bit of water from a plastic juice container. She motioned to me to help myself while she took a long pull of her drink and then lit a cigarette. I noticed the ashtray was overflowing with long butts. While I poured a modest amount of rye into the glass, which caused her to raise her eyebrows, she talked.

"You known how I spotted you as a writer...?"

I shook my head no, as I took my first burning swallow.

"Risk! I read 'Hum Me a Few Bars'... and I said, here's a guy who takes risks.... He writes from his gut... and that's what it's all about. Then I wrote Jane and she told me you were a bank robber. I laughed like hell. But it makes sense.... The two can't be much different... in the risk department."

I handed her the envelope.

"It's a story I wrote in the joint," I said. "The same night I finished *A Jest of God*...I was so...taken with the book. It was like my head, my heart, came unglued. I felt like I was spinning...and it was wonderful. So I sat down and wrote this.... I did it in about four hours. It just came rushing out."

She peered at me through her thick lenses, waiting for me, I suppose, to make some point. I felt like a nut case. She took a large swallow of her drink and pulled the story from the envelope.

" 'Ring Around a Rosie,' " she said, and smiled. "I like that."

"I should have known that you get inundated with stuff to read. I

just thought.... Well, maybe sometime you'll have a chance to look
at it.... I wrote it because of you...for you in a way. I don't know. It's
hard to explain."

She took another deep gulp of her drink, lit a new cigarette from
the old and put the story down. She reached out and took my hand
and squeezed it firmly. She emitted a short and what seemed like an
anguished chortle.

"Listen kiddo," she said. "You don't have to explain anything to
me.... We're in the same tribe."

There was something native about Margaret's face. The high
cheekbones. The way her eyes really looked into you as though
searching out your spirit. But I knew she was of Scottish ancestry.
From Neepawa, Manitoba. A prairie woman. Used to looking across
vast spaces and spotting the smallest detail on the horizon.

"Go down and help Eleanor set the table or something," she said,
letting go of my hand. "Pour yourself a drink.... And don't be so
stingy. I want to read this."

"Right now.... Listen, it's yours to keep. I didn't mean for you to
read it now."

"Scared," she teased, giving me a wicked grin.

"Yes," I said.

"Well, it's a condition you gotta get used to. Quick, make a drink
and go."

I did as she instructed and went downstairs, opened the wine and
listened to Eleanor talk about the messy divorce she was hiding out
from. It was a long, agonizing twenty minutes before Margaret
appeared.

She had the story in her hand and there were tears in her eyes.
Eleanor appeared with a box of Kleenex. Margaret took off her
glasses, wiped her eyes and blew her nose, noisily.

She put her arms around me and embraced me fiercely. A bear hug
from a strong-armed woman, her legs solidly grounded, squeezing me
with a passion that filled me with warmth.

"Thank you," she said when she released me.

I was astonished.

"You liked it...?"

"Yes," she said. "Where have you sent it?"

"Nowhere," I said.

"Try *Tamarack*," she said, "Or *West Coast Review*. *The New*

Yorker, even! It's a damn good story. Unusual. Funny and sad. Get it out the door so it can make you a buck."

"I don't want to publish it yet," I blurted out.

Margaret laughed deeply from her chest.

"A working writer can't afford to be sentimental," she said. "Thank God I've got an agent to do all that. I hate the selling part. But in the early days I had to do it all myself."

"Weren't there things you didn't want to let go of? Things that were personal?"

"Sure! Everything I do is personal. I care about it all. When I'm writing about them, my people are as real as my kids...but the time comes for them to leave home. You gotta be practical!"

She turned to Eleanor, who was hovering. "It's time we fed this young man. Is the food ready?"

"Yes. And Don opened all the wine. All four bottles."

"Then let's get to it," Margaret said, pulling out a chair and indicating where I was to sit. "What're we having?" she shouted into the kitchen.

Eleanor appeared in the doorway of the kitchen with a platter of steaming food.

"Cabbage rolls," Eleanor announced.

Margaret and I started laughing. Eleanor served us and kept asking, "What's the joke...?"

"Me," said Margaret, "I told him what a great cook you are...."

Eleanor bowed her head modestly. It seemed a strange gesture from a woman in her late twenties or maybe early thirties. Perhaps it had something to do with the violent marriage she had endured.

"You are," Margaret insisted. "A wonderful cook even if that asshole you were married to spent more time decorating the walls with your food than eating it.... Anyway, the joke is that I told Don that we'd probably be dining on something stuffed with something. And we are...."

Eleanor smiled but it was a painful expression.

"Am I so predictable?" she inquired.

"You're a jewel of invention," Margaret said, and then looked at me for confirmation. My mouth was already stuffed with food so I nodded vigorously.

"It's delicious," I managed to sputter.

Eleanor smiled, for real this time. I knew whatever competitive tension there was between the two women had diminished, for the moment. Margaret stood up and held our her two hands to Eleanor and me. We both stood and in the next instant our fingers united us in a tight circle.

"A brief grace," Margaret said. "Thank you God…for these your gifts, friends, fellowship…and your greatest gift and mystery, this power to love…."

A moment's silence passed and then abruptly Margaret released us and sat down. She poured wine for us all and then looked over at me with a sly expression.

"So tell us, Don Bailey," she said.

"What?" I said.

She grinned over at Eleanor.

"Everything," she said.

Eleanor leaned forward and giggled.

"Yes," she said. "Everything."

I grinned back. I knew where I was. I felt that funny, strange tingle of being accepted. Of belonging. Of being home.

Ring Around A Rosie

(This is the story that Margaret read during our first meeting.)

Shape up, Roger. This is it. The train's stopped. People are leaving. Get your crummy cardboard suitcase and go. Go where? Never mind that crap, just follow the crowds. Just like prison; follow the crowd. But I'm out. This is it. Gotta move it.

Union Station. God, it looks like a flea circus. A busy little beehive. Buzz, buzz go the little people. Phone-booth. Where the...? Ah, there they are. Now to announce the great news to the waiting world. My arrival. Hah! Roger boy, just be cool, eh? None of that nasty bitterness. Be nice. Okay.

"Hello, is Steve there?"

"No, who's this?"

A good question, lady, but I haven't got all day to explain.

"Roger Blair."

Anyway, that's the label on the can. Lists of contents aren't required by the law so we won't bother with that.

"I thought it might be you," she says, and am I mistaken or is the voice suddenly very chilly? Don't jump to conclusions. What are you, paranoid or something? Maybe she's just defrosting the fridge.

"Yeah, it's me. Who's this, Joan?"

"Yes. What is it you wanted, Roger?"

After six years she's curious about what I want. What does she expect, a grocery list? Right now I think I want my dime back. Humour the girl. Be patient. Rome wasn't built in a day and all that. And anyway, what the hell do I want?

"Well really, Joan, I don't want anything except after all this time I thought it'd be nice to give Steve a call and see how he's making out. You know, stoke the fires of old friendship and all that." Chuckle.

62

Roger, for God's sake stick that chuckle somewhere. The broad'll think you're nuts.

"Roger, if there's anything I can do...well anything, I will. Anything Roger, only please leave Steve alone. You could come over now. There's no-one here. We could...talk about it."

My God, the woman's hysterical. Offering a starving man holy bread. She has no right. What did I do to deserve this? Am I some kind of disease she'd expose herself to, to save her precious husband? Call me cancer or maybe the plague that breeds in rats. Hey, this isn't fair! Anything! This broad is on tilt.

"He's restless," she says. "Doesn't seem satisfied with anything. Like before, Roger. We have a daughter now, ya know."

"Is that right? I didn't know that, Joan. Well look, I don't wanta cause trouble. The last thing in the world I wanta do. Look, just forget I called eh? Okay?"

"Yes, Roger, thanks. And I'm sorry."

"That's okay. Goodbye."

"Bye."

Just forget I called. No, that won't work. Better you should forget I ever lived. But I don't have to tell you about that, do I, Joan? You know all about self-preservation. So Steve's a father now. A daughter. A new weapon to defend the fortress with. Well, Joan, my lady of stone, I guess you forgot. I've got daughters myself. Somewhere. So what? They're weapons for somebody else's fortress now. Just be cool, Roger, and figure out what you're going to do. First thing is to get out of this phone-booth before somebody comes along and locks it. Go have a coffee. See, there's a coffee shop.

God I wish that waitress wouldn't bend over like that. Can see right to the top of her stockings. She's got a behind on her like a juicy pear. Didn't Eve use something like that to tempt old Adam? Something like that.

"Yes?" she asks, and gives the happy toothpaste smile.

"Coffee and...."

"Yes?"

"I don't know. I'm hungry for something different. Any suggestions?

"Whatever you want, sir."

That's the second time today. Do these broads know what they're doing to me?

"How about a nice juicy pear?"

"We have canned pears. No fresh ones. Will that be all right?"

Canned pears. That's funny. I should tell her, hers look pretty fresh to me.

"Sure, canned pears'll be great."

Ah, that tasted good. A little warm spot in the belly. Just what I needed. She's watching me. Do I eat funny? Well, when your only eating companion for six years has been a toilet bowl, you're bound to act a little strange. She's smiling. Maybe it's the clothes. They're not bad but I guess she can tell. I gotta get outa here. Don't panic. Pay the bill. Keep smiling. Leave.

"Hey mister!"

It's her. What the hell...? Ah, the bloody suitcase. My life's blood.

"Thanks."

Grab it and run like a purse-snatcher down the tunnel into the subway. Pay the fare. It's a lot more expensive than before. Before when? You know. On, yeah. Safe now sitting in the subway car, going someplace. Where? Christ, I don't know.

Dundas. I'll get off here and go up to the Derby for a beer. Man, look at all the people on the platform. Where are they all going? Flies circling the corpse. Aha, so you're going to get poetical now. Roger Blair, jailhouse poet at large. Wanted for lousy metaphors. I'm sweating. What am I so nervous about? They can't hurt me. They're only people. Listen to that guy jingle the change in his pocket, just like a new guard with his first set of keys. Jangle, jangle up and down the corridors. Drive a guy nuts. Aw, stop that crap. Grow up. It's all over. Live it up. Laugh it up. Ho, ho.

Up the stairs to the street. I know this corner. It's hardly changed. Same lousy signs everywhere. Pictures of bands in the windows that nobody's ever heard of. Everything suspended for the last six years, waiting for the conquering hero's return. Hah, Roger, you're a scream. Go get drunk, for God's sake.

Look at the beautiful sun. Grey. It's actually grey. The Toronto sun. The only city I've ever been to that has a grey sun. How many cities have you been to, Roger? A few: Montreal, Hamilton, Windsor. Not many I guess, but I know it's only Toronto that has a grey sun. You're sure about that, eh? Sure I'm sure and I love it. Hah? Look, you sonofabitch, stop bugging me. I thought I left you back in that cell. You've been bugging me the last six years. Leave me alone. You don't belong out here anyway. Sure I'm going to make it. Just you watch. I"m going for a beer.

Man it's dark in here. The waiter coming at me. What should I have?

"Ah, Old Vienna please."

"Yes sir."

God, boy, you handled that great. Stop sweating. Nothing to be nervous about. Everybody calling me sir. Gives me the creeps. Calm down. Nobody's watching you. Hardly anybody here to do any watching. Oh, oh, look at that at the bar. Gotta be a hooker. She's turning. A little rough in the face but still. Should I ask her over? Maybe she's just waiting for someone. She's saying something to the waiter. Keeps looking over here. What? Here he comes. Clomps down the beer. 75¢. Wow! It's an expensive world out here.

"The lady at the bar asked if you'd mind her sitting in your booth. The races are coming on in a minute and it's easier to see TV from here."

No, no, I don't mind."

Is the guy nuts? You just won the Irish sweepstakes. Would you mind signing your name to this slip of a hundred thou? Hate to bother you and all that. Would you mind? I guess not! Probably the broad's pimp. Here she comes. About 35, maybe 40. Hard to say in this dark. All smiles. A little chubby too. Still.... What? Well, she's company.

"Hi," she says. Sits down. Heavy makeup, but nice hair. Reddish brown. Soft looking.

"Hello," I say. A great line that. I've been waiting six years to use it.

"I hope you don't mind me sittin' here. I usually come in and sit here right away so I can see the TV later. Today I got shootin' the breeze with George, he's the bartender, and before I know it, it's race time and someone else is sittin' here: you. This is the best spot to see the TV from," she whispers like it's a big secret or a piece of important information. Maybe it is.

"I don't mind a bit. I'm gonna finish this beer and blow anyway."

Now why did I say that? She may look a little tired but you're no ball of fire yourself. Cultivate her. Nurture her into bloom like a delicate plant. What am I, a horticulturist? What was it that writer called it? The black rose. That's the only flower I'm interested in. You don't get a green thumb from fooling around with them. I'm 28 years old and for six years I haven't been laid. That's my problem. You sure, Roger? What about...you go screw?

"I don't want you to leave on accounta me," she says. Sounds serious, like she meant it. Careful.

"I've gotta find a room anyway. Just got into town."

"Yeah, I saw the little suitcase there. I thought maybe you were a salesman or something, ya know."

Or something? Well hell, lady, I am something. Stop laughing you. It's just a grammatical error. That's all.

"I'm just one of life's vagabonds." Oh, that's cute, Roger. You idiot.

"Yer what?" she says.

"Just a little joke. Actually I just got out of a mental hospital. Really."

"Suicide kick?"

See that, Roger, she knows all about you. Probably clairvoyant. You can't fool her. I'm not on a suicide kick, man. What're you talking about? I want to live. Yeah?

"No ma'am, mine was just a simple case of lost identity."

"Oh." She sounds disappointed. We can't all be winners, lady.

"I was in once myself," she says. "Started drinkin', ya know. Went at it steady for two weeks. Started thinkin' about everything, my daughter...gettin' depressed, ya know."

"You got a kid?"

"Yeah, she's in a foster home. I go see her sometimes, but it bugs me, her being there. Anyway I got real depressed this one time and cut myself. See."

Thick white ridges across each soft-looking wrist. God, lady, I wish you wouldn't show me your scars. I'm a believer. If ole Jesus himself came up to me and asked do you believe I'm the guy, I'd say sure. I'm no doubting Thomas. Who am I to question anybody and go feeling all over them for nail holes? You just don't want to get involved, Roger. Admit it. Okay, so I admit it. I've got my own scars. I don't want to bother anybody with them. Because you're ashamed of them. Aw, will you go to hell. Please.

She puts them away. Good. Beer's almost finished. I'll soon go. Where though? I had it all planned. Steve and me, a few drinks, call up a few broads. Well that's out, bright boy, so what now? Phone Mamma? Wouldn't she love that?

"Didya find it when you were there?"

"What's that?"

"The identity thing. You said you lost it. Is that like amnesia?"

"Sort of. I kept thinking I was somebody else, like God sometimes or Santa Claus in the middle of July. But I've got it all fixed up now. That's what I carry in the suitcase. Rolled up in my socks."

"Hey, ya know, you're all right kid."

You hear that Roger? The lady says you're all right. Yeah I hear. The waiter again.

"Another for you folks?"

I should go. You're weak, Roger. Yeah I know.

"Come on kid, have another. Watch the races with me. Ya might bring me luck."

"The same," I say and he shuffles off. Tired feet.

"I've got a real good thing today," she says. Squeezing my arm like I'm a rabbit's foot. Can hardly pay attention. Head's buzzing. After one beer. Not acclimatized. What's she saying?

"...he's in the fourth, a friend of mine told me to go heavy. I got him twenty across. Ships That Pass. He hasn't won this season. You follow the nags?"

"No," I say. An honest answer. Lots of guys in the joint did but safe old Roger is cautious of those pitfalls. Much too smart to gamble.

"He should go off at least ten to one. I'll tell ya what, if he wins I'll buy ya a steak supper. You look like ya could do with a good meal."

Sharp laughter, like somebody stabbed her in the gut. Is she drunk or what? Or nuts? Or just friendly? What have you got that she could possibly want? Skinny-bone wreck, two inches away from being a midget. Smashed-in face. Bad teeth. Hair falling out. Ho, you're in great shape. Just great. Yeah, well I've got one commodity money won't buy. Yeah? Yeah! Youth. I can't argue with that, Roger. Especially where your thinking is concerned. Yeah, well maybe. But my poems are young. Somebody told me that. Mercy, Roger, your jokes choke me. Shut up, you.

"Whaddaya say?"

"I was thinking of a poem."

She moves closer. Can feel her warm leg. She really is nice. She listens.

"My daughter's good at poems. She knows them all. Which one it is?"

"Number 69," I say.

That was nasty, Roger. Yeah, I know. Sorry. Always sorry.

"Which one?" she asks again. The patience of a saint.

"It goes: Funny little fella/wears his sister's clothes/don't know what to call him/but I think he's one of those."

A peal of laughter. She laughs like a milkweed pod breaking open. A cultured woman. Knows good art when she hears it. Calls the waiter.

"Tell him," she says.

Repeat it for him. Face remains stolid. Doesn't crack a smile. Years of practice. No appreciation of true poetry. Doesn't affect her, though, she moves closer, still laughing, almost in my lap. I've made a friend…maybe. Order more drinks and the waiter shuffles off.

Darrel Wells's voice from the ghost box over the bar.

"Good afternoon racing fans… ."

What about me, Darrel? I'm not a racing fan. I'm an ex-con looking for whatever it is that ex-cons look for on their first day out. Don't I get a good afternoon too? Oh God, can the melodramatics Roger. Be quiet and concentrate. She's talking to you.

"Mine doesn't come up till the next race."

You get any closer lady and mine'll be coming up through the table. Have to keep calm. Be cool.

"You bet them every day?" I ask.

"No, I couldn't afford that. Sometimes twice a week. Whenever I got the money, ya know."

"What do you work at?"

Now there's a stupid question Roger. Besides, it's none of your business.

"Oh, this and that, ya know?" A shrug of the shoulders. A perfect answer though. Uncommitted. What's life all about? A shrug of the shoulders. Oh, this and that. What are you doing today, Roger, and tomorrow? Oh, this and that. Yeah, I like that. It's got style.

Darrel Wells's voice again. The race is running. Not hers but she watches, transfixed. Pumps my arm as if I contained oil. All excited. Rosie used to be like that too. Remember? I don't want to. You're a big scaredy-cat Roger. Yeah I know.

Race over. Tensions released for a minute at least. Drinking in silence. Wonder what she's thinking. The next race? Her daughter who knows all the poems?

"Were you there long?" she says.

That's a touchy subject, lady.

"The hospital I mean.

"A few hundred years at least. I lost count."

She laughs again. Soft. It's nice to hear a woman's soft laugh after all the sneers in there. If music be the food of life, play on, play on, laugh on. Feed me that soft sound. Sign here for a Care package.

"It's boring, isn't it?" she says. "I remember when I was down on Queen Street ya know, there was this ole lady who never said a word to anybody but one time she blew her top and almost wrecked the whole TV room. Smashed everything, ya know."

"Yeah, it happened where I was too." It's true, only there it was men. Putting their heads through windows because a girlfriend writes a bad letter. Acres and acres of men growing wild as thistles and every so often some well-meaning soul harvests them. Bales them up in nice neat suits and sends them out the chute. But then it's too late. Their thorns scratch everyone and they have to be returned to the field. But not you, eh Roger? No, not me. My thorns are too blunt to hurt anyone.

"Did you get that suit from the hospital?" she asks.

Astute eyes this girl has.

"Yeah, does it show that much?"

"No, its not that bad ya know, it's just that ya need a few meals to fill it out."

Mother instinct rearing its ugly head, but still it's nice. Even the idea that someone cares. Comforting. You maudlin sonofabitch, Roger. Probably.

Darrel Wells droning on, announcing the second race.

"There's mine!" Excited again like a kid. "Look at 'im. He's going to win. I know it. I can just feel it."

"They're at the gate. They're at the post. They're off!"

My God, look at the dog-meat she picked. It's a wonder he didn't die of a heart attack coming out of the gate. So small and scrawny. Sitting second last. First turn: he's keeping up with the bunch. Moving a little on the outside. He's got a chance. Might make it.

Jockey's pounding the piss out of him. There's a hole. Get him through. Go! Go!

"He's coming! He's coming!" she yells.

In the stretch. He's really moving, right up front with the lead runner—ah, he blew it. Close though. Should be a photo. Still, second's not bad, considering.

She sighs.

"I thought for sure he'd win."

"I thought he did pretty good. He pays enough for place and show, you get your money back anyway."

She wears real disappointment. Still clinging to my arm. Like it was a log. We're past the rapids, lady. You're safe now. Swim on your own.

The announcer's voice again.

"The inquiry signal is up. A protest has been launched."

Don't understand. What's happening?

"Number six, the winner, is disqualified and placed last for interference. Number four is declared winner... ."

The rest is gibberish. Her scream. "He won! See, I tol ya!"

The prices flash up on the board.

"I've got to phone Harry," she says. Squeezes out of the booth and hurries away, her rear end flashing like a signal.

I should leave now. I never could stand a winner. Even by default. Wasn't that what Rosie said in her last letter, three, four years ago? "You're a loser Roger. The worst kind. You lose by default. You don't even show up to play the game." That's me all right, I guess, but since I lose by default I think I should have the right to hate those people who win by default.

Rosie was a winner. She beat polio, and the clanking leg-brace she dragged around was like a trophy. She could dazzle anybody. She even made mincemeat out of me and I'm supposed to be a tough guy. A bank robber. A piggy-bank robber. Jello-tough. All that's childish, Roger. Why? Because she loved you. You know she did. Well where the hell is she now? No answer eh? You were the one who insisted that she not wait. You Roger, the tough guy. Didn't need anybody. Yeah but did she have to listen? You called off the game. Not her, Roger boy, so stop crying. Go screw willya?

Here she comes, the winner. All smiles.

"Come on," she says.

"Where?"

"We're gonna collect the money. Come on." Tugs at me as if I were the main attraction at a taffy pull.

"Okay," I say. Why not? Grab the suitcase, 40 pounds of six years' poems. Can't lose that. Do your share for pollution, Roger, drop it in the nearest sewer. Get off my back you!

Outside the sun is still a grey globe. People are hurrying past, going to important places. And us too, going somewhere on this lovely spring day. So warm they wouldn't give me a topcoat when I left this morning. Just this morning. Already it seems eons ago. Just a few hours. When you're free time has no significance. Don't get profound, Roger. Follow the lady. Get in the cab.

"Over $200," she bubbles. "Imagine, I haven't won for months and then bang—just like that, over $200."

Hugs me. Woman smell. I see the mask of makeup. More like 40, but still... .

"I tole ya you'd bring me good luck."

"That's me, Roger Rabbitsfoot."

"Is that your name?"

"What, Roger Rabbitsfoot?"

"No silly." Giggling like a little girl. "I mean Roger. Is that your name?"

"Yeah, but you can call me Rabbitsfoot if you want. Some of my best friends do."

"I'm Elly," she says.

This is getting too involved. In a minute we'll be showing each other pictures of our daughters. Telling lies and not caring if the other believes them or not, just so somebody listens. I like you Elly, but somehow I thought there would be more today than just meeting you. Stop trying to live out your illusions, Roger. Just enjoy yourself. Yeah for once I think you might be right.

"Where did you get those godawful shoes?" she says.

What's wrong with them? They're new joint shoes. Rounded toes. Feel funny with the light socks I'm wearing for the first time in...well, six years. Do they look that bad? I guess so. They're different. Don't go with the brown suit.

"I guess they do look a little strange, eh?"

"You wanna believe it!" Pats my thigh. "That's okay Roger. We'll soon fix them up."

So now we're a team. Where are we? The taxi's stopped. Don't know. Things have changed.

"Just hang on a minute Rog. Won't be a minute," and she disappears into a variety store.

"Nice day for April, eh?" the driver says as if he wants confirmation of his own senses.

"Great," I agree. Not much sense in arguing a fact. Suddenly I've got this feeling that I'd like to tell him everything. Shake him up. Just say, look fella this nice April day you're babbling about is the first one I've spent outside prison walls in six years. How does that grab you? Looks like a nice guy. A family man, wearing the sweater his wife knitted him for Christmas two years ago. Give him something to tell her in bed tonight though: I had this guy in my cab today, just got out of prison... Mary, you listening?... just got out of prison after six years. Imagine that eh? She wouldn't be interested, Roger. Neither would he. Can't you get it through your moss-covered brain that nobody's interested? Nobody? Nobody.

Here she comes. Face all rosy. God, get that name out of here. Slides in beside me. Purring like a cat.

"I got it. Over to Bloor and Bathurst," she says.

"New shoes for you," she squeals and rubs my stomach as if expecting a genie to appear. Suddenly I'm kissing her. In broad daylight with people looking in the windows, but what does that matter? She pushes back at my mouth, holding, squeezing me. I'm alive at least.

"My, my, you're a frisky one," she says, letting go. There's no answer to that.

The cab stops and we're on the street again. She pays the driver. What's wrong with you, Roger? That's your job. You pay. Yeah, I know but it's been so long I forgot.

She leads me into the store like she was my mother. People looking at me. Don't start that crap about your mother, Roger. You never went shopping with her a day in your life. Yeah well maybe that's so but it's none of your business. Everything you do, Roger, is my business.

"Look Elly, this is nice of you but I've got money. I'll buy shoes later. In a few days when I get settled. I mean.... ."

She's hurt now. I've hurt her feelings. Look at her face. All crumpled. Rosie was like that too. Always doing things for me.

"I just want to," she says. So vulnerable looking. Soft. What's wrong with you Roger? Go along with the program. Why do you always have to rebel? Just for once accept things the way they come to you. Yeah, man.

"I'm sorry Elly. I'm just not used to presents. Go ahead, you choose. Which pair?"

"These are nice," she says. Smiling now. Face all shiny. Pointed toes. Polished leather. Clerk watching me as if I'm going to run away with them. Just your imagination, Roger. They feel good. Nice and light, comfortable.

"What do they look like, Elly?"

"Very nice," she says. Timid smile touched with shyness.

"Look in the mirror," the clerk says.

Yeah, that's you, Roger. Suit doesn't look too bad. That'll soon fill out. Fresh air, a little tan, I might look human. Yeah but will you act it?

"I really like them, Elly. You've got good taste."

That's it, Roger, be pleasant. Look at her face, beaming like a flashlight with a new set of batteries.

"We'll take them," she says. Pays the money. Brisk and efficient like a little housewife. Like Rosie. Happy in her work. Stop with the thumbscrews, Roger. Don't play masochist.

"Keep the old ones," I tell the clerk. "Burn them".

Outside again. Crowds of people squirming like maggots over a cadaver. What day is it? Friday, of course. People probably getting off work. Doing their shopping. It's getting late. Everybody will be locked up back there. So what Roger? Well...I don't know. I just thought of it. I've got an investment in the place. Forget it. Write it off as a loss. Yeah, I suppose.

Shoes feel great. They squeak. My shoes squeak. I could write a poem about how they squeak. Will you stop that, Roger? You make me sick.

"What're ya gonna do about a room?" she says. A slippery question.

"I don't know. Get a hotel room, I guess. Take a look around later and see what I can find."

"Why not get one at my place?"

In a minute she'll be doing my laundry. Don't be sarcastic, Roger.

She's just being nice. Yeah, I know.

"I haven't got too much money," I say, which is true, a little over $300.

"Oh, you can get a room there, a nice room, clean ya know, for sixteen a week. Why not come over and take a look anyway? I got a bottle of rye up in my place. We can have a drink and you can decide, ya know."

Standing on the streetcorner with this dumpy little woman, old enough almost to be my mother. What happened to all the great plans? I used to stay awake nights lying in that cell dreaming of this day. Is this it? 'Fraid so, Roger. If I go with her, I know what will happen. I don't want that. I mean, not just that. I want... Yes, what? More. Like waking up beside somebody you care about. Like love sort of. You're kidding, Roger. Why? Remember the Irishman, Roger? "How can we know the dancer from the dance?" Yes but.... You ask too much from the moment, Roger. Be patient. Who knows, there may be something in the dance. If not... . Yeah? Change partners. Find a new location. Yeah, I suppose.

"Are you all right?" she says. Worried frown in the heavy face. Anxious expression. Worried about me? Why?

"I'm okay." Timid smile again. Twenty years ago she must have been gorgeous. Still some of it there. Especially in the hair.

"Elly, why are you doing this? I mean it's great and everything but you don't even know me. I might be a nut or something!" Good line that, Roger. "I mean it doesn't make sense."

Big smile now. I never noticed the nice teeth before. Nice and small and white.

"You're my rabbit's foot, remember. Don't be so tense. Don't worry so much."

Takes my arm, leading me. I'm tired of being led. Jerk it away. Start running, legs pumping, bumping into people. Stop. Where are you going Roger? I don't know man. I wish Rosie was here. I wish....

But that's just it, Roger. She's not, and you are. Remember how she stuck to things? Diligently, you used to say. The most menial tasks. She even persevered with you. That's what you couldn't take about Rosie. You never stuck to anything, couldn't cope with someone who took delight even in sweeping floors. Admit it, Roger. Be honest. Maybe you're right, but so what? Rosie's not here. I'm alone. No, Roger, you're wrong. Rosie's still around. Even old Willy knew about that: "But if the while I think on thee, dear friend/All losses are restored and sorrows end."

See what I mean, Roger boy? You want me to go back? She needs a friend too, Roger. Stick it out. She asks nothing, like Rosie. Surely now, you can spare something.

She's waiting. Patience of a saint.

"See I told ya. I'm a nut."

"Me too. Let's go."

In a cab again going God knows where, but I feel better, more relaxed. Like after a rough game of handball. I remember that crazy game we used to play, where, in kindergarten? Standing in a circle holding hands, just like now, warm and protected and protecting too.

ring around a rosie
pocket full of posies
hush a, hush a,
we all fall down... .

And we did. We all fell down and it was such harmless fun because there was always somebody there to catch you, to pick you up. Always somebody. That's the boy, Roger. Now you're beginning to get the idea.

Common Ground: Divorce

During that first dinner it became clear to me that Margaret had an amazing capacity to take on other people's pain. As I told stories about my days in the orphanage, tales that I intended to be comic, or entertaining, she wept. The facade of humour I tried to create was penetrated by a will determined to find the wounds. I felt embarrassed. I had not set out to solicit sympathy. I wanted to entertain.

"You talk pretty good," she said, and then took a Kleenex from the box that Eleanor had set beside her. She blew her nose loudly. "But you shouldn't try to bullshit a bullshitter."

Eleanor laughed and began to clear the table.

I was shocked. Did Margaret think I was lying to her?

"What I told you is true," I said defensively.

"Of course it is!" she thundered, giving the table a hefty whack. "So why make a joke out of it?"

"It's easier," I responded.

She smiled, her dimples creasing deeply. She patted my hand and reached for the last of the red wine. I was amazed at her capacity for the grape. Eleanor and I had polished off the white wine and when that was gone, I'd had a couple of glasses of red. By my reckoning, Margaret had knocked off at least two bottles by herself. And she seemed fine. A little weepy perhaps, but clear and coherent in her thinking and speech. My mind was getting a little foggy so when Eleanor offered coffee I accepted gratefully.

"I'll be in my study," Margaret said, and rose from the table, taking the wine with her.

I went into the kitchen and offered to help Eleanor with the dishes.

"No," she said, "Margaret wants to talk with you. You go ahead. But be careful."

Careful? Of what?

I looked intently into Eleanor's very beautiful, child-like face for some hint of an explanation and was buffeted away by a coy, mysterious smile.

"Of what?" I asked.

She busied herself with tidying up. I couldn't see the expression on her face but I sensed anger.

"I love Margaret," she said. "But you must understand that she's like a vacuum cleaner. Everything you say...and do is sucked up."

So what? I thought. I sort of did that myself. Watching people all the time. Listening to what they said.

"She's working on a novel now...about a woman just like me. She's using me, picking me apart and sticking me back together again the way she wants. On the page."

She turned to me and I saw her eyes were frightened. I thought of a actress in a horror movie who is being stalked by a maniac with a long, sharp knife.

"Sometimes I catch her staring at me," Eleanor said. "I feel like she's siphoning off my spirit. And then she goes upstairs and works at her desk. Writing it all down."

I felt sorry for her but didn't know what to say that would be comforting. She solved the problem for both of us by giving me a quick, brisk hug. Then she poured my coffee and pointed to the stairs.

"Be careful," she said.

Strange woman.

Margaret was scribbling in an exercise book when I entered the study. She closed it quickly and held up her pencil.

"Number 4HB. Buy them by the gross. Same as these exercise books. Always buy the same kind. I like the blue covers best.... I'm sort of superstitious about them. Everything I've ever written has started out this way.... What about you?"

I noticed she had switched back to scotch.

"I type on to the page," I said. "In prison I wrote everything out in longhand first but now that I've got a typewriter, it's easier."

"I'm not much of a typist," she said, offering me a little rye for my coffee. "Fortunately someone always shows up and offers to do it for me.... And I never turn them down."

She seemed to find this funny and gave a short, snorting laugh.

" 'Course I have to do the first draft myself. No one could read my writing. And it takes me forever.... It's the hardest part, typing that damn draft, but when it's done I always feel the greatest satisfaction. I know the shape is there. Then it's up to the editor."

She lit a cigarette and for a moment looked like she had drifted into daydream and was seeing the end of her present project. I felt like an intruder and I guess she sensed my restlessness. She picked up her scotch and took a deep drink. The scotch was darkly coloured, hardly any water.

"Eleanor says you're working on a novel," I said.

"I've started...something," she said with a laugh. "I don't quite know what it is. Plus I'm working on a piece for the *Star Weekly*. A Christmas piece. I don't like writing to order but the dough's good. The heating system at Elm Cottage is just about ready to give up the ghost."

"Your home in England," I said.

"Yes, I can't wait to get back.... I miss my kids."

Suddenly she began to cry. I thought of my own children and envied her the obviously strong connection she had with hers.

After a few moments she removed her glasses and soaked up the tears with Kleenex.

"It's the damn divorce," she said. "It'll be final in a couple of months.... What a word, eh...final. How can a court say that all that went on between us is now done and over?"

Letting go, I thought. Shaking it off. The world is full of people, puttering along in their little boats, trolling the waters with their emotional grappling hooks. They hook you, haul you in, and then use you until they're finished. Then they abandon you. Toss you back into the cold water. You've got to be strong, tough. A curse on the fishers of men. Women. Who needs them?

Who was I ranting at? Margaret or me?

But I didn't dare say any of this. Her pain was too powerful to be deflected. Maybe that's why other people's pain engaged her attention. It was a way to avoid her own.

"Eleanor's a little strange," I said in an attempt to change the subject.

Margaret gave a hearty laugh.

"You and Jack would've gotten along," she said. "My husband.... Soon to be my ex.... No one could change a touchy subject better than Jack...or wait it out. Silence was golden. Just like my grandfather. Two of a kind. But you're right, Eleanor is peculiar. She's had a hard time of it."

"She thinks you're writing about her," I said.

"Of course she does. She won't allow herself to be photographed either. Just like the Indians. Afraid someone is going to steal her spirit. But I write fiction, not tragic documentaries. The sad thing is, her life isn't that interesting. She married a military guy. An officer. Rich, old family. Lived in a big limestone house of Lake Ontario just outside Kingston and she got to play house while he was away. But then he'd come home and whatever she'd done is his absence was never enough. Or good enough. And then she began to write. He abused her and she had to put the pain somewhere so she kept a diary.... And one day, she foolishly showed it to him. That resulted in her worst beating."

She paused to light another cigarette.

"He burned her diary and in a way that was good. For her it was the worst invasion of all and she got the nerve to leave him."

"So what's she doing now?" I asked.

Margaret took a hefty pull at her drink and glared at me. Rage had displaced her earlier maudlin mood.

"Hiding out. Trying to write. Waiting."

"For what?"

She sighed.

"I don't know. What do beautiful thirty-five-year-old women, who've been insulated all their lives and suddenly discover brutality, wait for? A knight in shining armour? A warm safe place? I just don't know. Maybe if she waits long enough, something of herself will catch up.... You know what I mean?"

I laughed nervously.

"I'm a runner," I said.

She laughed loudly.

"I know," she said. "I know all about you.... What about this divorce your wife wants?"

"It's not surprising," I said. "All that time apart."

"Do you still love her?"

I hesitated. I wasn't used to talking with anyone about how I felt. Feelings were private things. In prison, emotions were kept under lock and key. They were a luxury few of us could afford. Rage fueled a person's will to live in prison. Anger made it possible to rebel against the system. Sadness and despair were suicidal states.

I guess I spaced out because suddenly Margaret roared at me.

"My Gawd man, either you do or you don't!"

"I guess I still do," I said, "but it's a love from the past. A historical love. Based on the way things used to be. Except now things are different. I've changed. So has she. I think I'll always love her but we couldn't ever live together. I don't know who she's become. I don't know what I want from my life so I can't tell her."

"Jack's an engineer," she said, and gave a feeble laugh. "He builds bridges. Funny, isn't it?"

I knew exactly what she meant.

"That's what you do," I said. "In your work. You build bridges, emotional bridges that connect people...make them feel more real, alive, part of the world instead of isolated in a swamp, or stuck up a tree someplace."

She gave me a hard, evaluating look. It was getting late. Both of us had knocked back a lot of hooch. Was this booze talk, she was probably wondering.

"That's what I try to do," she said. "Sometimes I wonder though.... I sweat blood and the books get written. A publisher puts them in the stores. They sell and people read them, but do they do the job? I wonder about that all the time. Are they really bridges?"

I was stunned that she would have any doubt. She seemed to want reassurance. I felt like a poor choice of consoler.

"When I read *The Stone Angel* I realized getting old was just as horrible as I'd imagined, but I loved Hagar. And I loved how she loved life and wanted to squeeze every last drop of juice from it that she could...so in a weird way, the book made me feel better about getting old."

"She is one tough old broad, isn't she?"

I nodded while Margaret poured some more scotch and then emptied the overflowing ashtray into a tin cigarette can. She saw me watching her screw the lid on tight and smiled.

"Paranoid about fires," she said. "This young poet used to drop into Elm Cottage. Stay for a day or two. Just to get away from the noise of his children.... Gawd knows why he came to our place. It's an absolute zoo! But he always managed to find a corner for himself. He'd have dinner with us but it only took about three glasses of wine to get him drunk as a skunk...and one night he set the couch on fire. Passed out and his cigarette dropped out of his mouth. It terrified me. The whole place could have gone up. I smelled the smoke, thank Gawd. Threw a bucket of water on him, on the couch. No real harm done. Except the couch."

She sighed and I could sense she was homesick.

"I should go," I said. She reached out and touched my hand.

"Pour yourself a small one to face the night," she said.

I did and added some water.

"So what will you do?" she asked.

"Springboard," I said. "And write."

"A book?"

"No, it's too early. I'm not sure what I want to write about. Certain things pop into my head and I write about them. It might be a poem or a story but nothing large that would fill a novel."

"You've got the voice," she said. "Now you have to stake out the territory."

"Yes," I said. "Something like that."

"And what about this young woman, Anne?"

I laughed.

"Not much is going to happen there," I said. "To her I'm just an irritant."

"A grain of sand that sneaks its way past an oyster's shell is the beginning of a pearl... ."

We let that sit there for a few seconds and then both of us burst out laughing.

"Nice thought, Margaret," I said, "but this lady has guys showering her with pearls. Diamond, baubles, bangles and beads. I'm not even capable of competing at the bead level."

"But you like her."

"Yes...for some weird reason."

"There must be a special quality about her.... I mean the people we end up loving have something our spirits reach out to, something we crave and can't live without.... It was like that with my Jack. When I met him I thought, oh no, not another silent Englishman, too stingy to say a word, but I felt a tugging inside whenever I was around him. I lusted to have his children...and I did. I guess I was lucky. Jack was the only man I ever met who I wanted to be the father of my children."

"I don't think I want to be a father again," I said. "I don't think I should."

"Because of your girls?"

"Yes, I really messed up."

"Sure you did, but you were just a kid yourself. Besides they aren't finished with you yet. Even if your wife remarries and they have a new father, they'll know. You're their real father. Their blood is yours. No one can change that."

It's difficult to describe the kind of intimacy Margaret could create. Part of it was her voice. It had the seductive quality of a doctor with a good bedside manner. The tone made me think of a priest dispensing forgiveness. She spoke with an energetic conviction that had a strange soothing effect and made me think of a mother I'd never known, but had often imagined, wooing me into safe sleep with a lullaby.

Margaret made me feel more brave. Or maybe it was the booze.

"What about you?" I asked. "You don't sound too happy about the divorce. What will you do?"

"In the love department?"

She laughed her bitter snort, lit another cigarette.

"I'm forty-two, kiddo, and in case you hadn't noticed, no raving beauty. Never was . . . . My daughter Jocelyn is gonna be a knockout but that's because she got more of Jack than me. David takes after me more. But that's okay. A broody look in a man is attractive . . . makes them mysterious. He'll do fine. Me, I've got my work . . . ."

"That's all?"

A small smile flickered across her face.

"If some presentable man appears who's determined to sweep me off my feet, I'll pay attention. But I'm not gonna hold my breath. So, let's talk about this Anne. Why don't you bring her to dinner. Let me take a gander at her."

All night I'd wondered what would happen when this evening was over. Would I ever see Margaret again? Was this just a one-shot friendly gesture she was making to some poor ex-con who happened to write a story or two, and whom she thought it might be nice to encourage? No. She was inviting me back again. And more than that. She wanted to meet the woman for whom I'd developed a desperate appetite.

"Anne would be thrilled," I said. "She's a Canlit nut. In fact she thought I was putting her on about coming here tonight. She thinks you walk on water."

Margaret clapped her hands together gleefully.

"Terrific!" she exclaimed. "Let's set a date."

She pulled out her date book and we found a suitable time that I wrote on the back of my cigarette package. Then I stood up. It was time to go.

"You really don't mind?" I asked. "Anne's kind of... strange."

Margaret stood up and embraced me in a fierce hug.

"Aren't they always," she said into my ear. "Anyway, all's fair in love and war."

Fall 1969

Anne Louise Walshaw. Her birthday was October 5th. In 1969 she turned twenty-three. My birthday was two days later. I was turning twenty-seven, and I was broke. Money flowed through my life more quickly than time. To celebrate the festive day of her birth I took her for a walk. She had a romantic weakness for large houses, especially those built around the turn of the century. So we strolled through Rosedale and every so often stopped in front of a building that she found attractive, and discussed how we'd renovate it. We speculated on the decor and how we would change it if the place was ours. It was a harmless game that allowed us to learn about each other's secret dreams. But it was just a game, so it was safe. As multi-coloured leaves fluttered down from the trees I sang every Gene Kelly song I could remember, off-key. Occasionally we even held hands.

With no particular destination in mind, we ended up at Casa Loma. We stopped at the retaining wall that surrounds the castle and I showed Anne the spot where I smashed up my car during a getaway from a bank hold-up. My last bank robbery. If only I'd made the hair-pin turn, my life would have turned out different. For one thing, I wouldn't be with Anne.

I'd come down Spadina Avenue doing ninety, nothing could stop me. I'd already run a road block on St. Clair Avenue by taking to the sidewalk. I was feeling hot and high. But a squad car was right behind me, a young hot-shot cop behind the wheel. I could see his face in my rearview mirror. He looked scared. I know I was. A sign cautioning drivers to slow to 15 MPH appeared. The cop braked. I accelerated. Going into the turn I tapped the brakes. Nothing happened. I slammed my foot down on the pedal. The brakes locked. The car plowed into the wall. On impact my head was propelled forward and shattered a hole in the windshield but the steering wheel exploded into my chest, pinning me and probably saving me from sailing right out the window.

I wasn't in good shape. Breathing was difficult. I tasted blood in my mouth. Pain swept over me like a wave of lethargy. I just wanted to sleep. Then out of the corner of my eye I saw the young policeman approaching me. He had a gun in his hand. For some bizarre reason I felt compelled to get my head back inside the car. The second I moved I heard a loud, echoing crack and felt a searing pain engulf my left leg. It was as though someone had set me on fire.

In the hospital the last rites were administered by a priest Stella had called. I remember finding this hysterically funny, laughing out loud as the doctors probed at me. Then I drifted into a state of serious concentration as I tried to remember the lyrics to "I Don't Want to Set The World on Fire."

A long time ago. It's hard to forget those days. Especially when the weather's damp and the old bullet wound on my left leg begins to throb.

I didn't share these details with Anne. Our relationship was tentative enough without my telling her horror stories that would scare her away. Instead we gathered chestnuts, breaking open the prickly green pods that blanketed the ground and admiring the brown nuts encased inside. We began tossing them at each other. Soon it was a pitched battle with both of us hiding behind trees. Finally I called a truce. Her aim was too good.

We sat on a hill at the south end of the grounds and looked out over the city.

"Someday when I grow up," I said, "I want... ."

"What?" she asked.

"Some day when I grow up... ." I started again.

She jumped to her feet and stomped around in a furious circle.

"That's the trouble with you, you know," she said. "All the guys I know that are your age have grown up. They've got careers going. Goals set out. You're going to flop around like a fish out of water until you suffocate or find your way back to a lake."

"That's not so bad," I said.

Her face was a tight mask of distress. What was she so afraid of? Disorder? Uncertainty? Her fear seemed to smolder within her, creating a smoke that I inhaled and experienced as a kind of aphrodisiac.

I too was terrified. Each morning I woke up in my fenced-in bed expecting to find myself back in prison. But I was free. And after a soak in the bathtub on the second floor I'd dress and go over to Parliament Street and have a leisurely breakfast of coffee and toast at the Parkway restaurant. Instead of feeling relaxed, though, I walked around in a tense sweat, wondering what I was supposed to do from one moment to the next. I missed the routine of prison, the rules and orders that regulated my life. Freedom was scary.

"Listen," I said. "Last week when I had dinner at Margaret's she invited me back and suggested I bring you."

"That's right!" she said, flopping herself down beside me again. "You were supposed to tell me what happened. You've been avoiding me."

I laughed.

"Anne, every time I call your place Jenny tells me you're out on a date. During the day I'm trying to organize Springboard, do a bit of writing...and get a job."

"A job?"

"Yes, an activity that pays money."

"What kind of job?"

"I got one yesterday. I start tomorrow. Ontario Hydro."

"Doing what?"

"I'm not quite sure but it pays nine bucks an hour."

"That's good," she said, but I could tell from her expression that I was somehow diminished in her sight. Here I was trying to pass myself off as a writer, a saviour of my fellow ex- cons, but in the end I was still Joe Lunch Bucket punching a time clock to make a few bucks for the groceries.

"It's just a temporary thing," I said defensively.

"Sure," she said. "Hey, did I tell you where John Kneale's taking me tonight?"

I didn't want to hear about another fancy supper club where she planned to dance away the night with one of her successful suitors. I grabbed her and pulled her to the ground. She was very strong and in seconds had managed to flip me on to my back. She sat on my chest and laughed.

"I had lots of practice growing up with two brothers," she said, and her face was split with a grin that made me think of a satisfied fox. Suddenly she leaned down and pressed her mouth against mine. I opened my mouth and felt the tingle of her tongue against the roof of my mouth. I began to drift into a sexual fantasy in which we made love among the leaves, but before the images could focus she was off me and bounding down the hill.

"Race you back to Bloor Street," she shouted.

Running. Always running. From me? Herself? What? I got up and tore after her.

The following week I returned to Margaret's with Anne on my arm. She was radiant with excitement. Her long blonde hair had been carefully fashioned into a bun at the back. Old-fashioned but sexy. She wore a lovely brown paisley dress. I was proud of her. Exhilarated to be sitting on the bus beside her. She raced me to Margaret's front door and won. We arrived breathless. Margaret answered the door and stood for a second looking at Anne. Scanning is perhaps a better way to describe it.

"So you're Anne Walshaw," she said finally. "I'm so pleased to meet you."

She took both of Anne's hands and held them for a few seconds. The two of them laughed at some shared but unspoken joke.

"Come in, come in," Margaret said.

We crowded into the small vestibule. Margaret snatched Anne's coat from her and nudged her toward the stairs.

"We're going up to my study," she said. "Give Eleanor a hand, will you, Don?"

I went into the kitchen and found Eleanor poking with a fork at a chicken in the oven.

"About ten more minutes," she said, closing the oven. She flashed me that radiant, childlike smile that was disturbing in its intensity. It was as though she lived her life walking an emotional tightrope. The evidence of the strain this caused her was in that smile. Beautiful, beckoning, but also desperate.

"Stuffed chicken?" I asked, as I began to open the wine.

"Yes," she said.

We worked side by side for a few minutes; I opened the wine and Eleanor tossed the salad. I felt nervous about Anne being upstairs with Margaret. Like all egotists I assumed they were talking about me. But then I thought, no, Anne is well read. They're probably talking about books, discussing authors. Why would they talk about me?

"You think they're up there talking about you, don't you?" Eleanor inquired.

"I doubt it," I said.

"They probably are," Eleanor said with assurance. "Margaret loves to gossip. She enjoys the role of earth mother, listening to people's problems, giving good advice. Interfering, really."

"I thought she was your friend."

Eleanor smiled.

"Of course...but that doesn't mean you shouldn't watch out...Margaret's very persuasive, don't you think?"

"Yes," I agreed.

"What if she decides that your girlfriend would be better off without you in her life?"

I laughed. What she was saying sounded so preposterous.

"What if she doesn't approve of her?" she hissed.

"Margaret's not my mother," I said. "What she thinks or feels about Anne is between them. It's got nothing to do with me."

Eleanor giggled, then chuckled loudly, finally bursting into loud laughter that bordered on hysterics.

"You are naive," she sputtered.

And you, I thought, are paranoid.

Suddenly Eleanor stopped laughing. She wiped tears from her eyes on the apron she was wearing over her dress. Her face was alert, listening. The sound of shared laughter drifted down from Margaret's study. We both looked toward the stairs.

"My parents were like that," Eleanor said. "Laughing together at their private jokes. Even my husband with his buddies...laughing together until I walked into the room. Then they'd stop. I'd ask what's so funny? And he'd say nothing.... Nothing!"

Then I understood. Eleanor was jealous of us. Of everyone who took Margaret's attention away from her. How hard it must be to be so lonesome.

I did something I've never been good at: I opened my arms to Eleanor and she snuggled up against me, just for a moment or two. I didn't hug or even really hold her, my hands barely touched her back. The contact was uneasy, a gesture that had little substance. I had a rare insight: basically, I was afraid of women. I didn't understand their rhythms, their sudden shifts of mood, the openness with which most women shared their feelings. I was a control freak. Shirt tucked in neatly along with most of what I thought and felt. That's why I liked to write. I had power over my characters. I could get them to do what I wanted with no consequence to me. Most of the time.

"Don't you find it odd," Eleanor said, as she withdrew from me and went back to making salad, "that we're often captivated by the very people who reject us?"

"It's because we feel unworthy," I blurted. "So we choose people to care about who will prove how unworthy we are."

"Do you really think so?"

"Sure," I said. "I can't explain it but I see it all the time. Look at Margaret. She knew she was going to be a writer. Even when she was a kid, she knew. Then she chooses to marry a guy who'll be threatened by the very thing she does best. I'm willing to bet he sabotaged her every step of the way...but part of it is how she felt about herself.... You know what I mean?"

"I do," Margaret said.

She and Anne were standing in the doorway. I felt like a fool. Here I was worrying about them sitting upstairs and talking about me.

"Jack is a good man," she said. "He was the best husband he could be. And a good father."

"I'm sorry, Margaret, I had no right... ."

She waved away my apology and led Anne and me to the dining room. She poured herself a glass of red wine and stared at me over the rim as she downed half of it.

"Because men are so often the aggressors, they get the mistaken idea that most of the choices in life are theirs. They have a right to think that way. I don't know of any war in history that's been started by a woman.... But in matters of the heart... ."

She looked over at Anne and smiled. Eleanor entered with several platters of food.

"Women hold the cards," Margaret said. "That's why we're more tolerant, emotionally speaking. When a man behaves like a fool, betrays us, we're hurt, yes...but then we remind ourselves, I chose this guy...I knew this was a possibility...and so we cope with the knowledge that we knew all along that he could hurt us. When men are betrayed, most of them come unglued, like they never considered it a possibility."

She lifted her glass and finished the wine.

"Let's eat," she said.

I felt like an idiot and was grateful when Eleanor asked me to carve the chicken. Who did I imagine I was that I could ramble on about anyone else's life, making judgments, when I didn't have an inkling about the nuts and bolts that held my own together. I was ashamed of myself as though I'd betrayed Margaret in a way that I didn't understand. I looked up from the chicken and she smiled at me.

"Anne says you're working," she said. "When do you have time for the writing and Springboard?"

I laughed but I knew it sounded weary. I was tired.

"It's shift work," I said. "So today I worked from six this morning till three this aft...but tomorrow I go back on nights. Ten at night till six in the morning... ."

"You must be exhausted!" Margaret exclaimed. "No wonder your complexion's the shade of mashed potatoes. What do you do at this job?"

"He won't tell me," Anne said. "He acts like it's something he's ashamed of."

Margaret squinted her eyes and looked at me closely. I was being scrutinized.

"So what's the big secret?" she asked.

Eleanor waited with a half smile on her face. I felt embarrassed. The job I had was awful. I didn't know how to present it without humiliating myself.

"Actually it's the weirdest job I've ever had. Ontario Hydro is paying me vast amounts of money to be a human pipe cleaner... ."

"What? Explain," Margaret said.

"There's just six of us on the crew," I said. "When we get to the Hearn plant, you know, the big one down near Cherry Beach, we go to the locker room and change from our regular clothes into these white overalls and hip waders. The first couple of days they gave us rain capes and hats but no one uses them, they get too hot. Then we go over to the stack we were working on and start cleaning it. Except after about twenty minutes everyone is down to their underwear and bare feet. It's against the safety regulations but you try crawling up inside a thirty-six-inch pipe with a wrench, or a fire hose squirting pressurized water. It gets damn hot fast."

Margaret looked bewildered.

"I'm missing something," she said.

"Me too," Anne said. "What exactly are you doing to these stack things?"

"The Hearn plant has these coal-fired generators that produce electricity. The stacks are the chimneys that release the smoke high in the air. There are four of them and they each stand over a hundred feet tall. From what I've learned they were erected in the thirties and haven't been cleaned since being put into operation. The thing is that each stack has a filtering system so when the smoke goes up these little metal cups inside, the system catches the big pieces of pollution crap so they won't be released into the air... but after so long all those cups are jammed with grunge, and so we have to climb up inside the stack with a pneumatic socket wrench, remove the cups, drop them to the guys below and they clean them... ."

"It sound barbaric," Margaret said.

"Something out of Charles Dickens," Eleanor chortled.

"You mean you're actually inside the chimney stack itself?" Anne said.

"Yeah, two guys at a time. The first guy goes in with the fire hose. He uses that to blow crud off the cups so the second guy can find the bolts to unscrew them."

"How do you hang on?" Anne asked.

"The guys inside the stack have to wear safety harnesses. They attach under your arms and are controlled by a winch out on the floor that the foreman and one of the other guys look after. You just shout if you want to be hauled up, or lowered. It's kind of a dirty job. All this black stuff that's been clinging to the walls and traps for thirty years is flying around."

"Do you at least wear masks?" Anne asks.

Margaret glared at me. I didn't know if she was angry at me or the circumstances. She hadn't touched her food but the wine was disappearing quickly.

"Goggles," I said, "to protect your eyes. And they give us these little masks to cover our nose and mouth but they've got a paper filter in them... thirty seconds in the stack and they're soaked. You can't breathe. Nobody wears them. The way we work it nobody stays up inside for more than half an hour in a three-hour cycle."

"This is not a job any human being should be asked to do," Margaret said.

"It pays good money," I said.

In a strange way I enjoyed her fuming indignation. I hated the job and almost quit the first day. Several guys had walked away when they were asked to climb inside the chimney. But I'd stuck it out for the week as though it were some kind of endurance test. It was good money and the reality was I hadn't completed grade eight. They were not a lot of jobs open to an uneducated ex-con.

"How long you think you have to work at this before you prove your point?" Margaret asked.

"What point?"

"How tough you are!" she yelled. "Good Gawd man, when you finish the chimneys.... How long's that going to take?"

"Three, four months."

"So then you get them all spanking clean, what're they gonna do, have you climbing inside the furnaces, cleaning up the ovens where they burn all this messy coal...."

"Well...."

A palpable tension had developed in the room. Eleanor was smiling as she ate quietly. Anne looked worried, embarrassed, her eyes darting back and forth between Margaret and me.

"He's got to have a job," Anne said timidly.

Margaret roared with laughter.

"You call what he's describing a job! Japanese kamikaze pilots had more pleasant jobs.... And they didn't get as dirty."

Eleanor let out a tinkling laugh. Anne looked shocked. I smiled.

In the short time I'd known Margaret, I had concluded that she was not a person who went out of her way to find and appreciate the funny things in life. She was very serious. She laughed when something struck her as comic, but she laughed less than most of us. For her it was not a social release. And she did seem to have a large reservoir of anger that bubbled up more easily than laughter.

"How many different ways do you have to be told?" Margaret asked. "You're a writer. Your first responsibility is to that.... Sure, you've gotta eat. Make dough...but not by such a macho suicidal mission where everybody wonders when they'll get the call about you being scraped up off the floor!"

Eleanor laughed. Margaret gave a small smile and patted my hand.

"We know you're a tough guy, Bailey. You made your point."

She then dug into her food and was quiet for the rest of the meal.

Anne had a late date with one of her suitors so we had to make it an early night. Before we left Margaret took me aside.

"I'm up to my ass in work," she said. "Revisions on the new book, the Christmas article. I haven't even started it. I owe the *Star* a book review. And I'm going home next month. I do this to myself all the time.... Call me at the university...maybe we can have lunch if I can get away from the cannibals long enough."

"I will," I said.

"But if it doesn't work out, don't be peeved with me. I've just taken on too much. And I'm coming back late spring, early summer. Trent University has offered me some kind of writer-in-res thing. I want you and Anne to visit me **at** the shack.... It's just outside of Peterborough."

"Sure," I said.

She squeezed my hands tightly.

"Get on with your own work...the writing. And Springboard. You need to do that and it's needed. Go now...and write."

It was like a benediction. She hugged Anne, got a little weepy, and we left, shouting our goodbyes to Eleanor.

On the bus home, I asked Anne what she thought.

"I like her," Anne said. "But I found her kind of bossy."

Bossy. Yes, that could describe a certain aspect of Margaret.

I worked one more week at Hydro and quit. The money I'd earned was enough to live on for a month, if I was careful. But I was never good at that.

The fall flew by. I went to John Robert Colombo's reception for the Russian poet and found myself moving among the Toronto literary crowd with a tray of hor-d'oeuvres. Now I knew why he told us to dress up. We were the clean and neat unpaid help. Later I traded places with Doug Fetherling who was tending bar and did my darnedest to get everyone roaring drunk. But writers seem to have an enormous capacity for booze. The highlight of the evening was when Colombo gathered everyone in a circle and asked the better-known writers if they had happened to bring something they could read. I saw Miriam Waddington reach into a colossal purse and pull out a hundred-page manuscript. I hadn't brought anything and I was pretty sure I wouldn't be asked anyway, so I made a quick exit.

I called Margaret several times and we chatted on the phone but she was too busy for anything but her own work. We promised to write to each other and meet again next year.

Springboard was beginning to take shape. I had applied to the Atkinson Foundation for some money to help run the organization. As a result, an editor from the *Toronto Star* called me, and suggested they do a story on me. I countered by asking him to let me write my own story. He agreed and I did five hundred words on the Hydro job. He was amused, paid me twenty-five bucks and told me to write something else. I did—a little piece about living in Toronto on twenty-five bucks a week. He thought this stuff was hilarious. I was in business. Living from week to week. But surviving.

Christmas 1969

Freedom sometimes means isolation. As Christmas approached I felt lonely for the prison community I had left behind. During my years of incarceration I had avoided the disappointing promise of Christmas by organizing concerts. I wrote skits for my fellow inmates to act in, cajoled the resident musicians into performing their imitation of Johnny Cash singing "I Walk The Line," and hustled the shop instructors into giving us scrap wood and paint to make scenery. Over half the prison population was involved in the Christmas concert my last year at Warkworth. The show ran three nights: a performance for the staff and their families, one for people in the outside community, and the final one for ourselves.

Although I was terrified of public speaking, I MC'd the three-and-a-half-hour show. It was held in the gym which had been decorated with enough crepe paper to give the most blasé firefighter nightmares. Folding chairs accommodated the audience and the show featured a music group called Purple Banana, jugglers who dropped things, singers who couldn't carry a tune, and actors who forgot their lines at the critical moments. But as awful as it was, the concert provided us with a huddle formation that overcame our day-to-day grievances with each other. Screws who appeared with their families became real people, and at intermission we all mingled, drinking coffee, talking with each other and forgetting the boundaries that usually separated us.

As snow blanketed the ground I longed for the warm security I'd found in prison. I missed the seasonal fellowship that emerged miraculously in the midst of confinement. I realized that in my twenty-seven years, fifteen Christmas seasons had been spent in various institutions. Faced with the choices that freedom provided, I didn't know what to do. Everyone else seemed to have plans. Anne had a parade of admirers trooping through her life in shifts, starting Christmas Eve. She had made it clear to me that I was not part of her plans. Stella, my soon-to-be ex-wife, had obtained a legal separation that stipulated I was not to visit my children without her permission. Because of my criminal past, the courts were convinced I would be a bad influence. When I asked her to let me drop by Christmas Day, she told me my presence would just confuse the kids.

A certain desperation set in. I had to do something. What was the point of being part of the larger world if I couldn't participate? Then I began to think that maybe my freedom was temporary. Maybe God was playing a joke on me, allowing me to think I was a real person when in truth I was just another institutional zombie.

The second week of December found me in the Winchester Hotel, up in the Alpine Room, sipping rye and water and consulting with Carlos the bartender about the folly of mankind's compulsion to create ritual and perhaps order out of chaos. We concluded that life was a series of random events and though we might struggle for control over our destiny, the efforts we exerted would have little effect. Time was the constant. It flowed in one direction—forward.

Fortunately we were interrupted by the arrival of Barry Morris, who took the stool next to me and ordered a beer.

"So, all set for the holidays?" he asked.

"Sure," I said. "Wall to wall parties. What are you doing?"

"The Regent Street Youth Corps are having a dinner for single roomers. A lot of old people who live alone come. They get served a big turkey dinner with all the trimmings. It gets them out of their places for a few hours at least and for some of them, it'll be the best meal they'll have all winter."

"Where is it?" I asked.

"Over on Huntley Street. A big insurance company picks up the tab for the food and lets us use the cafeteria. Two, three hundred people show up. Interested?"

An idea was forming in my mind but its shape was like a wind-blown cloud.

"What could I do?" I asked.

"I start rousting people out of their places about noon. You could help me. A lot of these people are reluctant to come. Pride. Despair... . They get paralyzed."

Strange, the same thing happened in the joint. Christmas dinner was served in the gym, the one time a year when we ate together, but some guys wouldn't leave their cells. Better to be lonely alone than in a large gathering. Also it was an easier way to nurture the rage you needed to live in confinement.

"What time's the dinner?"

"Around four or so," he said. "It's all volunteers who do the cooking and serving. They work in shifts so they won't be away from their families the whole day."

"What about entertainment?" I asked.

He laughed.

"They've got each other's company...believe me, that can be pretty entertaining."

"But what if I could round up some real entertainers?" I asked, the earlier vague idea now fully formed in my mind. A community Christmas concert for those who had no community.

"You'd have an appreciative audience," Barry said, "but how...?"

"Leave it to me," I said, energized by the challenge.

The next day I went into the Christian Resource Centre, closed the door to my small office and started to make calls. I let my fingers do the walking through the yellow pages of the telephone directory. There were hundreds of listings under Entertainers.

My first call, to someone named Abe who advertised himself as a violinist and fiddle player, was answered by a quavering male voice. When I explained what I was trying to do, he laughed.

"My wife tells me I'm a fool to waste the money on the ad," he said. "I've only had three calls all year but I like to keep my hand in."

"So you'll come?" I asked.

"I'm seventy-eight years of age," he said. "I had to stop driving two years ago when I couldn't make out the difference between pedestrians and telephone poles...so I'd need a ride."

"No problem," I said, "I'll pick you up."

"Also, I wonder if Ethel could come. My wife. She was the soloist with our church choir for forty years. She hasn't got the volume she once had, but if you have a microphone she'll fill their ears with some of the sweetest sounds they'll hear this side of heaven."

"Wonderful," I said.

"And then there's Ray," he said. "His daughters plunked him down in one of those nursing homes when his health got bad but he still plays a strong accordion.... Except the staff won't let him most of the time. Says it bothers the other residents. He'd come if I asked. We'd have to pick him up too."

"Call him," I said. "Ask."

"I like the sound of this gathering," Abe said. "Me and Ethel know how fortunate we are to still be chugging along.... Near sixty years we've been married. At our age it's plain luck not to be dead...what?.... Excuse me."

He went off the line for a moment and I thought of how lucky I was to stumble across this guy.

"Hello, still there?"

"Yes," I said.

"Ethel had a good idea...she's got this friend Libby. Spinster lady. Taught piano since before the ark. We usually have her over for Christmas so she doesn't have to spend it alone...if you could get your hands on a piano...."

"I will, Abe."

He issued a short laugh.

"I know another guy," he said, "plays great bass...haven't talked to him in years but I'm sure I could track him down. Used to play in a big dance band."

"You're a gold mine, Abe."

"It's a pleasure to get involved," he said. "Who knows what might come of it all."

And so it went.

Jo Jo, the juggling magician, agreed to donate his time. Doodles the clown said she would come and give an exhibition of balloon sculpting.

There were refusals. Some people were insulted that I asked them to donate their time, but I was amazed at how many were eager to be part of the festivities.

The days flew by in a flurry of deals. An electronics company loaned us a sound system. An old piano was found in a church basement, moved to the insurance company by a group of the local back alley drinkers who rounded up a truck someplace. The CNIB sent out a blind piano tuner who somehow breathed new life into the old instrument.

Christmas Eve I was feeling buoyant, hopeful, and I suppose most important, useful. I went shopping in the afternoon and spent most of my cash on presents for the kids. A toboggan, stuffed animals and a couple of board games. My plan was to deliver them that night. Late, after they were asleep. I would appear just like Santa Claus, drop the stuff off and disappear.

An open house was held that evening at the Christian Resource Centre. The place was mobbed by community people. All the members of the writer's group did their literary circling around the sandwich tray. Lou was noisily present, banging his head against the radiators and communing with the water spirits, who he said were particularly active during the Christmas season. It was too much for me so I slunk away to my retreat in the Alpine Room of the Winchester.

Over a stiff rye and water I counted my blessings. But my solitude was interrupted by Anne who sidled up to me, looking radiant, vibrating with the energy of someone on the verge of cracking up.

"You drink too much," she said.

"True," I said. "Some day I'm going to write a poem about it."

"When?" she asked.

"When I've drunk enough."

She laughed, but the sound was hard and brittle.

"What's wrong?" I asked.

"Brian came," she said. "The guy from Ottawa I told you about."

"Sure, I remember. I thought you and he were doing the town tonight."

Again the harsh laugh.

"He stopped by just long enough to ... ." Her voice broke. She started to cry. "He made me feel like a hotel room. Check in. Dirty up the sheets...check out."

What could I say? I hated the guy, sight unseen, but he was my competition. Anne seemed unclear as to what she wanted. Maybe he was just protecting himself.

"It's still early," I said. "Why don't we go to a movie?"

She nodded agreement and I took her hand. We walked over to Yonge Street and were just in time to catch the last showing of *Midnight Cowboy*. We both cried when Ratso, the slimy character, played by Dustin Hoffman, died on the bus just as he reached the land of his dreams in the company of the troubled, strangely innocent Jon Voigt.

Outside it was snowing. We decided to walk back to Anne's place.

"Movies like that are depressing," Anne said. "They make me feel that I don't have any control. I mean, if I care about somebody, I'd better be careful because I may screw up my own life just to please somebody else."

"Are you happy?" I asked.

"No.... I mean sometimes I am...but no."

"Who are you trying to please?"

"Me," she said, and then laughed. "And my mother...she has such fantastic ideas of how my life should be...whatever I do, I'll disappoint her."

"That's sad," I said, "but it's good to know, because now you can do whatever you want."

"It's not so easy," she said. "Not with my mother...speaking of which, I mentioned this dinner thing you and Barry are doing tomorrow. She was impressed and asked me to invite you over when you're finished. For coffee and dessert."

"That was nice of her."

"Will you come?"

"If you want me to."

"She knows about you being an ex-con. It'll be kind of interesting to see how she reacts when you're sitting in her living room."

"Sounds like an experiment," I said.

She laughed.

"Maybe it is...at least you know."

When we reached her house she hesitated on the walk.

"You want to come up?" she asked.

I wanted to. Desperately.

"Yes," I said, "but I've got to deliver my kid's Christmas presents...so not tonight."

"You're weird, Bailey," she said. "For months you chase me and then when you catch me in a moment of vulnerability, you back off. Scared?"

"Yeah, I am," I admitted.

"Why?"

"The timing," I said. "Tonight I'm the consolation prize, the runner up. I want to be the winner..."

"You are definitely weird!" she said and stomped through the fresh snow toward her door.

"See you tomorrow night," I yelled as she slammed the door behind her.

I walked the few blocks back to my place thinking she was right, I should have taken the opportunity she offered. I was being stubborn at my own expense. Besides, she was lonely, hurt. If I really cared for her wouldn't I respond to that instead of my own selfish need to win?

In my room I opened a bottle of brandy and tried to write a poem that expressed my agitation.

Then it was time to play Santa Claus. I put the stuffed animals and games in a green garbage bag so they wouldn't get wet, and loaded them on the toboggan. It was still snowing and the toboggan slid along easily. The night was bright with an almost full moon. I felt pleased with myself but I knew the feeling was a bubble of my own making that could burst any second. I was faking it. Conning myself that everything was all right but in my gut, I burned. Christmas Eve and I was alone. At least I wasn't locked in a cell.

I walked to the end of Carlton Street and arrived at Riverdale park. The steep slopes were empty for the moment. In a few hours though the hills would abound with young children, yelling and screaming as they zipped along on the sleds that had arrived under their Christmas trees. Perhaps even my own kids. They only lived a couple of blocks away. I stood there, trying to imagine myself playing with the girls, laughing, tossing snowballs. Normal everyday things that seemed so remote. Why was that, I wondered.

I made my way to Stella's apartment. The windows were dark so I jammed the stuff between the doors and rang the buzzer several times. I heard someone inside yell and then footsteps coming down the stairs. I ran for home.

The next day I was up early. Using a car that Barry borrowed somewhere, I picked up the sound equipment. I found an army of volunteers busy setting up the tables for dinner in the huge cafeteria. A group of teenagers was decorating a massive tree. Another group was hanging holly and streamers of crepe paper. I set up the microphones on the small stage, pleased to see that there was a clear space left for dancing. Then I joined Barry in the kitchen where he was helping prepare the meal. The air was already heavy with the smell of roast turkey.

"Everything seems in good shape," I said.

"You sure these entertainers are going to come?" he asked. "I told a lot of people..."

"Sure," I said. "I'm gonna head out shortly and pick some of them up."

Barry looked around at all the activity.

"I just hope our shut-ins come out. It's supposed to snow again. It would be just like them to boycott us because it snowed a little."

I took his arm. It was as rigid as steel.

"Relax," I said. "We'll go out and haul them in if we have to."

"We will," he said gloomily, looking out the window at the first snowflakes.

I took the car again and started to do my rounds. Jo Jo the Juggling Magician had a huge trunk of props that I had to tie to the roof.

"I hope the pigeons don't catch cold," he said, as I drove him back to headquarters.

Doodles the Clown was a woman of about fifty. She looked like she was dressed for church. She patted a small suitcase by her feet.

"Everything I need's in here," she said. "Gimme an hour and you won't recognize me."

Both Abe and his wife Ethel were as gracious as I imagined them to be. We drove the few blocks to their friend Libby's place and she too was eagerly waiting. Getting Abe's friend Ray out of the nursing home proved more difficult than any of us had anticipated. The staff insisted he stay on the grounds and enjoy the wonderful Christmas dinner that would be served. To ensure his presence they took away his clothes and we had to sneak him out to the car in his housecoat and slippers. Then we went back to Abe's place and found some clothes that almost fit him although he had to stick with the slippers.

Tommy, the guy who played bass, was in Sunnybrook Hospital for veterans. Abe wasn't sure if his friend would be allowed to leave. Apparently he'd just had surgery but Abe didn't know how serious it was. When we got there, though, Tommy was sitting in the reception area, his bass case beside him, all ready to go. He was wearing full parade dress, including his regiment's beret and all his medals. Then I noticed the crutches. And the missing leg.

"Wonderful thing," he said to Abe in a loud voice so staff could hear, "having a Christmas get-together for us old vets."

He picked up his crutches and began to make his way toward the door. He saw me staring and pointed his thumb at the bass. I had to run to catch up with them at the car.

"I'm glad you've come," I said, "but how're you going to play without…"

"Without a leg to stand on?" he laughed. "No problem mate, the damn leg used to go numb after half an hour anyway. Now I just use my instrument like it's a cane."

Who was I to argue?

By four in the afternoon, Abe and his motley crew of musicians were set up on the stage ready to go. Abe was wearing an old tuxedo and looked quite smart as he handed out sheet music to Libby at the piano. As the first shut-ins began to straggle in, the small orchestra began to play "O Holy Night."

Barry came running up to me in a panic.

"They're pouring in," he said. "We're not going to have enough food!"

I went to the entrance doors with him to greet people who were arriving. Lou, our worshipper of waterways, was unwinding his mane of hair from under a plastic shower cap. Many of the people were old and frail. They needed help taking off the numerous layers of clothing they'd worn to combat the cold. One tiny, elderly lady wore a snowsuit that would have fit a twelve-year-old. Another woman removed a bulky coat that had been lined with carefully folded newspapers which she placed in a shopping bag so they could be used again when she went home.

Almost everyone had bags of one sort or another. I quickly learned that these were for holding slippers and sweaters. After the heavy winter boots came off, hardly anyone wore shoes. Sweaters and slippers were the order of the day, except for a few people who made do with getting around in their sock feet.

The meal was served immediately. Abe and his group played muted classical music while people ate. And the people kept coming. The organizers had figured on two hundred but over three hundred showed up. The volunteers in the kitchen performed a fishes and loaves miracle and everyone was fed.

When it looked like most people had eaten I approached the stage and introduced the entertainment. I made the mistake of announcing everyone, with the result that Doodles came out doing back flips and immediately launched into her balloon sculpting, creating bouquets of flowers, weird and wonderful animals which she launched into the crowd. Not to be outdone, Jo Jo the Magician pulled six pigeons from his hat and began to juggle them. Abe and his crew struck up the band and Ethel belted out a raunchy rendition of "Making Whoopy."

Chaos reigned. Several women rose from their chairs and began to dance. Some with each other, some alone. An old fellow got up and performed a jig. I stood at the microphone trying to orchestrate the madness and after a minute realized that I was the only one bothered by the disorder. So I sat down and let it happen.

By eight o'clock everyone was winding down. But there was no weariness in the crowd. Small groups were forming. The buzz of talk and laughter grew and the band had to play louder. When Ethel sang the opening bars to Vera Lynn's "Until We Meet Again," the room went silent. Then after a few seconds people began to sing along until by the end of the song, everyone was part of it. It wasn't the choir of Westminster Abbey but the sound was powerful and full of feeling. As the last note died away, the crowd began to move toward the lobby.

The small groups remained intact. Those who had larger rooms invited others over. Winter clothes were slowly layered back on. At the doorway everyone received an unexpected present. One of the volunteers was an executive with a local wine company and had arranged for everyone to receive a box that contained a half bottle of wine, two glasses and a package of cheese and crackers.

"I don't think that was such a good idea," Barry said. "Some of them will get drunk."

"So what?" I demanded.

I thanked the performers and offered to drive them home.

"We called two cabs," Abe said. "A whole crowd of us are going back to our place."

He was glowing.

"Thanks again," I said. "You were wonderful."

Ethel walked up to me and took my hands.

"We feel wonderful," she said. "And if the Lord is willing and we live another year, we'd like to do it again."

I stayed around another hour and helped clean up. I felt good about the day. I realized my contribution had been motivated by my need to do something, to be part of an event that gave meaning to the day, and that need and a lot of luck had helped me stumble into what turned out to be an occasion of joyous fellowship with other humans.

As I was leaving I noticed there were still some of the wine and cheese gift packages left. I took one, decided I'd be on my own later, and took another. Then I headed over to the subway and Anne's.

Her family lived in Etobicoke, a two-block walk from Royal York station. Her mother answered the door. She was a handsome woman in her fifties, her blond hair now grey.

"You'll be Don," she said, taking my hand in a firm grip and giving me a well-tuned smile. "Everyone, come and meet Don..."

Everyone came, as she commanded, all of them huddling in the small vestibule with the door behind me still open. I handed her one of the wine and cheese packages.

"You shouldn't have..." she said.

Her husband, Bal, a tall thin man with a pot belly, thinning white hair and a sour expression, took my hand for a second, and then reached behind me and slammed the door closed.

"Why don't you let the poor guy in the house before you bombard him?" he said. He then nodded at me and turned back to the living room.

I saw Anne standing behind her two brothers, Mike and Doug. She was grinning. Did her family act like this all the time I wondered, or was this just social awkwardness because I was an ex-con.

Michael, blond like his sister but with his father's blurry features, stepped forward and spoke with a booming heartiness.

"Real nice to meet you," he said. "Our sister's a bit secretive about her work. Maybe you can fill us in." How, I wondered. Was I supposed to be one of her cases? He didn't shake my hand so much as grasp it, and then cover it with his other hand. I'd experienced ministers doing that. And undertakers. He wasn't more than twenty and it seemed an odd gesture. But finally he let go and the other brother shuffled forward. He looked like Anne, with her fine features, but his fair hair was two feet longer.

"Hello," he said, and then paused awkwardly. "Ah, welcome..." He remembered to put out his hand but it had the vitality of a piece of starched rope. I looked at him closely. Younger brother was stoned.

"I'll bet you never had a chance to eat," Anne's mother said, putting her hand to my back and propelling me through the living room and into the dining room. "You just sit here and I'll make you up a plate. White or dark meat... .?"

"A little of each," I said.

Anne sauntered in and sat down across from me.

"What do you think?" she asked.

Brother Doug sidled up to me before I could answer.

"If you want to do a toke, I've got a spot in the basement that's private," he said.

"Thanks," I said. "Maybe later."

He grinned and wandered off. To the basement, I presumed.

"He blows the smoke into one of the heating vents," Anne whispered. "The smell goes through the whole house and drives my mother crazy."

Bal came into the room rubbing his hands together.

"I'm making myself a rye and ginger. Can I get you one?"

"Sure," I said. A stiff one, I wanted to say.

Michael came in and sat beside me, turning his chair so he faced me.

"Anne says you're working with ex-convicts," he said.

Anne's mother came into the room with a plate heaped high with food which she set in front of me.

"Just eat what you can," she said, "but if you find your appetite, there's plenty more...would you like me to open the wine you brought? We're not big drinkers ourselves but a little wine is nice once in a while..."

"Mrs. Walshaw..." I said.

"Call me Audrey...please."

"Here you go," said Bal, putting the whisky in front of me. I wanted to grab it and chugalug it.

"Oh, that was a good idea," Audrey said.

"Why doesn't everybody stop hovering and let the guy eat in peace," Bal said as he exited.

"We're just having a little conversation with our guest," Audrey called after him. "When you have a guest it's only common courtesy to keep them company...I think I'll make some tea...would you like some tea, Don?"

A valium, I thought. Am I going crazy?

Suddenly Audrey stiffened and went over to the heat register.

"Bal", she called into the next room, "that smell is coming from the furnace again."

Sure enough, the sweet odour of high-grade grass smoke began to permeate the room.

"Probably just the new filter, mom," Michael said.

I looked at him. He seemed serious. I took a quick swallow of my drink. It was stiff. Very little ginger ale. Bless you Bal. I decided my safest bet was to eat. So I dug in. Audrey went back to the kitchen and began to bang pots around.

"Anne says you're an ex-con yourself," Michael persisted.

My mouth was full of food so I nodded.

"Could you leave us for a few minutes, Michael?" Anne asked.

"Hey, sure," he said, bounding from his chair. "Guess you've got things to talk about...but I'd sure like to hear about this Springboard thing..." He stood in the doorway to the kitchen, smiling. I nodded some more and he left.

"This isn't how I remember it on 'Leave It To Beaver'," I said.

Anne laughed.

"They're nervous," she said.

"Because of me...why?"

"I think you scare them," Anne said.

"Do I still scare you?" I asked.

"Sometimes," she said. "But not tonight. How'd it go today?"

Audrey entered the room at the end of the question and waited for the answer.

"Speaking for myself, I'd say it was a great success. Food was supped, songs were sung, people danced...it was a triumph of the spirit. I know that sounds hokey, but..."

"These were mostly old people," Audrey said.

"Yes," I said. "And most of them live by themselves...I think what they enjoyed most about today was the socializing."

"It makes you wonder about their families," Audrey said. "I know some people have no family...through no fault of their own, like you. Anne told us you were orphaned, but you'd think they'd have somebody..."

Suddenly I remembered my own kids. It was late, but they might still be up. Surely Stella wouldn't mind.

"May I use your phone?" I asked.

"You've hardly eaten anything," Audrey observed.

"I did nibble at the banquet," I protested. With an expression of disappointed weariness, she took my plate back to the kitchen. I felt guilty and I guess it showed. Anne reached over and touched my arm.

"If you'd eaten it all, she'd have been unhappy because you didn't take seconds...there's a phone in the front hallway. I'll see you have privacy."

As I dialed the number I realized I took privacy for granted. Even in prison the eight by twelve space of your cell was respected.

I looked through the French doors into the living room. There was nothing threatening about the room but it had a certain stiffness and an orderly drabness to it. Is this what it meant to be middle-class? I hadn't been in many middle-class homes. Was this representative? If Anne and I were to co-habit in some form, is this the kind of home she would expect?

Finally someone answered the phone. It was Rebecca.

"Hello Becky," I said. "It's your dad..."

"Who?" she asked, and then a squeal..."Daddy! Mommy, it's Daddy!"

Stella was on the phone immediately.

"A little late to be calling," she said.

"The kids seem to be up."

"Just getting them to bed. They're beat."

"They have a good day?"

"Pretty good. They didn't get everything they wanted but what they wanted was everything. They took the toboggan over to the park for an hour."

"So can I talk to them?"

Silence.

"Carmello's there," I said. "Right?"

"Right," she said.

"Well, give them my love."

"I will," she said. "And thanks for bringing the stuff by."

She hung up and I listened to the dial tone for a few seconds. Then I went back to the dining room and found the whole family gathered around the table drinking tea. I took a quick drink of the cup that had been poured for me.

"I should be going," I said.

"I'd sure like to hear about Springboard," Mike said.

"Some other time," I said.

"Well, I think what you did for those old people was a fine thing," Audrey said. "It shows the rest of us how selfish we are."

"He did it, Aud, because he had nothing else to do," Bal said.

He looked at me for confirmation. I nodded agreement and finished off my tea. I stood up and so did Anne.

"I'll walk you to the subway," Anne said.

"I'll drive you," Mike chirped, "if my dad will loan me the car."

Bal frowned.

"Ask your mother...it's her turn to pay for the next smash-up, I paid for the last."

"I'm happy to go on the subway," I said.

Mike's bright smile collapsed into blankness and a hint of anger. I edged out of the room and made it to the front hall. Anne was right behind me. In a few seconds the other family members had gathered to see us off.

"Thanks for having me," I said.

I shook hands all around again.

"You're welcome anytime," Audrey said.

Bal made a snorting noise, then Anne and I were out the door.

We walked through a tunnel of snow-covered elm trees for a block without speaking. I realized I'd forgotten my wine and cheese. I started to laugh.

"What?" Anne asked.

"Your family," I said. "Are they always like that...kind of trampling all over each other?"

"They don't know any better," she said.

"Your father does."

"Yeah, he's the weird one."

I took her hand. My hands were bare and she was wearing woolen mittens. I noticed she had on a scarf, wrapped around her throat. A sensible precaution against the cold. I didn't even own winter boots.

"I like your dad," I said.

"Me too," she said. "He pussyfoots too. Just like the rest of them but then he reverts to his natural self, which is blunt."

"Like you," I said.

"I wish I was...more that way," she said.

We arrived at the station and stopped. I wanted more than anything to convince her to come home with me. I wanted her to want me in her life as much as I wanted her.

"You want to come back to my place?" I asked. "I've got an alarm clock.... You could get back in time. I've got a poem I wrote after our movie the other night I could show you."

She laughed.

"Is that the writer's equivalent of etchings?"

"Hell, I've got better than that," I said. "My walls are covered with real paintings...not exactly the ceiling of the Basilica..."

"Do you think you'll ever be a famous writer?" she asked. "Like Margaret?"

"No," I said.

"Why not? She thinks you have talent."

"I haven't got her obsession," I said.

"So what will you do?"

"You mean when I grow up?"

"Yes," she said.

"I dunno...marry you, maybe."

"That's spooky," she said.

"Why?"

"Because it's not enough...I guess I want someone who's obsessed."

"I am," I said, "with you."

"Worse! I've got my mother for that!... Are you cold?" she asked abruptly.

"Frozen," I said.

"Kiss me," she said.

I did and then she turned me around and shoved me toward the entrance to the station.

"I'll see you in the new year," she said. "And don't need me so much...you'll have better luck."

On the subway home I though of what she had said. I wished there was someone I could talk to. I thought of Margaret, of Hagar in *The Stone Angel*, of Rachel in *A Jest of God*. Of how those women needed to be needed, and to declare this need. It was one of the things I loved about those characters, their needs made them so human. Their need to be connected to other humans on this strange planet Earth, their struggle to achieve intimacy, wasn't that what life was all about?

I arrived home and as I climbed the stairs to my room, a wave of exhaustion rolled over me. I felt grateful for the day. Tomorrow I would figure out the meaning of life, the ground rules for love, and other important questions concerning the universe. Now I needed to sleep.

As I climbed into bed my eyes were drawn to the picket fence along the wall. I read the caption again. DON'T FENCE ME IN.

Maybe that's what Anne was talking about.

David Helwig

Barry Morris

Maggie Nistad

Ed Laboucane

Me, Anne and Jane Rule on our first meeting

Jane Rule and Helen Sonthoff on Galiano Island

Dale Zieroth and Jane Rule

Margaret and Tommy Bell, godmother and godfather

Tommy Bell, Anne, me and John Metson at Daniel's christening

At Margaret's 50th birthday party

Me and Daniel

Anne and Daniel

The three of us

Tommy Bell, Anne and Daniel on his second birthday

At Margaret's Lakefield home on Daniel's third birthday

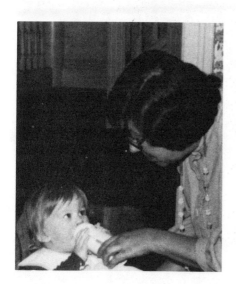

Margaret tending Daniel

A pensive moment

Margaret's magic treehouse

Ms. Turtle

Greta Garbage

At peace watching the river go by

With Daniel in front of our Toronto
house shortly after Anne's death

Daniel leads the way as I escort Daile
from the altar

1970: Tightrope Walking

Early in 1970 I attended a staff meeting of the Christian Resource Centre at which a man from the St. Lawrence Centre made a pitch for us to stage an event at their soon-to-be-opened Town Hall. He suggested a political rally, or a panel of experts who would discuss some pertinent social issue.

I though of Springboard. The authorities had finally given me permission to go into the institutions. I'd held several meetings with inmate committees, asking them what they needed. The overwhelming consensus was that they wanted a transportation system so their families could visit them. A reliable transportation system that was cheap, preferably free.

I drifted back to the meeting and listened to the guy's pitch.

"A variety show," I suggested.

"What?" he asked.

"A huge variety show, with people in the community coming out and showing off their talent. I'll bet we could find hundreds of people who sing and dance, tell jokes. Cabbagetown's full of talent."

"I like it," the guy said.

"I'll bet we could get Hugh Garner to MC," I said.

The guy was bouncing in his seat.

"Great!" he said.

"Who's going to organize it?" John Metson asked.

"If nobody else wants to, I will," I said.

"I'll help," Anne said.

I looked at John, expecting him to veto that idea, but then Barry spoke up.

"I think that's a terrific idea...Annie's wanted to get more involved in the community and this sounds like a great opportunity."

"Okay," John said. "As long as it doesn't interfere with your other duties…"

He was looking at Anne. She nodded at him and smiled across at me.

The next two months were frantic. I appeared on television and radio shows to pitch for volunteers for Springboard. Then I raced to auditions that Anne had organized in church basements and libraries. Hugh Garner had agreed to MC the show and insisted on coming to all the auditions. He required a certain amount of hand-holding as the number of participants began to grow.

"The damn cast's gonna be bigger than *War and Peace*," he said one night. "And you gotta get those old dames who dance and blow kazoos on and off the stage faster."

Volunteers began to trickle in for Springboard. I had to set up a training programme for them. What did I know that they needed to know? I didn't know—I faked it. Letters were pouring in from the prisons. Men writing, sending me information on their wives, girlfriends and mothers, phone numbers, addresses, wanting me to contact them. Arrange rides. I needed someone to help me who could follow up the letters, find out if these women needed other help. Anne was too busy with the concert. I didn't feel right doing it myself. But then one day just when I thought a fatal flaw had appeared in the scheme, a red-haired bundle of energy bounced into my office and declared she had all the free time in the world and she wanted to help out.

Her name was Maggie Nistad. Her husband, Warren, was a minister who counselled draft dodgers who fled to Canada. They had both left their home in the United States to protest the Vietnam War. She was twenty-two years old and brimming over with love for all humanity. Except the American administration. I put her to work immediately and within a week she had our transportation system underway. It was shaky at first, and sometimes volunteers backed out at the last minute and we had to scramble for someone else, or fill in ourselves. But it was functional.

During this period I called Margaret several times. She too was busy. Too busy for lunch or dinner. She urged me on in my writing and I told her I'd mail off some stuff that I'd been working on. She sounded frenzied on the phone but had a curious interest in the variety show.

"It's really going to happen?" she asked.

"Sure, Anne's got it all organized."

"And Hugh Garner is really going to MC it?"

"Absolutely. We're in rehearsals now and he never misses one. I think he's scared we'll change the programme..."

She laughed.

"You get yourself into the damnedest things," she said. "But I want to see this extravaganza, so call and remind me."

I promised I would.

One morning I woke up and found Anne in bed with me. The rehearsal had run late the night before and without any prompting, she had just come home with me. But we hadn't made love. We were both exhausted. I watched her sleeping and wondered why I wanted so much for her to be part of my life. I leaned over and kissed her. She woke up.

"I love you," I said.

"You'll say anything to wear a person down," she replied.

Then we did make love. It was awkward. I banged my head on the slanted ceiling. The bed was too small. We got tangled in the sheets and blankets. But we laughed and that gave us the grace to be tender and generous with each other's vulnerability.

"This doesn't mean what you think," Anne said later.

"What's that?" I asked.

"I'm still keeping my options open...I mean this is nice but I don't want to be pinned down to anything."

"Understood," I said.

I didn't understand. Not really. But then I was doing with my life what I wanted. Anne wasn't sure yet. She didn't want to be swept along by my enthusiasm and mistake it for her own. There was still a gap between us. A pass with no bridge. I yearned to cross it, it hurt to stand on the other side. It would be many years before I learned that love allows us humans to wave at each other, sometimes touch, but never close that gap. That only happens in our imaginations.

The night of the concert, I picked up Margaret in a cab an hour before the show was to start. By the time we got to the theatre the sidewalks were jammed with people waiting to get in. We used the stage door and I took Margaret to the dressing room so she could meet Hugh Garner. Unfortunately, he was half in the bag with a forty ouncer of vodka close at hand.

"I'll go get a seat," she said. "Looks like you may be needed."

But the show went smoothly. Hugh rambled a little as he told stories of his childhood and growing up in Cabbagetown, but the audience thought he was wonderful. We used the extra time to get the Regent Park Go-Go band on, which was made up of thirty elderly ladies, all dolled up in Parisian gowns, who played toy kazoos and danced the can-can. And then there were the twenty-four tap-dancing checkers, all children under ten who had to be lined up properly on the board. There was a big set change near the middle of the show and I'd written a skit for Anne and me. We sat on the edge of the stage pretending to be in a cab. She was the driver and I played a mouse trap manufacturer attending a convention, who was out to find a hot time for himself. We got a few laughs.

But the biggest hit of the night was a lady named Rosie. She didn't come to auditions because she was crippled with arthritis. She lived in a small Ontario Housing apartment in St. James Town. She sang for us in her small kitchen and was thrilled when we asked her to be in the show.

She knew exactly how she wanted to do her number. The stage was dark. A spot slowly revealed her sitting at a small table with a glass and a bottle of whisky. The music came up and she hoisted herself up on crutches. Painfully she stepped forward and softly began to sing, "My Man." Her voice grew in volume and depth until it broke through everyone's defensive barriers, and she threw down the crutches, wobbling and warbling her heart out. The audience went wild and demanded an encore. So she did the same song over again. I learned later it was the only one she knew by heart.

The last act was a calypso band. When they launched into "Age of Aquarius," the audience surged forward and filled the stage. People were dancing and embracing each other. We called out the hundred-and-fifty performers to take a bow, and they too joined in dancing.

I looked around and found Margaret hugging Rosie.

"What guts" she said, wiping the tears from her eyes. She hugged me. "I hate crowds but this...this ain't a crowd, Bailey. It's a goddamn tribe!"

Anne came over and Margaret put her arm around her and began to steer the two of us backstage.

"You two were hilarious," she said. She spotted Hugh heading toward the dressing room and waved.

"Let's go see if he has any of that bottle left. I could sure stand a drink.... Even vodka."

Life became a juggling act. The pressure from Springboard's presence in the prisons was mounting every day. Letters arrived with requests for us to help one guy's wife find an affordable house big enough for her and their three children. She didn't have a car so it needed to be downtown. Could we get Mother's Allowance to put a guy's common-law wife and kids on provincial welfare? Did we have volunteer families for guys who had no one in the outside community?

The volunteers themselves required support and nurturing. Maggie Nistad was working sixteen, eighteen hours a day, and like myself was not being paid. We had no budget to compensate her for the gas she burned in her car, the lunches she bought for distraught wives. I took on more and more luncheon engagements, speaking to the Rotary club, church groups, Daughters of the Empire, making my pitch that they could help by volunteering time and putting in money. Some days I'd come back to the office with two pounds of change, the result of passing around the large leather hat that I'd taken to wearing. We'd stack up the coins and see if we had enough dough to finance another trip to the Kingston area so we could visit the prisons. Or should we use it for the postage on the return letters to the guys inside?

At night I wrote. One of the small publishing companies that were mushrooming up everywhere, the House of Anansi, accepted ten of my poems for publication in an anthology that was to appear in the fall. I suggested to Dale Zieroth that he send them some stuff. To my mind he was a real poet. I just sort of dabbled in it. He sent in some material and it was immediately accepted.

I got lucky with a review I wrote for the *Canadian Forum* of David Helwig's book, *Streets of Summer*. The editor of the magazine, Abe Rotstein, liked my work, and asked me for more. There was no money involved but, as Margaret said, the publishing of my work gave me a presence in the writing community. She claimed this was important.

I had a relationship with Anne that included sexual union but was barren of future commitment. She was still seeing other men, and it seemed to me I fit into her life like a spare part held in reserve in case there was a system breakdown. I tried not to think about it and I certainly had enough activity to keep me occupied, but I was still bothered. I called Margaret at Massey College to see if she had a little time to dispense some advice. Fortunately a student had canceled the next day and she could see me during lunch. She told me to bring sandwiches.

A secretary showed me into a huge, wood-paneled office with leather couches and chairs arranged into a sitting area. It was a dark, cool space with twelve-foot-high bookcases, the shelves pulsating with leather-bound volumes of literature. It was the kind of room I imagined all real writers had, a place big enough to pace, with vast amounts of material to induce intellectual foreplay before one actually sat down and wrote.

Margaret had created a small fortress area in one corner of the room. She had moved her desk as close to the wall as possible and it was stacked with numerous piles of manuscripts through which she could peek and not be observed. But I knew she was there because of the cloud of smoke.

I went to the sitting area and took the corned beef sandwiches from their bag.

"Lunch is served," I called.

"Oh kiddo," she moaned, and appeared from behind the barrier. She was holding a sheaf of pages and was looking at them with distaste. She walked over to one of the couches and plunked down.

"I need a moat built around me," she said. "Anybody and their dog can drop stuff off for me to read.... Some of it's dreadful...but what do I say to the poor soul when they want to know what I think? This women here has written a two-hundred-page female family tree. Everything you never wanted to know about her Aunt Matilda...."

She laughed and put down the pages.

"Can't you just be honest?" I asked.

"You mean tell them they're wasting their time?"

"And yours," I said, handing her a sandwich.

"That's what I'm being paid for, kiddo. Besides, what she's trying to do is sort of interesting...it's just so badly written."

We ate and she poured us coffee from a big urn.

"They think of everything here," she said. "I'm complaining but I'm treated very well.... If I really don't want to see someone, the secretary writes them a nice polite letter and returns their manuscript.

I just feel so guilty turning anybody away."

"I imagine there are some insistent people."

"You bet... one guy managed to get my home number and he just hounds me. Poor Eleanor keeps expecting him to show up on our doorstep... of course it'll happen when I'm out and she'll have to handle him herself."

"Sounds creepy."

"I've run into a couple like him before," she said. "One in London and then another when we lived in Vancouver... you'll get them someday... PPPs I call them: public people parasites. They just want to attach themselves to you for a while, feed off you and whatever glory it is they think you have. If you're a woman and they're men, they're usually not happy unless they can screw you... then you get to be a scalp they can hang from their lodge pole."

"It doesn't sound healthy," I said.

She lit a cigarette and I realized the cream-coloured pant suit she was wearing was made of a polyester material. It was a strange thing to notice and I started to giggle. She shot a startled look my way.

"I'm sorry," I said, "I was sitting here feeling worried about this weird guy who calls you but it doesn't seem to bother you, then you light a smoke and I notice that what you're wearing is highly inflammable.... It just struck me as funny. As if everything we do is dangerous."

She pinched some of the material of the suit between her fingers.

"True, it is," she said. "And I think we respond to danger in proportion to the convenience factor."

She smiled.

"Take this suit.... I love it. It gets dirty, I throw it in the washer for ten minutes, put it in the dryer for another ten and whammo! Clean, no wrinkles. I take it when I'm travelling and I can rinse it out in my hotel room in the bath tub, put it on a hanger and there it is, all fresh and ready to go in the morning... you see. Convenience... who cares if it's dangerous... besides I never set fire to myself. In fact I'm pretty sure I was wearing this one night in London when I was a guest at a church supper. It was right after I won the Gov Gen for *Jest of God*. Anyway, it was a ladies' auxiliary group and in those days, when I was asked to something, an occasion designed to honour me, I felt obligated to attend. It was a church basement, with a bunch of long tables set in a square... probably the same tables they used for bingo or cribbage so they'd covered them with paper table cloths so we wouldn't have to read all the graffiti inscribed by generations of bored youth…Toby loves Tony…Tony loves Ted…Ted loves Toby…actually I love to read that stuff. Anyway, the meal came and went…no booze, of course. The woman in charge asked me how long I'd be speaking. Migawd! I was speechless. Totally unprepared…I thought showing up was all I had to do…. I told her no more than five minutes and then instantly that seemed like an eternity…what could I say. I needed a cigarette to think but no one else was smoking. I asked her could I slip off to the can for a fast puff and she said oh, please, don't trouble yourself, no one will mind. But of course I did…my Presbyterian upbringing reared its ugly head, so I ducked down like I'd dropped something and lit my smoke. Then I held it under the table while I frantically thought of what I could talk about…literature…Canadian literature…writers…women writers…what? And then the chairwoman was introducing me. I went to put out my cigarette and saw to my horror that I'd touched it against the paper tablecloth and the damn think was smouldering…So what did I do?"

"You blew on it," I said.

She burst into a fit of laughing and coughing.

"That's exactly what I did…with the usual results. A small, flickering flame began to make its way along the tablecloth. I was paralyzed. I had visions of the whole place going up, and stood there trying to remember if Cromwell or some other great historical figure was buried behind the furnace room. I was convinced we'd all die and my children would have to live with the inheritance of forever being known as the offspring of Pyromaniac Peggy. I saw my own obituary: Margaret Laurence, author of *The Fire Dwellers*, and other books, ignited herself and eighty-two members of the Wycliffe Anglican Church Ladies Auxiliary early last evening…I was transfixed…stunned into inaction. Suddenly the lady introducing me noticed the flames heading her way. As calm as a swan she picked up the pitcher of water beside her and poured it all over the table…I swear not one eye blinked in the place."

"So what did you talk about?"

She laughed at the memory.

"Household dangers. I told a story about how I hated to darn, but I was always leaving clothes around that needed repairs to remind myself to do them...David ended up finding a loose button from a shirt when he was three and of course he swallowed it. Almost choked to death and after that, I never again pretended to be a sewer. A weaver of stories maybe, but no darning for this doll."

We sat in silence for a moment. I was feeling nervous about my mission. Margaret had enough on her plate without being hassled by me. My problem was really just inaction. If I felt as strongly about Anne as I told myself, I would demand that she make a commitment. But I hadn't. Maybe I didn't want her to.

"So what's happening with you and Anne?" Margaret asked.

"I don't know," I said. "I feel like I'm in the bull pen most of the time, warming up in case the designated pitcher falls apart."

"No one's keeping you there except yourself," she said.

"That's true, but when I push her for more, she backs off."

"What do you want from her?"

I laughed.

"Everything," I said.

"I'll bet you do...you're a guy in a rush to do everything, see everything, have it all. She's more cautious, but practical too. You live like you've got a fire inside you."

"I've got a lot of time to make up for."

"Sure. But she doesn't...No wonder you frighten her. She doesn't know what you're going to do next. Nobody does. You coralled her into helping you with that community show and look what happened."

"It was a great success. The St. Lawrence Centre offered me a job to organize other community events."

"But you didn't take it...Any guy in his right mind would've. A normal, settled type of guy would have seen it as a great opportunity, but instead you're trying to save all the ex- cons you can get your hands on, doing it with spit and baling wire. I'm not being critical, Don. I admire your passion and the energy of your enthusiasm but looking at you strictly from a female perspective...a young woman seeking a partner in life who will be the father of her children...you wouldn't be my first choice. Oh yeah, and the guy fancies himself a writer too."

There was passion in her voice. Anger too.

"So what should I do?"

She lit another cigarette and gave me an exasperated look.

"Just accept her. For who she is to herself...she's not the mother who walked out on you...she's not your first girlfriend who humiliated you at the school dance...she's not the social workers or teachers who messed you around. She's just herself. She doesn't owe you a damn thing!"

"I know that."

"Sure you do, but everybody brings their own history to a relationship...you don't have a good history with women and you bring that distrust. You want Anne to compensate you for the pain you've experienced elsewhere...it's not fair, Bailey. To you or her. I'm talking from experience, kiddo. I'm going to live out whatever old age is granted to me, alone."

"Come on Margaret, you're still young. You'll meet men."

She laughed and got up from the couch. She began to pace.

"I've met them...let me tell you, they're no bargain. It's ironic. I was a feminist before it had a name. What I want from a man right now is distraction...some entertainment...a nice dinner...followed by an energetic romp between the sheets."

I laughed.

"Nothing wrong with that."

Margaret stopped pacing and glared at me.

"Let me tell you what I get.... Men of my generation are frantic that life has passed them by...those that have the energy dress and behave as though they're ten years younger...they hang around the meat-market bars trying to latch on to one of the young women dispensing what they think of as free love...but nothing's free. They discover those young women have performance expectations...in bed...and these guys can't cut it. They want to be comforted. They want a woman who understands them, who soothes and forgives them for just being men, and so they come to women of my generation for all the things missing...never imagining that we want the same things as our younger sisters...or daughters. I'm damned if I'm going to spend my later years serving as a comfortable chair for some man to lounge around in...every man I meet wants to curl up to me...put up his feet like I was an old hassock...I'm not furniture...shit!"

Tears were running down her cheeks. I didn't know what to do. I got up and put out my arms but she waved me away.

"Sorry," she said after a few minutes. "It's a sore spot.... I'm trying to put it all in the new novel."

She went to her desk and found a Kleenex, blew her nose loudly and wandered back to the couch.

"It's the hardest thing I've ever tried to write," she said. "Probably because it's the closest thing I've written to my own life. It's too close.... I'm having a tough time with it."

"I know what you mean," I said. "I wrote to Jane Rule and I guess I was moaning and groaning about how tough it is. She reminded me that no one had asked us to do this...you know it's not like we write on command from God or something."

"We do it because we have to," she said. "It is our destiny...and our responsibility...and yours now, too, because you're a member of the tribe."

She looked deeply into my eyes and I felt she had the power to see things in me that I was oblivious to. I was just a guy trying to make sense out of my life. I wasn't a member of any tribe. I wanted to belong somewhere, but so far the place where I had felt the most real was prison. I hungered for roots but remained feeling rootless. Maybe my need to belong was seen by Anne as a threat to consume her.

"Margaret, how do you know when a guy wants to turn you into furniture?"

"It's not hard to figure out...he tells you how restful you are. He calls you his oasis in the turbulent sea of life...crap that's meant to be complimentary but it communicates what he wants...a soft place to lay his weary head."

She looked at her watch.

"Migawd, I've got somebody coming in ten minutes."

She sprang up from the couch and gathered up the sandwich wrappers and coffee cups. She caught me smiling at her actions.

"Women's training," she said, and smiled back. "But you brought lunch, so it's fair."

"Is that what it comes down to?" I asked. "Who takes out the garbage...keeping everything in balance?"

"Partly," she said. "No one wants it taken for granted that they'll do all the crummy jobs, male or female. But what I want from a man is to be treated as though I'm at least as much of a challenge as his golf game...or some big business deal he's trying to pull off.... I'm not a fucking reward he gets for bringing home the bacon!"

She was angry again and she lit a cigarette to get it under control. "You understand?" she asked.

"No," I admitted, "but I'll think about it...I mean I understand what you're saying but I'm not sure how it comes about. I don't think I want Anne in my life as some kind of reward... ."

She smiled, took a deep drag of her cigarette and looked for a few seconds much older than her forty-three years.

"You do though. She's the golden girl, the brass ring that will prove Bailey is finally making it."

God, how close to the truth was that, I wondered. Pretty close.

"I'll keep it in mind," I said.

"If you two get together, it'll be her decision."

"So maybe I'm wasting my time worrying."

"Probably...so go write something, but first give your old Aunt Margaret a hug."

I embraced her. She didn't feel old, with her slim body pressed against me. She astonished me by putting her mouth against mine and kissing me deeply. I was light-headed, disoriented at my own powerful response. Then she pulled away gently and held me at arms' length.

"We all have needs," she said.

Before I could respond she was leading me to the door.

"I'm going out to my shack in June," she said. "I want to get in a couple of months writing time before I go back home. Give me a call and we'll arrange for you to come up on a weekend. I don't work then."

Her cheerful smile waned.

"Go," she said. "And don't think that everything that happens is within your control."

I didn't see Margaret again until that summer. In the meantime many events unfolded. Ed Laboucane was released from prison. He came and worked with me at Springboard even though he didn't agree with my approach. We spent a lot of time arguing, which was difficult since Ed was not a big talker. He made statements and let me chew at them by myself.

Ed was a loner. In the joint he had amassed money and power by taking control of contraband. He set up card games and pieced off the range guard so the cell became off-limits and was not raided. With another guard, he arranged the delivery of small amounts of booze.

He loaned money to guys who gambled and lost. He dealt dope and pornography. But he wasn't a typical jail house merchant. Ed had a small group of guys who carried his cash, delivered merchandise, and took the risk in all his transactions. He was a broker. He arranged things, took a percentage cut of the transactions, but managed to keep an arms' length distance between himself and being caught.

Ed was Métis. He had grown up on a small ranch south of Edmonton where his family raised quarter horses. In 1970 he was thirty years old, three years older than me. There was also a three-year difference in our educations. I was a grade eight drop-out, but Ed had left school before completing grade five. In the joint, though, he'd taught himself to read and speak French. He married a Ukrainian women five years his senior, when he was twenty-two. Her family owned a large, lucrative ranch in Alberta and since they had no sons, Ed imagined someday he would run the place. But after four years and the birth of a male child, it was apparent to him that the family would always view him as an interloper. He left and became a fraud man. Using stolen ID that he purchased, he wandered the country cashing bogus cheques, lived in hotels, developed a large thirst for whisky, and kept his ears open for high stake poker games that he could buy his way into.

He was a con man. The best I ever met. But who was he conning? The world or himself? It was impossible to tell. But working together in Springboard, we were a good team. Ed wore expensive suits that he purchased in second-hand stores. He had a great eye for finding hand tailored garments that fit his five-ten, one-hundred-and-sixty-pound body perfectly. I wore jeans. Ed wore his black hair short, mine was long. In meetings, Ed rarely spoke. His handsome face remained impassive, impossible to read. I pitched non-stop.

The breakdown of our roles suggested that I was the bird dog and Ed was the hunter. I flushed out the quarry and Ed bagged them. Neither of us understood what made the combination work. But it did. One of the things we agreed on was that we needed to find some kind of work for ex-cons to do when they came out. I came up with the idea of delivering flyers. I went to several drugstore chains and convinced them to let us distribute their door-to-door advertisements. Now we needed a truck. Ed and I canvassed the neighbourhood around the Christian Resource Centre and found a beat-up half-ton parked on the street. We knocked on the doors of the nearby rooming houses and located the owner. He was an old, alcoholic reprobate by the name of Wes. He agreed to be part of our scheme as long as we arrived at his room at five every morning with a bottle of wine to get his system going. Ed and I took turns. Wes was from the east coast and along with his ration of wine in the morning he insisted on cooking up a couple of pounds of salt cod. The stuff stank, and how he could function fueled by that combination I never understood. But it worked. Within a week we had the Springboard Flyer Force in action. Word got out and we always had enough guys fresh out of the joint ready to work. It was a simple and effective way for guys to get a few dollars in their pockets without stealing.

Shortly after the Flyer Force was underway, John Metson arranged for me to meet Norman McLean, who was chairman of Canada Packers. He was a short guy who within a minute of meeting me was bumming cigarettes. He was eighty-two, and his doctor forbade smoking. I told him we were trying to find permanent jobs for men coming out of prison. My proposal was that Canada Packers take on guys who had worked consistently for a month in the Flyer Force. Norm liked the idea and said he would arrange a meeting with the board of directors and union representatives.

The meeting was held in a plush boardroom. I talked for forty-five minutes. When I finished, one of the union officials commented that ex-cons were not known for their reliability. He asked Ed how he planned to deal with this. Ed rose to his feet, cleared his throat, and swept the room with his pale blue eyes. He stood tall, his brow knitted slightly as though he were choosing his words carefully, thinking of exactly the right thing to say. Fifteen or twenty seconds of silence passed. Tension filled the room like a cloud of humidity. Then he spoke.

"Any guy we send to you will be answerable to us."

He sat down.

Later over lunch, Norm was chortling at our success.

"Your partner doesn't say much," he remarked as he smoked one of my cigarettes, "but what he does say, is effective."

Ed smiled and made no comment.

I was extremely busy. More and more guys released from prison made their way from the bus terminal to our office. Ed sometimes handled them but he didn't have a lot of patience with their anxieties. Besides, he'd secured a job as head doorman at the Le Coq d'Or hotel, and days when he wasn't with the Flyer Force he liked to sleep until noon.

So much of the time-consuming activity of just being with an ex-con when he first got out fell to me. It didn't leave a lot of time for Anne and I to explore and develop our relationship. I saw her during the day and sometimes we had lunch. She still attended the writers' group on Wednesday night and usually we arranged to spend Friday evenings together. Sometimes she'd make dinner at her place, or we'd go out to one of the inexpensive restaurants on Parliament, and then we'd walk over to Yonge Street and take in a movie. Afterward we'd go to the Winchester for a few beers, lots of talk.

Anne was an unhappy woman. She'd been brought up with the notion that her role in life was to find the right man, marry him and make a home. What she wanted, though, was to make a career for herself. She'd applied to Carleton University's School of Social Work and been turned down. The interviewer said she didn't have the maturity needed to be a professional helper. This infuriated Anne but it didn't help her clarify what it was she wanted to focus her energy on.

I suppose my fondness for her, the love that pushed its way into the recesses of my soul and took root, was in part based on her rage. Something had gone horribly wrong in her years of imagining a life that was soft and gentle. She had been bruised and wounded. I imagined myself as a healer, someone who could soothe and comfort the hurts. Through that, I would be healed too, and comforted.

One Wednesday she did not appear at the writers' group until the meeting was breaking up.

"I can't make Friday night," she said.

"Okay."

"Brian's coming into town. I've been talking with him a lot lately on the phone. He suggested I come to Ottawa. I could enrol at Carleton, take some courses and apply for graduate school next year."

"Sounds like serious planning," I said.

"He's still got two more years of school before we could get married."

Her face had a pinched expression. Was I supposed to talk her out of this rendezvous? Did she want me to paint a picture of some promised land where she and I could live happily ever after?

I was mad. Brian. John. They all seemed like fantasies to me. If nothing else, I was real and would include her in whatever journey our mutual lives took. Wasn't that enough?

"I've got a lot of history with him," she said. "I feel I owe it to him to give it another chance. And to myself."

"Fine," I said.

"You're angry," she said.

"No, I'm not. Resigned is the word that comes to mind."

"Don't be angry," she said, and left.

Dale Zieroth was standing a few feet away and must have heard the exchange.

"Wanna go for a beer?" he asked. "I've got an idea you might be interested in."

We were joined at the Winchester by Barry, who served as confessor to us all, so he knew what was going on between Anne and me.

"You should stick with your own kind," he said.

I'd had a few beers and his remark didn't sit well.

"Sometimes you're full of crap, Barry. You're telling me that Anne's out of my league, that because I'm an ex-con I should hook up with some reformed hooker? Find myself a fellow downtrodden soul that I can relate to?"

Dale lifted his glass and made a toast.

"Women and pain," he said.

Barry got up from the table.

"Some day, Bailey, the world's gonna catch up to you. You'll have to face who you are or drown your sorrows in a pail of booze."

He headed out the door and I ordered another round. Maybe I did drink too much. Booze relaxed me. It opened up a clear space in my mind where I could wander through my memories at will, and the alcohol dulled the rage that sometimes threatened to explode, or maybe implode. I was afraid it would blow me apart and I'd disappear into the air in a million fragments.

"Marge and I are thinking of getting a farm," Dale said.

"What a great idea," I said. Dale had grown up on a large prairie farm and much of what he wrote was concerned with the land. I also knew the city made him uneasy.

"We were wondering if you'd come to dinner Friday night and talk about it."

"Sure," I said. My Friday was open.

"We were hoping you might want to come in on it with us."

"Live with you?"

"Yeah."

I laughed.

"Sounds crazy, eh?"

"No, it's just that I've never thought of it before. When I was a kid I lived in a foster home that was on a farm. It was great."

"So you'll come."

"Sure," I said.

He left a few minutes later and I sat there until last call, ruminating on the random direction my life seemed to be taking. I sat by myself, content to be alone watching the couples and gatherings of people at the other tables, their voices animated. The babble of talk made me think of kites, dreams looking for the right current to sail them high into the sky to dance among the clouds.

Dale and Marge lived in a modest apartment on Metcalfe, just a block from the Christian Resource Centre. I arrived with a bottle of wine and a strong sense of trepidation. I'd only met Marge a couple of times and I sensed that she felt threatened by my influence on Dale. She was a quiet, shy person. Warm and welcoming but somewhat hesitant about new ventures. We talked little during dinner but finally after a second bottle of wine was opened it was Marge who did most of the talking.

"We want to find a place close enough to the city so we can commute," she said. "We've talked to a number of real estate agents and there are plenty of places, forty, fifty miles out. Some of them are abandoned and need work."

"We'd need a car," I said.

"We figured we could pool our money and buy a clunker," she said. "Just something to get us back and forth. None of us have to be at jobs right at nine."

Dale was a teacher at a free school called Point Blank. Its structure was pretty loose. Marge worked at House of Anansi publishers, and they too had flexible hours. Springboard's Flyer Force was in a profit situation and I'd hired a guy to run it so I didn't have to be in the city at five a.m.

"I like the idea," I said. "I'm curious as to why you asked me."

Dale was a bit tipsy. With his thick, droopy mustache he looked a bit foolish as he grinned, shrugged and said: "We like you."

I looked over at Marge who was sitting in a chair on the other side of the small living room. She held my gaze and then rose and walked over to me. Instinctively, I rose and she put her arms around me. It was a warm, solid embrace. I felt tears dripping on my neck.

"You'll drive us crazy with your antics," she said, and then began to laugh softly.

I was touched by their generous gesture. I hardly knew these people and yet they had invited me to be part of their lives. Why? I couldn't figure it out. But I knew that I wanted what they were offering.

Suddenly there was a loud knocking on the door. Dale sprang up and opened it. A young woman entered. She was dressed in a long, black, billowing skirt and a black silk blouse with puffed sleeves. On her head she wore a black kerchief tied at the corners so it sat like a skull cap. A gypsy, I thought. Her long silver earrings tinkled as she strode into the room. The silver bracelets on her wrists jangled. Her movements were musical. Marge appeared and the two women embraced.

"This is Denise," Marge said. "She's thinking of coming in on the farm with us."

The young woman held out her hand to me. Her eyes were black. Not dark brown. Pure, mysterious black. I felt myself pulled into their depths.

"You're Bailey," she said, and smiled. "I've heard about you."

Dale and Marge stood there grinning. This meeting was a set-up.

"Sorry I'm so late," Denise said. "Have I missed everything?"

Dale yawned.

"We talked about the farm, and Don's in."

Denise turned to me. She looked young. Eighteen maybe. Bubbling with energy. Eyes sparkling with pleasure at everything that came into view. She glowed, and I thought, if I were a moth I would gladly annihilate myself against the light she radiated.

"I've got an idea," she said. "Why don't we let these guys pack it in and you and I go for a beer at the Winchester."

"Sure," I said, "but maybe we should all talk about the farm thing together."

Marge yawned.

"We aren't nighthawks like you guys. So you go ahead."

It was eleven o'clock. I couldn't believe they were serious. No one goes to bed that early. They just wanted to force us to spend time together. Fine with me.

The Winchester was just a block away. The minute we were out the door, Denise took my hand and began to skip along the street. I'm not a skipper so I had to run to keep up with her.

She insisted we sit in the live music section. The country and western band destroyed the songs of Buck Owens, Waylon Jennings, and Charlie Pride indiscriminately. They were loud, so we danced.

I've never been a great dancer but in Denise's embrace I experienced a fluidity in my body that flowed into the current of her rhythms. I felt aroused. Touching her was erotic. My heart pounded. I wanted to devour her.

When the band took a break, she left our table and approached the leader. She spoke with him for a few minutes and I saw him laugh and nod his head.

"He's going to let me do a song," she said.

The band reassembled and she ran back to the stage. A short conference was held with the musicians. She stepped up to the mike and began to sing, her voice soft and throaty..."Oh once there was a tavern..."

The band was restrained, letting Denise's voice provide the energy. People began to clap to the rousing rhythm. Then the place settled into a hushed silence at the melancholy conclusion. She allowed several seconds silence and then broke into the spirited chorus again. When she finished, the audience clapped and clamoured for more. But she left the stage and came back to the table.

"That was great," I said.

Her eyes sparkled.

"You wanna do something?" she asked.

"Sure."

In seconds we were out the door again running down Winchester Street. She ran up to a door and pounded.

"Mary!" she shouted. "It's me...open up."

In a few moments, a woman wearing an old bathrobe opened the door. Obviously she'd been asleep. Denise pushed past her into the ground floor apartment. There were paintings and half-finished canvases piled everywhere.

"Look," Denise said, "Isn't this great stuff? Mary's going to be famous someday... .Look at the colours!"

I looked. I couldn't make sense out of any of the images but the colours were great: bright and bold.

Mary, the artist, slumped into a chair.

"You guys know what time it is.... I gotta work in the morning."

"Tomorrow's Saturday," Denise said.

"I'm filling in for someone."

Denise ignored this.

"This is Don.... I wanted him to meet my best friend...share a glass of wine...you know, like communion."

Mary held out a weary hand but she wore an amused smile.

"Hi," she said.

Denise was already off in the kitchen rummaging around. She returned with three glasses.

"Couldn't find the wine," she said.

"Fresh out," Mary answered.

"That's okay, I'll go upstairs and bang on Tony's door. He's always got plenty."

I stood up to stop her but Mary waved me to a chair.

"When she's got an idea, she's like a runaway freight train. Nothing can stop her."

"I'm sorry for barging in on you like this."

"It's okay. With Denise I'm used to it.... She must like you a lot to bring you here. She's never brought another guy."

"We just met a couple of hours ago. I feel like I'm caught up in a tornado."

Mary laughed.

"Don't fight it."

"Where do you have to be in the morning?" I asked.

"I'm a nurses' aide over at the Wellesley."

"How do you know Denise?"

"She took art lessons from me when I taught at Point Blank. She's a natural but she bounces around from one thing to another. She's doing pottery now."

"Success!" Denise shouted as she entered with half a bottle of wine held high. She poured us each a glass.

"To friendships," she said, clinking her glass against ours. "To the new ones, to the old ones, and the ones we haven't imagined yet."

We sat for a quiet moment sipping our drinks.

"You look beat, Mary," I said. "We should go."

We all gulped down our wine.

I looked around at the paintings again. Would I ever see them in a gallery? The colours were bright and bold but they made me think of old ladies who wear too much makeup.

Mary saw me looking.

"You want to buy one?" she asked.

I tried to laugh my way out of it.

"I'm too poor," I said. "And I don't have a wall big enough to hang one on."

She wheezed harshly.

"Don't feel bad," she said, "I'm forty-three, got a degree in fine arts and I've been painting for more than twenty years. In all that time I've only sold five pieces. And all of them to family members. Each of them lugged the painting to their cottages.... I get to see them when I visit because they all hung them in their guest rooms."

"Someday, somebody's going to discover you, Mary," Denise said. "And then you'll be rich and famous."

Mary smiled and the two women hugged each other. I felt sad and helpless.

"Nice to have met you," I said.

Out on the street, Denise took my hand and began to tug me along.

"Isn't she great?" Denise asked.

"Yes," I said. "Brave."

She pulled hard on my hand.

"Where are we going? It's gotta be two in the morning."

"The best time to visit the zoo," she said and started off running.

The gate was closed and had a substantial lock on it. No problem. Just climb the chain link fence. I went first and helped her over.

It was dark and we couldn't see much but the air was filled with sounds of birds and beast, bleating, chirping. Noises of sleep. Or signals to a mate in the next cage. Cries to ancestors thousands of miles away on other continents.

"I love it here at night," Denise said. "All this caged fury...but it's peaceful too. You know what I mean?"

"It reminds me of prison," I said.

"Didn't you ever want to escape?"

"I did," I said. "In books. I read. Wrote. Dreamed a lot."

We were leaning against the fence that enclosed the giant sea turtles. In the moonlight we could see their large humps on the cement edge of a small pool.

"You suppose turtles dream?" she asked.

"If they do, they dream about being turtles."

"That's sad," she said. "I think they should dream about being whales, or eagles, so they could fly away."

"They're too smart for that," I said. "I suspect turtles know they're turtles. They know they're stuck with it. Maybe they're smarter than people."

"What do you dream about?" she asked.

"Being a turtle," I said.

"That's cheating!" she shouted, grabbing my arm. "Come on, 'fess up."

I started to walk back toward the entrance. Suddenly I was tired. And I felt old. I stopped and turned toward her eager, smiling face. She was very pretty. There was something magical about her, uncontrollable. It frightened me. I felt like I had been playing a childhood game for the last few hours, but now I realized playtime was over.

"I do dream of being a turtle sometimes," I said. "I wish I had a shell that I could retreat into...sort of hide out until it's safe to come out again."

"Was that what prison was like for you?" she asked.

What a terrible question. I thought I might cry. But before I could answer she put her arm around me and whispered in my ear.

"Let's go back to my place," she said, "and fuck our brains out."

When I woke up in the morning I was disoriented. Whose bed was I in? Why was my body so sore? Particularly my groin. Then a soft hand reached over and stroked my hair.

"Hi," Denise said. "Remember me?"

I started to laugh.

"How old are you?" I asked.

"Twenty-one," she said.

I laughed some more.

"What's funny about that?"

"Nothing," I said. "I just realized we never exchanged a word last night about the farm."

"Forget the farm," she said. "Let's just stay here forever."

I scrambled out of her grasp, found my clothes on the floor and began to dress.

"I've got to get going," I said.

"Sure," she said, her voice muffled by the blanket she pulled over her head. "Wham, bam, thank you ma'am.... So long.... See ya around."

"No," I said, hauling the cover off her. "It's not like that. There's things I have to check on...."

It sounded lame but the truth was that I was feeling emotionally feeble. For months I'd been living on the left-overs Anne dispensed to me and suddenly this young woman had appeared and presented me with a feast. It was too much.

"The world will continue without you," she said.

"Maybe that's what I'm afraid of," I said.

She pulled herself up in the bed, face pensive.

"Probably," she said. "So when will I see you again?"

"Later," I said, edging my way toward the door. "Today. I'll come back later today."

She beamed a wan, wise smile in my direction as I sidled out the door.

Out on the street I felt relieved, as if I'd been arrested for a crime I hadn't committed, placed in a line-up, but then released because the witness could not identify me. It didn't take a genius to figure out that something was seriously wrong with the way I thought of myself.

I walked the few blocks to my place. Sitting on the steps of the porch was Wayne, the brewmaster from the joint. He stood up quickly and handed me a note. His hands were shaking.

"She was just by," he said. "A blonde woman. I forget her name."

I read the note.

Dear Don:

I've got to see you immediately. Come to my place.

love,

Anne

I stuffed it in my pocket and turned back to Wayne who was shuffling nervously from one foot to the other.

"Somethin' important, eh?" he said.

"What's up with you?" I asked.

"I need a favour but it can wait."

He turned as though to walk away and I grabbed him and sat him down on the porch. I pulled out my cigarettes, offered him one and we both lit up. I sat down beside him and we both looked at the bright sun light bouncing off the dew drops on the blossoms of a crab apple tree on the next lawn.

I sensed fragility in Wayne, as though his years in prison had caused his soul to atrophy so that now it rattled inside like a clay ball, vulnerable to the slightest jostle. He might explode or simply shatter.

"When did you get out?" I asked.

"Two weeks ago yesterday," he said. "I was gonna come and see you right away.... My parents' place is just a couple of streets over, but then my parole officer said I shouldn't be associatin' with other ex-cons.... My parents got on me...my dad's retired from the CNR and he just wants to sit in his chair, drink a little beer and watch his game shows... . No hassle, ya know?...My mom's gotta have something to worry about but just one thing at a time.... The thing is my sister moved back in with them a couple of months back when this guy she married tried to turn her into wallpaper.... She's got two kids. Little kids, crying all the time.... Mom's going nuts and I don't know shit from Shinola... ."

We both laughed.

I got up and hauled him to his feet.

"Let's go get breakfast," I said.

We went to the Parkway on Parliament Street. Over bacon and eggs he told me what he wanted.

"Seventeen years is a long time," he said. "I kept telling them at my parole hearings that I needed a gradual release. But they wouldn't listen. Then suddenly they have a special board meeting and all of a sudden I'm out on the street."

We finished eating and set off down the street.

"So the thing is, I'd like you to help me get back inside," Wayne said.

We had been walking for a couple of hours and were standing outside the ferry terminal.

"Let's take the boat over to the island," I said.

"You listening to me?" he asked.

"Sure. You want to go back to the joint."

"It ain't so great out here," he said.

I nodded agreement and pointed at the ferries. The *Thomas Rennie* was loading. The expression in Wayne's eyes was blank. It was too big a decision for him to make so I took his arm and led him through the turnstile. We stood on the top promenade of the boat talking and looking back at the city. Wayne pointed at the skyline.

"Half those buildings weren't there before."

We docked at Centre Island but Wayne didn't want to leave the boat. Instead we remained at the rail. The waves lapped against the side of the boat and seemed to act as a gently prod to Wayne's memory.

"When you're a kid," he said, "you got it made...stupid things like finding flat stones on the beach and skipping them over the water are great. You can spend hours doing stuff like that and you don't think anything of it. The days go by and you think this is the way it'll always be."

The ferry pulled away from the dock and churned its way to Hanlan's Point. Wayne continued to wade through his turbulent recollections, trying to make sense of the grief he felt.

"The shrinks used to ask me when it started...you know the feelings...being pissed off with the world. Was there a dog that died...did my mom start giving me enemas?"

We both laughed.

"The crap they asked me wouldn'a made sense to a monkey."

The boat lumbered its way back toward the York Street terminal. When it docked, Wayne and I waited for the crowds to exit before we took our leave. We left the boat and walked along Front Street. The day had become beautiful, the warmth softened by a breeze coming off the lake. The sea gulls circled, their screeching adding ominous overtones. We hoofed it over to Jarvis and walked north. When we reached Carlton, we turned east again and headed back to home turf.

I was getting hungry and suggested that we stop in at the Winchester for the buck and a half luncheon special and maybe a few cold draft.

Wayne grinned.

"You're gonna get me in trouble," he said. "I've got an abstinence clause in my parole."

"Me too," I said.

We had barely tucked into the daily special—shepherd's pie— when suddenly Barry Morris stormed through the doors. He stomped over to our table, his bushy black beard twitching with indignation.

"I should've known you'd be here," he said. "Anne's in a real state trying to find you."

"Where is she?" I asked.

"I just left her at Dale and Marge's."

"Okay, we'll go over as soon as we finish eating."

Wayne scrambled out of his chair.

"I don't mind. We can go now."

I pushed him back down.

"Eat," I said, and turned to Barry. "This is Wayne. He just got out after doing seventeen years solid...he's shaking a rough day."

I smiled at Wayne while he and Barry shook hands.

"Sorry to barge in on you guys," Barry said. "But Anne's in rough shape too."

He turned and left.

"Is that the guy you told me was a minister?" Wayne asked.

"Yep...listen, you going to drink that beer?"

Wayne looked at the beer with alarm, as though it represented a potion that turned his nightmares into reality. I moved the two glasses over to my side of the table.

"I want to drink it," he said, "but I'm afraid...I keep hearing those shrinks tell me that I'm an alcoholic...that everything I did was because of the booze."

"In the joint, you were the brewmaster. You made and drank gallons of that horse piss. I never saw you get into trouble. You were always the first guy to go to his cell and sleep it off."

He smiled at the memory.

"I mixed a lethal mash, didn't I?"

"Sure did," I said, as I finished off his first beer.

He stopped eating his food. I picked up his second beer, offered the glass to him but he shook his head no. I chugalugged most of it and got up. He followed me out the door and along Winchester to Metcalfe Street where Dale and Marge lived.

"Where we going?"

"To some friends."

He ran to catch up as I headed up the walkway to Dale and Marge's.

The apartment door was flung open by a white-faced Marge. I introduced her to Wayne.

"Oh, Don..." she sighed.

Dale came into the room with a pleased smile.

"We haven't even moved in together and already our lives are filled with excitement."

I introduced him to Wayne and tried to read Marge's troubled face.

"What's happening?" I asked.

"Anne's been here three times," Marge said. "She's hysterical...you tell him, Dale."

"In a nut shell, she's convinced you've dumped her...."

"For Denise," Marge said.

"I just met Denise," I said. "How could she even know about her?"

"They collided," Marge said.

"Anne came looking for you twice and we suggested you might be at the Winchester...." Dale said.

"She came back and said you weren't there, so...." Marge said.

"We suggested she try the office," Dale continued.

"But you weren't there either," Marge groaned. "So she came back here again."

"And she arrived just two minutes after Denise got here looking for you and Denise started going on and on...." Dale said.

"About last night," Marge said in a hushed voice.

"All the gory details," Dale said.

"My advice is to track them down and get this resolved quickly," Marge said.

"Yes," I agreed. "I'm sorry you got caught in the middle of this. Actually I'm surprised Anne's upset. She's been telling me for months to go out with other women.... Kept saying I was putting pressure on her by always waiting for her."

"Something happened last night," Marge said. "With her and the man she saw. Whatever it was, it upset her. I think she wanted you to be there as her friend."

I nodded, then said, "I hope this doesn't mess up our farm plan."

For the first time, Marge smiled.

"No" she said. "We expected some commotion in our lives when we invited you into it."

"Just not so quickly," added Dale.

They were both grinning. Strange how people's moods change so fast.

"We'll head out. Thanks for everything."

"Where are you going first?" Dale asked me.

"Denise's."

"Ah, the easiest first...work your way up to the tough one," he said.

"Don't count on it," Marge said. "Denise is quite a determined person."

We waved goodbye and headed for the street.

It was a short walk. Denise lived just a block away.

"This is strange," said Wayne. "You sure I should come along? I'm not my best around girls...women."

"You ever been laid, Wayne?" I asked him.

He stopped walking and looked at me with his head tilted to the side as though he was watching an airplane coming in for a landing. He stared at me like that for a few seconds and then straightened his shoulders and pointed a finger at me.

"That's getting pretty personal," he said, glaring.

"I'm sorry...it doesn't matter. I just had this funny idea."

"Like what?"

"No, it's too crazy." I said, and started walking again.

He skipped along to keep up with me. I've always been a fast walker.

"If I wasn't a virgin when I went in the joint," he said, "I am now. I mean after seventeen years a guy loses his touch, you know what I mean?"

"Sure. Actually I was thinking of a favour you could do for me."

"Yeah, like what?"

We were just a few houses away from Denise's place. I stopped and looked up at the open window of her second storey apartment. I could hear music playing inside. Wayne stopped and looked up also.

"This woman we're going to see, Denise."

"Yeah."

"She's pretty lonely," I said.

"I can relate to that," he said.

"She's bright, fun, talented...but I don't think she has a lot of close friends. Particularly men. I just met her last night. We had a few beers and already the next day she's wondering where I am."

"And you have this other girlfriend who's going bonkers looking for you."

"Right," I said. "So I thought...I dunno, maybe you could show a little interest in Denise. I know you've decided to go back inside, and I'll help. But it's got to wait until Monday anyway, with the parole office closed and all."

"Right," he said. "But she might not like me."

"That's true," I said. "The idea I had was just to play it by ear.... If she shows interest maybe you could invite her to a movie or something."

"Do you know what movies cost now?" he asked. "When I went in the joint...."

I waved away his tirade on economics.

"I'm just asking you to be open to the possibility," I said.

"How come you asked about me being laid?"

"I don't think she's had much experience," I said.

"Did you...?"

"I told you, I just met her last night!"

"Right," he said. "Sorry. So you mean she's...sort of shy."

"Yes," I said. "And a guy would have to go easy...not be pushy."

"Sure," he said. "I know what you mean. It's almost like teaching her. I mean, if she wanted to."

"Right," I said.

"You know its's strange, Don," he said. "I don't feel so bad right now."

"You seem a lot more relaxed," I said. "The first few months are hard. A person gets used to belonging in the joint. I still miss people calling me Beetle."

He laughed.

"Hey yeah, I forgot that was your nickname...but yeah, I miss the place."

"So let's go see Denise."

"Okay," he said. And we started along the street again.

Bob Dylan was playing on Denise's stereo. I knocked on her door and she flung it open and greeted us with a smile that could melt asphalt.

"Saw you on the street. Looked like you were having a little meeting...not about me I hope. Hi, I'm Denise."

Wayne took her hand and mumbled his name. He looked like someone had just injected him with a massive dose of valium.

"Come on in," Denise said. "I'm just pouring myself a glass of wine, but I've got beer."

"Beer," Wayne croaked.

I followed her into the kitchen.

"He's cute," Denise said.

She opened two beers, poured herself a glass of wine and set them on the counter top. Then she turned and pulled me into her arms in a savage embrace. It only lasted a few seconds and then she slid away from me.

"I ran into your girlfriend," she said.

"Listen, Denise...."

She held up her hand to stop me.

"Don't explain. Last night was...last night. I knew about Anne from Marge and Dale so it's no sweat. You didn't deceive me. And wasn't last night great?"

"It was wonderful," I said.

"Was it really?" she asked in a soft voice.

"Someday I'll write a story about it," I said, and tried to grin my way past her penetrating stare. She smiled and her eyes clouded over with sadness.

"You won't just forget me?"

"Are you kidding, we're practically neighbours. I'll drop in every day to borrow your toilet plunger...."

She brightened a little and touched my face with one hand. I thought, I must be nuts. Here was a woman who really liked me. No questions asked. Unconditional acceptance. She had warmth. She exuded sexuality, was uninhibited. Full of life. What was I doing?

Then she laughed.

"You look so serious," she said.

"I'm just realizing what I'm doing."

"Too late," she said, mocking me. Then seeing that I was troubled, confused, she stopped.

"Last night was the most free I ever felt in my life," I said. "I felt like I was walking on firm ground with you, feeling every step I took but at the same time, I had the sensation of floating."

"But it scared you too, didn't it," she asked.

"Yeah, it did."

She handed me my beer and picked up the other drinks.

"Drink your beer and go find Anne," she said.

"How come you know so much?"

She laughed.

"Certain things are obvious. Anne's got something I could never give you, something you'd kill for."

"What?"

"Respectability. Now tell me about your friend in the other room."

I felt outraged. Betrayed. Was I so transparent?

"Respectability! I hate respectability. It's everything I'm against."

"Something wrong in there?" Wayne called nervously.

"Be right there!" Denise shouted back, and then turned to me. "You may hate it but you lust after it. Accept it. Tell me about Wayne."

"He just finished seventeen years of a life sentence," I said. "He's only been out a couple of weeks and is feeling shaky."

"What was he doing life for?"

"Murder. He didn't do it, but he was with a guy in a robbery. The other guy committed the murder but Wayne was there."

"He must have been just a kid."

I nodded.

"He looks so vulnerable."

"One of his problems is he hasn't been around women much...the fact is he's never had a real girlfriend."

"You mean he's never....."

I nodded again.

"You can order quite a few things on canteen, but not girls."

"Wow. How old is he?"

"Thirty-three."

"That's incredible. A thirty-three-year-old virgin. He should be put in a display case."

"We better get in there. He's probably ready to climb the walls."

We both entered the living room and startled Wayne, who was looking through Denise's record collection.

"I hope you don't mind," he said. "You've got a lot of records. Most of them I don't know. But I like the Doors."

"A lot of it's South American music. Most people have never heard of it but I like it. If you want I'll play some."

Wayne took a big swallow of his beer and choked. Denise patted him gently on the back. My beer was almost drained and I put it down in preparation for leaving.

"Sit down," Denise said to Wayne.

He gave me a questioning look.

"I've got to find Anne," I said. "It sounds like Denise is inviting you to stay a while...I can come back later if you want."

"We'll be fine," Denise said, taking a seat beside Wayne on the couch. The poor guy looked like a rabbit surrounded by a pack of wolves, his eyes darting around, looking for a hole to plunge himself into.

"Well I'll be back at my place in a couple of hours if anybody needs me," I said.

Denise had risen and was holding the Doors album up for Wayne's approval. He shook his head in the affirmative and she put it on the turntable. To the two of them, I was already gone. Jim Morrison's voice followed me down the stairs and half a block along the street.

I walked over to Anne's very slowly. I wasn't up for a big confrontation. I knew no way to explain my actions of the night before. Anne would be angry. She had a right. I have no tolerance for disloyalty and I assume other people feel the same. In a peculiar way I felt ashamed of myself.

I rang her bell and heard feet running down the stairs. Anne tore the door open and embraced me in the most passionate hug we'd ever shared.

"Do you still want me?" she asked.

"Yes."

She took my hand and led me up the stairs. There were no more words. Instead we made love on the living room rug. It was a frantic coupling complicated by a fly that jammed, buttons that became tangled in loose threads, and one sock that decided to glue itself to my foot. God, sex can be so awkward. Sometimes when things are going badly I see myself standing in front of a Model T Ford, turning the crank furiously but the damn thing won't start. But it was lovely. I didn't even mind the tingling of the rug burn on my knees.

Later Anne asked me, "Why do you want me?"

"You're my ticket to respectability," I joked.

She laughed.

"Isn't that funny," she said. "I want to be with you for the exact opposite reason."

"You're attracted to all that is disreputable about me."

"Yes," she said. "I want to be part of the craziness that I know your life will be.... Do you love me?"

"Yes," I said. "More than you'll ever know."

"Oh, don't say that. I want to know. Tell me why and how you love me so I'll know a little. Then I want you to remind me. All the time."

"Being in love with you gives me the energy, the will to imagine my dreams."

"That's nice," she said, stroking my arm. "That's a nice start."

So we got the farm. Dale and Marge, Anne and I. We leased it for six months. It was an old clay brick house with gingerbread trim at the eaves and peaks. It had ten acres of land that included the ancient foundation of a barn that must have burned down years ago. The property was located near a small hamlet called Ravenshoe, about forty miles from Toronto. The peculiar thing was that I had spent a summer on a Ravenshoe farm when I was fourteen. On a whim I went to see if the same people lived there and sure enough, Henry Yeomansson and his wife Betty were still there. Henry even came over to our place and hooked up the stove.

Anne told her mother a bunch of us were sharing a house. Communes were popular then. Her mother's biggest concern was that Anne would have to drive on the highway alone. Still, Anne made me set up my office to look like a bedroom, with a few clothes scattered around just in case her mother made a surprise visit.

We cleaned and painted. Marge planted a garden. My kids were even allowed to visit for a day. They managed to release the parking brake on the old Anglia we'd bought for a hundred dollars. The vehicle was held together by lumps of molding rust and various pieces of cleverly twisted welding rod. The rear end was shot so we'd installed over-size tires to cut down on the whine. It was a miracle the parking brake even worked. Anyway it rolled down a hill, crashed through a split rail fence and stopped in the third row of a neighbour's corn field. Rebecca and Estelle wrestled for the privilege of steering and fortunately neither was hurt. The hood of the car never closed properly after that so we wired it down. When I returned them to their mother, the kids shared the exciting news that they'd had a bath with Anne and me in the over-size tub. Stella was enraged and I didn't see my kids again for almost four years.

Springboard was expanding in leaps and bounds. New volunteers were appearing daily. It was a good thing because requests from inside, especially for transportation for prisoners' wives, were pouring in. Maggie Nistad was busy visiting wives, and screening volunteers. I oversaw the running of the Flyer Force, did the training of volunteers, and wrote proposals for money. Ed recognized the potential in home renovations and set up a contracting company to employ guys graduating from the Flyer Force.

Wayne never went back to prison. He and Denise became close friends. For a while he did some volunteer work with me at Springboard but then his dad got him a job at the CNR. He disappeared from my life, like a lot of people did when they didn't need me any more.

I was happy but restless. I worried that I didn't give Anne enough time. When I wasn't working at the office, I was pounding at the old Underwood. But at night, the four of us would often build a fire in a fire pit we'd found in the foundation of the old barn, drink a little beer, toast hot dogs and marshmallows. And we'd talk. Dream out loud. Sometimes sing. Dale and Marge would always go to bed first so Anne and I had some time to ourselves.

One night I asked, "Are you happy?"

"I don't think about that much," she said. "But I'm content. How about you?"

"I wish I knew more," I said. "I mean in my work. I think dealing with the bureaucrats would be easier if I understood more about the system. Then I wouldn't have to put in so many hours. A lot of what I do is wander down blind alleys. Anyway, I signed up for the Canadian Urban Training programme."

"CUT. They'll never accept you," she said.

"They already did. And the United Church is going to pay for it. Metson arranged it."

"Shit!" she said, and stormed off into the darkness. I got up and followed her.

"What's wrong?" I asked.

She was furious, the skin of her face stretched tight and forming a bitter mask in the moonlight.

"I asked John to sponsor me for CUT," she said. "I've got a

university degree for Christ's sake.... He said I wasn't ready."

"I'm sorry," I said. "You never mentioned it to me. I could have talked to John."

"I don't need you to fight my battles," she said and stomped off into the house.

Anne was very prickly when she felt her independence was threatened. And yet she wanted to be a community worker. In fact she was door-knocking in the neighbourhood of the Christian Resource Centre, talking to tenants, trying to persuade them to join a tenant rights group that was being formed by another staff member, Norm Brown.

To me community was people pulling together, recognizing that you couldn't do everything on your own. But Anne was fiercely independent. She didn't like to ask for help.

I took the CUT course. It was a two-week live-in situation. There were twelve of us. I was the only one who wasn't a member of the clergy. We were taught systems analysis and exposed to simulation games so we could learn about feeling powerless. I found the strategy sessions useful. My fellow classmates forced me to focus on the issues of prison reform instead of just how I felt. Theological reflection was a process that allowed me to learn how to digest my rage, using values I didn't even know I had.

The last part of the course was called the plunge. Each of us was given five dollars and sent out on the street where we had to exist for three days as skid row bums. We were instructed to live by our wits and make use of the skid row institutional system.

I cheated. My first day I managed to mooch over fifty-seven dollars by standing outside the Colonnade on Bloor Street, telling passersby that an insurance company had offered me a job if only I'd get a hair cut. Most people were amused. Some were indignant. The hippie era was on its last legs. Middle-aged businessmen were pleased to give me a buck if it contributed to my conforming.

I took my ill-gained money over to Yonge Street and prowled the bars, where I met an attractive teacher in her forties. I told her a variation of the haircut story but added that I was just in from Vancouver. She took me home and let me sleep on her couch. In the morning she whipped up a great cheese omelette and gave me ten bucks.

I came back to CUT headquarters early on the third day. But I wasn't the first to arrive. Over half the participants were sitting in the lounge looking dejected. For them it had been a horrible, devastating experience. They'd stayed at the Sally Anne hostel and eaten at the Fred Victor Mission and other soup kitchens around the city. I felt embarrassed to have had such a good time. I offered to throw a party at the farm and pay for it from the hundred or so dollars I'd brought back.

Anne was wonderful. She made tubs of potato salad, prepared a glazed ham and made everyone feel at home. But during the party she was distant, her eyes reflecting back the image of whoever she was talking to but revealing nothing. She smiled but it wasn't her natural infectious grin. She was hurt because although she played an important part in the festivities, she didn't feel she belonged. I felt sad for her but didn't know what to do.

In early July Margaret called and invited us all to her "shack" on the Otonabee river. Marge and Dale could only come for the day. We decided to drive the Anglia to the cabin so they could leave at their leisure. Anne and I would hitchhike home or take the bus.

Margaret gave very detailed instructions for finding her place. In fact the directions were so complicated we got lost half a dozen times. But finally we found the correct side road that led down to the river. We passed a farm and at the edge of the river was a row of thirty cottages. We drove until we spotted a wooden sign, nailed to a huge maple tree at the end of the lane, with the word MANAWAKA burned into it. This was the place.

As we parked the car, Margaret appeared. She hugged us all and herded us toward the front of the cedar A-frame.

"Come on in," she said. "I was just making us some lunch. I hope you all like tomato and lettuce sandwiches."

We passed through the heavily sprung screen door and the first thing I noticed was a sign on the wall that read BEWARE WRITER AT WORK. Margaret saw me looking at it and laughed.

"Jack McClelland had that made for me," she said. "I don't know if it's supposed to warn people off or remind me to get my ass in gear."

She took my bag and led me to one of the small bedrooms off the livingroom area.

"You and Anne'll sleep here. I'm next door. The washroom's across the hall. There's no shower and the toilet's finicky. It'll handle nature's own but will cough up anything else. Even a cigarette butt."

Before we joined the others, she gave me an extra hug.

"I'm so glad you're here," she said. "It's so good to see you and Anne together."

Dale, Marge and Anne had taken chairs around the huge oak table that sat in front of the floor-to-ceiling window that faced the river. Margaret went back into the tiny galley kitchen and continued to prepare sandwiches.

"Isn't that a great table," Margaret asked. "It's from an old library they demolished to build some new monstrosity. I got it from a fellow who sells guns and has an antique show up near Lakefield. He picked it up at an auction and refinished it. Didn't he do a beautiful job? I like how he left in the carved initials.... Probably carved by kids long dead by now. Just about everything here comes from his shop. The press backs, and the old rocker. Everything except the couch. That came right from the Sears catalogue. I'm going to have to order a new Franklin stove from them. It gets chilly at night and I like a fire but this one's just about had the biscuit. Its innards are rotted and I get terrified that some night I'll burn the place down."

Margaret brought the food to the table and we ate.

"The river's so gorgeous," Dale said.

"There's always a breeze blowing," said Margaret. "The current flows from north to south but the wind blows up from the south.... See, it's doing it now. It makes it look as though the river is flowing both ways."

We marvelled at the sight and for the next couple of hours sat outside on lawn chairs, under the shade of an old elm tree, watched the river just a few yards away and put words to the visions we had of our lives.

Margaret listened intently to Dale and Marge as they discussed their dream of returning to Invermere, British Columbia, where Marge's mom lived, and opening a bookstore.

"What a wonderful thing to do," she said. "Gawd, Dale, I just can't get over you being born and raised in Glenella. Twenty miles from Neepawa.... My home town."

We took photographs, and the afternoon flowed by gently like the river.

Marge and Dale left at about four. Anne and I went inside and tried to help Margaret prepare dinner but Margaret poured us drinks and insisted we sit at the table.

Suddenly, a tall old man appeared at the screen door. He tapped lightly and Margaret ran to let him in.

"Jack, come on in. I want you to meet some good friends of mine."

Anne and I stood up. Then I noticed the old guy was carrying something wrapped in newspaper.

"Brought you a fresh muskie, Margaret. Skinned and cleaned. Just stuff it like I told you last time and you'll have a real feast on your hands."

Margaret accepted the gift gingerly and quickly handed it to me. I took it into the kitchen area and put it in the sink. I opened the paper and saw that the carcass was huge. It must have been a ten-pound fish.

"Stay for a drink, Jack?" Margaret asked.

"A small one," he said and then arranged his large frame so that he teetered on the edge of one of the chairs.

"Jack's a diviner," Margaret said. "This is Don and Anne."

I got up and shook hands with him. His hands were massive but gentle. He nodded and smiled at Anne.

"Jack's divined all the wells around here," Margaret said, as she brought him a stiff rye and water. "Including the one we mix our drinks with."

"So I did," Jack said. His voice rumbled. "But I lost the gift.... Haven't found a well in over a year."

Margaret had a wonderful way of seducing people into talking about themselves. Jack was a man in his seventies and obviously a loner but within a few minutes Margaret had him telling us about being a Barnardo boy, sent out from England when he was just a child to work on a farm, almost as a slave. He told us about running away and how they'd come after him with a posse that included dogs. He was a wonderful storyteller and we laughed at his tales. Later I wondered about the pain he must be concealing.

Jack stayed and ate with us. His muskie had been popped into the freezer section of Margaret's fridge. The thing had to be folded over, it was so big.

Jack had the cottage next door to Margaret's and tottered home about ten, just as it was getting dark. Anne yawned and said she was ready to sack out. Margaret gave her a hug and Anne retired.

Margaret and I sat at the big table, smoking, drinking, and filling the air with endless talk.

"You seem more confident than when I saw you last," Margaret said.

"Things are going well for me," I said.

"The writing.... How's the writing?"

"Good," I said. "I'm thinking of applying for a small Canada Council grant so I can finish a book of stories."

"Great," she said. "Let me write you a letter of support."

"Would you? I didn't want to ask...."

"Of course," she said, and then her eyes narrowed. "But first you have to do something for me."

"What?" I asked.

She went into the kitchen area and located a flashlight. Then she took the fish out of the freezer. She motioned for me to follow her. She opened the screen door and held it so it wouldn't slam. Then we walked around the side of the cabin to a shed. Margaret opened the lock with some keys. She shone the light around the darkened interior until it illuminated a shovel.

"Get it," she whispered.

I grabbed the shovel and followed Margaret to a weed-infested area under some spruce trees, about forty feet from the cabin.

"Dig," she said softly, and shone the light on the ground.

It took me about twenty minutes to get a hole big enough and deep enough to accommodate the muskie. When it was buried we stamped the soil down and spread leaves around so no one would notice the ground had been disturbed. Then we ran back into the cabin giggling like school kids that have just pulled a prank.

Inside Margaret laughed until tears streamed from her eyes.

"I call that area my Muskie mortuary," she said. "There must be two dozen of the buggers buried out there. I keep telling Jack I'm not a big fish eater but every so often he brings me another one.... Have you ever eaten a Muskie?"

"No," I said.

"Tastes like baked mud," she said, and started to laugh again. "Gawd, I'm terrible, but I just don't want to hurt the old guy's feelings."

In the morning Margaret made us coffee and served bacon and sliced tomatoes with toast. Then she called a cab to get us into the Peterborough bus terminal. When it arrived she walked outside with us, hugged us many times and said: "God's blessings on you."

It would be a year before we saw her again.

Walking on Water

Late in July of 1970 Anne and I decided to hitchhike out to the west coast. We bought a pup tent and a couple of sleeping bags. Just before we left, Robert Weaver bought a story from me for CBC radio's Anthology series. With the five hundred dollars he paid me I purchased a couple of bus tickets to Vancouver in case Anne and I got stuck on the road.

It took us eight days to make the trip, the last leg through the mountains completed on the Greyhound. With no one to distract us we began to learn more about each other.

Anne felt my compulsion to replenish my liquor supply every day was a sign of a booze problem. I insisted that she enjoyed sitting around the camp fire at night with a glass of wine as much as I did. She said she could do without it so I bowed to her wishes. I wasn't happy about it though.

Several times we were approached on the highway by policeman who wanted to check our ID. Lots of people were on the road hitchhiking and I assumed the authorities were looking for runaways and criminals. I saw no harm in being cooperative with the police who were always polite and often cheerful and chatty. But Anne became indignant and refused to show her identification. One cop became so annoyed that he drove us back to his station and made us sit for an hour before Anne softened her position.

When we ate in restaurants, Anne was often cruel to the waitresses. I couldn't understand it. When I confronted her about it she said she had been a waitress for three summers at the Breakers hotel during her university years. The guests had treated her badly in order to get better service. She knew she responded to the mistreatment by trying harder, so she assumed all waitresses did.

Anne found me to be dominating. She complained that I felt confident to talk on any range of topics and this intimidated her. She had a degree in fine arts and psychology but when we visited the open air arts shows in Vancouver's Gastown, I started up conversations with the artists about style and technique. Anne held back, as if she lacked the confidence to voice her opinions.

While in Vancouver we stayed at the home of Jane Rule and Helen Sonthoff. They had a beautiful place on West Second Avenue that overlooked English Bay. Never before or since have I encountered two more loving, generous people. To be with them was a delight.

During the day, Anne and I explored the city while Helen tended her lush garden and Jane wrote. We'd meet again for dinner and over scrumptious meals and plenty of homemade wine, we'd talk. The talk would continue in the living room over brandy and often went well into the night.

Mostly we talked about people. Stories about how Al Purdy came in to do a reading with Charles Bukowski, and how the two men had competed to see who could drink the most before the performance and still stand, and about the initial tension on first meeting Margaret Atwood, and Alice Munro's shyness.

It never occurred to me to just listen. I contributed stories about Margaret Laurence, Robert Weaver, and Robert Fulford. None of these exchanges was made in a spirit of meanness. We all shared an affection for the people we talked about.

But Anne was frustrated. She felt demoralized at what she thought of as her limited ability to tell stories. Fortunately Helen noticed this and pointed out to Anne that, in their union, Jane was the storyteller.

What Anne and I learned about ourselves on that trip was that we were competitive people who needed to be sensitive about each other's territory.

After a restful, nurturing week with Jane and Helen, we headed back to Toronto on the train. Just before we left, Jane gave us an autographed copy of her new novel, *This Is Not For You*. We travelled coach and sat up all night, each of us holding half the book and reading it together. We laughed and cried at the same parts and the book served as a healing balm for any wounds our squabbles had caused. It has become one of my favourite books. No one writes about the struggle of humans to love one another with the power and grace that Jane brings to her work.

We arrived back in Toronto just before the Labour Day weekend. Ed and Maggie Nistad picked us up at the train station. They were warm but, I thought, restrained in their greeting. There seemed to be a tremendous tension between them.

The atmosphere in the car was explosive.

"Tell him," Maggie said.

Ed allowed himself a small smile.

"The Atkinson Foundation came through," he said. "Fifteen big ones."

"We can pay ourselves!" Maggie shouted.

We all hugged. As much as people can when you're driving through busy city traffic.

"That's wonderful," Anne said, but I detected a sour note in her enthusiasm. It was an indication of the dilemma we would experience for years. She was happy for my success but disappointed in her own inability to achieve whatever it was she wanted to do.

The Atkinson Foundation was the creation of the founder of *The Toronto Star*, so the grant of fifteen thousand dollars to Springboard was big news to the paper. I was interviewed at the Christian Resource Centre standing beside a beaming John Metson. That weekend my picture was on the front page. Labour Day weekend is notoriously slow for producing hard news.

A month later, the House of Anansi had a book launching for the poetry anthology *Soundings*. Anne and I, Dale and Marge drove in from the farm for the festivities. I was so exhilarated to be among the company of poets like Bill Howell, Sid Marty, and Tom Wayman that I got pie-eyed on the free flowing wine and beer. I approached Anna Porter, already a star in the publishing world, and suggested I might like to do a novel for McClelland and Stewart. Fortunately she was amused.

The farm was getting colder. We discovered it was not properly winterized so reluctantly we all moved back to the city. Dale and Marge rented a flat and Anne and I moved in with a friend of hers named Sue Roper. Sue was attending Ryerson Polytechnical Institute and studying photography. She was an attractive woman of twenty-five or so and multi-talented as a visual artist and photographer.

Springboard demanded all my time. Now that we had received such a large amount of money and so much publicity, the guys inside wanted more meetings and more frequent transportation. Maggie was pushing me to get involved with the prison for women. Next year, I said. My parole officer, Don Irwin of the John Howard Society, hauled me into his office and warned me off Springboard. He demanded that I bring Anne in to speak with him. When I did, he made me wait in the hall while he spoke with her. The gist of his pitch to her was, what was a nice middle-class woman like her doing with an ex-con like me. Since Anne was so anti-authoritarian, his little speech only made her more loyal to me.

We celebrated Christmas with her family. I made a complete jerk of myself by drinking too much and, after dinner, lying down on the floor and falling sleep. They were such a wacky family that no one said anything. Except Anne. She warned me I was drinking too much.

In the spring of 1971 Dale Zieroth and I received the astounding news that we'd both been allotted Canada Council grants. It was obvious that Margaret's influence with the Council had got us the funding. She was back in England but I wrote to thank her immediately. I think we received twenty-five hundred each. A huge amount of money, by our reckoning.

I went out immediately and bought a car, a 1965 Corvair from, of all people, Carmello, Stella's lover. He and Stella wanted Anne to cooperate in a divorce action so they could get married. I paid him $25 for the car and then spent another two hundred making it road-worthy. Anne and I shopped around and found a tent trailer. My dream was to travel west again, fishing along the way, doing a bit of writing.

Marge wanted to go home to Invermere, B.C. Her mother had multiple sclerosis and was confined to a wheelchair. As the only daughter, she wanted to return home and help out. Besides, she hated Toronto.

Ed was upset that I was taking off again. He felt I was leaving the burden of Springboard on his shoulders, but I needed rest. I'd been working long hours, seven days a week. I knew Maggie and the volunteers would carry the bulk of the load and she encouraged me to go, although I had to promise that we'd expand that fall to the prison for women in Kingston.

Just before we left, Ed fell in love. The woman was a Springboard volunteer named Wanda Manning. She was a young widow who had been married to the son of W.E. Manning. She had a young daughter and Ed was sufficiently hooked that in spite of his initial upset he hardly noticed my leaving.

We took ten days to reach the west coast, travelling in a caravan with Dale and Marge, stopping every day to camp and fish. I finished my first book of poetry in a two-day stop-over in the beautiful valley where Invermere nestles.

Dale and Marge had bought a Volkswagen Bug. Both the Bug and our Corvair had to be coaxed through the mountains. But we made it to Vancouver and spent five glorious days in the company of Jane Rule and Helen Sonthoff.

On the way back Dale and Marge stayed in Invermere. Anne and I continued on to Winnipeg where we visited Tim Sale, an Anglican priest I'd met during my CUT course. He promoted Winnipeg as a great family town. We had a pleasant visit but my impression of the city was of a giant swamp that someone had pumped out so that houses could be built, although the mosquitoes remained. Man-eating hordes of them.

Back in Toronto we were greeted by more good news for Springboard. The Secretary of State's department had given us a grant of seventeen thousand dollars. Ed, Maggie and I went out to celebrate at the Winchester. Anne declined our invitation and without her there I got so drunk I had to be driven home. She was furious the next day.

"Bailey," she said, "you're going to wreck your life if you keep up this drinking."

I ignored her warning. In the accumulated mail I found a letter from Margaret inviting us up to the shack. I called her immediately and arranged to go the next weekend.

Margaret didn't greet us when we arrived. We parked the car, walked around to the front of the cabin and found her sitting in a lawn chair. She sensed our presence, turned and held up a warning finger to her lips. We crept up beside her and saw she was manipulating a little device in her lap. It was a piece of red wood with a metal handle that she twisted. It made a high pitched chirping sound. Suddenly we heard a bird sing. Margaret pointed toward an ash tree growing on the shore of the river. We saw an orange and black bird, obviously answering the sound Margaret had created.

"A Baltimore oriole," she whispered. She gave the device several more twists and the bird answered again. Margaret laughed with delight. The throaty sound must have scared the bird because it flew away.

"Sit down," she ordered, and handed the bird call to me.

"Isn't it wonderful," she said as she got up to give Anne a hug. "It's an Audubon official bird call...made from birch and pewter. It really works."

She was obviously delighted with her new toy.

"I lured in a meadow lark this morning," she said. "But then a couple of jays came along and chased it away. They're very territorial. Like people."

She had a bird book in her lap and showed us all the different species she had attracted. Over two dozen.

"This is my idea of heaven," she said, picking up her glass from the ground. "A gin and tonic in one hand, my bird book in my lap and my little caller." She took a healthy pull on her drink and put it down. She pointed off to the left, to a field of thistles and overgrown weeds.

"My neighbour on the other side, Steve, he's from Yugoslavia. He's got a gorgeous garden...did you notice it on your way in?"

"I did," Anne said. "All those fresh vegetables made my mouth water."

"Well, we'll be eating some of them for supper," Margaret said. "He dropped me off some tomatoes and a couple of bunches of leaf lettuce.... Anyway he's after me all the time to cut down my little field there but the birds feed on the seeds, you know...and they use the dry grass for their nests.... I never tire of watching them. With my caller I sometimes feel like Jesus."

She laughed again.

"How's the writing coming?" I asked.

She gave me a disgusted look.

"I hate this book.... So many false starts, but I think it's underway now.... I'm putting in long mornings but the damn thing is pushing and pulling me so many places that I need my afternoons to recuperate with the birds. What about you?"

"I have a book of poetry coming out this fall."

"What about the novel?"

"He's too busy saving the world!" Anne broke in.

I tried to laugh it off but Margaret glared at me.

"You listen to this woman. She's got your best interests at heart."

Then Margaret got up and tottered inside. She seemed to be walking stiffly. Was it the drinks? I couldn't tell. I heard ice being banged out of the tray. Anne got up and squeezed my shoulder.

"I didn't mean that as heavy as it came out," she said.

"Another year and Springboard won't need me," I said. "Then it'll be writing full-time."

"You want a drink?" she asked.

"Yeah, there's a bottle of rye in our bag. Two bottles of wine too."

She went into the cabin and I sat there feeling the fear that always engulfed me when I imagined myself doing nothing but sitting at a typewriter all day. I had to DO things. My energy bubbled over and compelled me into action. Maybe my destiny hadn't cast me as a writer after all.

Anne came running out of the building shrieking with delight and holding up a book.

"Look what Margaret gave us," she said, handing me the hardcover.

It was a copy of *The Fire Dwellers* and it was signed "to Anne and Don/Don and Anne, much love, Margaret."

In a few seconds Margaret was back in her chair with a fresh drink. Anne went inside to get me one.

"It's funny, with young people today you have to be so bloody careful not to offend.... I mean I once signed this book to a couple I met and I put the guy's name first and didn't I get a nine-page letter from the woman about how hurt she was.... My Gawd! Anyway I hope you like this. You haven't read it, have you?"

"No," I admitted sheepishly. "I meant to pick it up...."

"Well now you have no excuses. It's a funny book. I don't mean humorous although I think it's got a few laughs. Stacey's funny I think, but it's one of the few things I've written that I pick up and wonder, so when did I do this.... I mean every book writes itself at some level but this one didn't demand to be written the same way *The Stone Angel* did. It just showed up one day. CBC is talking to my agent about it. Apparently someone there wants to make it into a movie of the week.... My Gawd, what have we come to, a book of the month selection now becomes a movie of the week."

She laughed at her own joke and then began to choke on cigarette smoke. I patted her back gently.

"Did I tell you that when Newman wanted to buy the rights to *A Jest of God* my agent's representative tried to talk them into letting me write the script.... My Gawd, I was horrified.... I don't go to movies. I don't even own a bloody TV.... Take the money and run, I said. And we did. Seventeen thousand dollars. Enough to burn the mortgage on Elm Cottage."

She beamed with delight. Seventeen thousand didn't seem like a large amount to me.

"Are you going to share in the profits of the film?" I asked.

"My agent was away when the call came. He told me later I should have held out for something like that but who knows, it may not make a dime. The apprentice in the office who handled it all was afraid the whole thing was a prank. So was I at first. But then Paul Newman himself called me, said his wife Joanne Woodward wanted to play Rachel. All I cared about was that a week after I signed the release, I'd have a cheque. Let them worry about the profits."

Anne returned with my rye and water.

"Did you know Margaret sold *A Jest of God* to Paul Newman? He and his wife are going to make it into a movie."

"That's wonderful, Margaret!" Anne cried and gave her a squeeze.

"Well good luck to them," Margaret said. "Newman told me he was going to direct it himself and I said that's swell. All the time I wanted to ask him, when will I get the cheque, Paul."

We all laughed, then sat for a while and watched the sun back-light the craggy trees across the river.

"Look," Margaret said, pointing to the opposite shore. I squinted but then I saw it, feeding at the shore: a blue heron. It stalked the shallow waters and then every so often gave a regal poke at the water with its long bill.

"It's beautiful," Anne said.

"There's several families of them living back there among the dead trees. They seem to come back every year...like me. Jack caught a hunter last year just after he shot one. Dragged the poor bugger into the police."

Suddenly the heron began to flap its wings. It glided over the surface of the water and then made a tight, swooping circle that led it back into the trees.

"I never tire of just sitting here and watching," Margaret said.

"It's so peaceful," said Anne.

"That reminds me," she said. "Come on, let's go inside and make dinner and I'll tell you all about this. I've got a favour to ask of the two of you."

"What I wanted to ask you," Margaret said as we ate, "is if you'd consider opening and closing the shack when I go back to England."

Anne looked at me with delight.

"You can safely stay out here 'til October," Margaret said. "It's not winterized but there are base-board heaters, and the Franklin stove.... I've ordered a new one and Dick Wiles is going to put it in for me later this summer."

I imagined myself sitting at the table, pounding away at my old Underwood, stopping to light a smoke and look out over the river. In my imagination I saw a blue heron gliding over the rippling surface of the water. I felt an expanding peace within myself as I daydreamed myself into this future possibility. But something was wrong with the picture. I studied it in my mind as Margaret and Anne talked. Something was missing. Other people. There were no other people in the picture.

"So it's settled?" Margaret asked.

"It'll be our pleasure, eh, Beetle?" Anne said.

Margaret laughed.

"I haven't heard that one before."

We spent the next couple of hours discussing various nicknames we'd all carried at certain points in our lives. When she was very young and known as Peggy Wemyss, Margaret told us that a group of kids had called her 'Piggy.' Until she smacked one of the kids across the face.

Anne had been the victim of all the derivatives of Annie. Names like Grannie and Fannie were yelled at her amidst gales of laughter. But Anne said she ignored the taunts and the kids stopped.

"Now I wish people would call me Annie," she said. "Anne sounds so hard."

She took a big gulp of her wine, shook back her long blonde hair and directed a crinkled smile my way.

"Annie is what I call myself," she said. "When I talk to myself. You know how you do when you're alone."

I was surprised at her candor. It wasn't often that Anne was so revealing. Margaret took Anne's hand and held it in a firm grip. There were tears in Anne's eyes.

"Then Annie it is," Margaret said.

They sat like that for over a minute without words, letting the physical bond of touch serve as a conduit for the love or energy that flowed between them.

Margaret got up and made a fresh drink.

"What about you, Bailey?" she asked. "What did they call you besides Beetle?"

"Foxy loxy hair face," I replied. I told her the story of how Mrs. Fox, my foster mother, sent me to school with my hair held in place by bobby pins because she didn't want me to get a haircut. As soon as I left the house I removed the pins and my hair fell over my face.

Margaret thought this was hilarious.

"Of course, when you're a kid, it's the most awful thing that can happen to you," she said.

I agreed.

Margaret was never a late-night person, in my experience. About ten she poured herself a nightcap and went off to bed. Anne and I decided to do the same.

"All this lovely fresh air's made me sleepy," Anne said, stretching and striking a seductive pose. It's amazing the little signals that people develop between them to communicate. Anne was feeling sexy. She hadn't said it but I knew.

In bed she kissed me passionately but as the ritual of lovemaking began, I withdrew from her.

"What's wrong?" she whispered.

"Margaret's in the next room...the walls are as thick as napkins."

"She won't mind," Anne said.

"But I will," I said as softly as I could, pulling myself up to a sitting position.

There was enough light from the window for me to see the expression on Anne's face. She wore a dimpled smile that seemed to express her amusement with me, but her eyes were narrowed, calculating, even angry. She gave me a playful but stinging slap and rolled over against the wall.

"You're such a poop sometimes, Bailey," she muttered.

I sat there for a long time. The rhythm of Anne's breathing became steady and I knew she was asleep. I got up quietly and went to the kitchen. I decided a nightcap would help, and poured myself a stiff rye and water. Softly I tiptoed outside, careful not to let the screen door bang. I sat down in one of the lawn chairs and stared up at the stars.

The sound and flash of a lighter startled me. Then Margaret was in the chair beside me.

"Remind me before you go tomorrow," Margaret said. "I've got a key for you and I wrote down Max Doughty's number. He's the plumber to call to get the water turned off."

"Do you understand men, Margaret?" I asked. "I mean do you understand why they do what they do?"

She took a deep drag of her cigarette and the red glow lit her face.

"I accept what they do," she said.

"Yeah, maybe that's it. The men in your books sometimes do horrible things to the women they encounter. Like Nick with Rachel. But you don't judge them."

"I'm a storyteller, not God."

"I'm always trying to figure women out," I confessed.

"I know," she said. "Men want women to come with instructions, as if they were cars. They want to be able to fix them if anything goes wrong."

I laughed.

"A funny image just flashed through my mind, of a guy getting married wearing cover-alls and carrying a tool box full of wrenches. The woman all in white, looking at the minister with a big smile on her face, oblivious."

"That's an offensive picture, but truer than you might imagine," she said.

"I don't think I'll ever be able to write well about women," I said. "The things they do...puzzle me."

"And offend you," she said.

"Sometimes," I admitted.

She patted my arm.

"Learn to accept," she said.

"I'm trying."

"We are a strange sisterhood, we women," she said and I heard the sting of reproach in her words. But directed at whom? Anne? Me? Who?

Anne and I rose early the next morning. We left a note for Margaret that we were going for a walk. We strolled along the riverbank for a mile or so until we came to a stand of fir trees. We sat in their shade and watched the starlings dart over the surface of the water, snaring insects. I kissed Anne and stroked her breasts.

"Not here," she said.

We got up and walked back. Accept, accept, I said to myself on the trek back to Margaret's place.

In the fall of 1971 I was in court again. This time it was because of the divorce action Stella had brought against me. I didn't get a lawyer. I didn't think I needed one. Anne and I had been asked by Stella's lawyer to appear at the Sheriff's office to have our photograph taken together. He told me this would be presented as the evidence of adultery, the grounds on which Stella was divorcing me. Anne and I thought the whole thing was a lark and were amused when a clerk produced a Polaroid camera from under the counter. We wanted to pose in a passionate embrace but the clerk wasn't amused.

When I got to court I didn't find the proceedings very funny. Stella's lawyer called me to the stand and went over my lengthy criminal record. He asked why I hadn't tried to see my children or to contribute financially to their well-being. In fact, I'd given Stella money anytime she asked. I bought all the kid's clothes. When I looked at Stella she shrugged and turned away. The lawyer accused me of not having a genuine fatherly interest in my daughters. He dredged up the story of Anne and I parading around nude in front of the girls. When I tried to explain we were having a bath, he cut me off.

The divorce was granted and Stella got sole custody of Estelle and Rebecca. I was ordered to pay all court costs plus two hundred and fifty dollars a month for the support of the girls.

I was so naive that five minutes after the case was over and I was out in the corridor being hugged by Anne, I invited Stella to the combined divorce and book launching party we were having that night. Fiddlehead Press had released my first book of poetry, *My Bareness is Not just my Body*. Stella accepted and walked away.

John Metson put an arm around Anne, who began to cry.

"Your ex-wife just gave you the royal shaft," he said.

"It doesn't mean anything," I said. "She is going to marry Carmello next month. They're talking about having a kid. It was all just a show."

Anne stopped crying and looked at me with disgust.

"God, Bailey, sometimes you are so stupid."

She headed off down the corridor toward the washroom. I turned to John for his observation.

"Her lawyer got away with saying some pretty nasty things about you. And it's all part of the public record."

I didn't think it mattered. After a couple of drinks at the party that night and even a dance with my official ex-wife, I forgot about it. I was too caught up in having a published book in my hands that contained my work exclusively. Sue Roper had drawn the cover so she was basking in glory too. I think Anne was happy for me but the divorce proceedings had made her uneasy.

Sue was moving out west so Anne and I had to get a new place. Maggie suggested we find something together. Then Ed, Wanda, and her daughter Laura asked to be included. We found a huge house in the west end of Toronto, on Runnymede. At the last second, David Remple, a community worker Maggie knew, joined us too.

We all had problems. Maggie's husband Warren had been laid off from his job. Springboard received a hundred thousand dollar Local Initiative Grant from the federal government so Ed, Maggie and I were all being paid reasonable salaries. The fact that Maggie was doing better than Warren caused real tension between them. Warren became despondent and hung around the house most of the day watching television.

David, who had the basement apartment, was simply lonely. And it was clear from the way he behaved toward Maggie that he saw her as the person to fill the void in his life.

Ed and Wanda were rarely home. Ed had a suite at Le Coq d'Or where he still worked, and they often stayed there. When they did come home they retreated to their third floor apartment and argued. Loudly. We seldom saw them at the dinner table.

I was very much in love with Anne, which meant I tolerated her untidiness and disorder. But inside it drove me crazy. She was busy working with Barry Morris, canvassing the Cabbagetown community about turning St. Enoch's church, which was closing, into a community centre. And she was taking night courses at York

University toward her Master's degree. She wasn't sure in what. But she was taking sociology with Ted Mann. Just in case she had a spare minute, she had also signed up at the Institute of Human Relations and was studying therapy techniques.

We were a busy household. Each of us was committed to saving the world from itself. Although sometimes I didn't think this was true of Ed. It was becoming more difficult to get him to join me in the accountability sessions we held with inmate committees in the institutions. He argued that each time we got more money, we expanded our services. He believed this made the system better but didn't change it. If Ed had had his way, we would have used the money for dynamite and brought the prison walls down. In retrospect he was probably right.

Maggie had persuaded me to form an official liaison with the Prison for Women. The first time we met with the committee I knew I was in trouble. One woman in her 30s directed all her questions at me.

"I'm doing a fin, five long years," she said. "I can't get outta here on any of the programmes. Half the joint's gone every day to school, working, even doing volunteer work. But I can't get dick."

"Why not?" Maggie asked, trying hard to be in charge.

"Cause I'm a shit disturber," she said. "If something stinks I'm not afraid to say so, whether it's the food, visiting privileges, whatever. The thing is in order to get outta here on a day programme you gotta get sponsored by Elizabeth Fry, and I ain't kissing their institutional ass."

The other women laughed. Maggie turned red. I found this peculiar. She had heard worse at the men's prisons but I guess it had never been directed at her. The men tended to be respectful around her, to curb their language.

"So can Springboard get me sprung?" the woman asked amid more laughter.

"What's your name?" I asked.

"Judy Bailey," she replied and gave me a lascivious wink. God, she smoldered with sexual energy. I felt myself squirming.

"If you're asking about sponsorship for a temporary absence, we do that all the time with our volunteers," Maggie said, still trying to establish control.

Judy pointed a finger at me and gave a James Cagney sneer.

"I'm talking to him," she said. "Don Bailey. Everyone knows he started Springboard. Some volunteer puts their name in to sponsor me, it means dick. It's gotta be his name."

"This is bullshit," I said, standing up. "Maggie is my partner. She's got as much clout with the administration as I do."

"Let's test it then," Judy said. "Next month, the Law Society is having a conference on justice. We got an invitation to send a delegate and the committee elected me."

The other women murmured agreement.

"I'll send a letter to the director saying we agree to escort you on a temporary absence," Maggie said. Her voice was tight. I knew she was angry.

"Make sure his name's on it too," Judy said. "If admin accepts you, fine, but I'm betting they'll want Bailey's signature on the pass."

Maggie and I stopped by David and Nancy Helwig's place for a beer when our session was over. David was still doing his informal writing/reading course at Collins Bay and Nancy ran a successful theatre group made up of inmates who wrote and acted in their own productions. Both of them had been around cons so long that they found Maggie's indignation amusing.

During the drive back to Toronto, Maggie was livid.

"She just manipulated me...the both of us. Made fools of us."

"Don't take it so seriously," I said. "She was testing us. Showing off her power."

"Thanks for backing me up," Maggie said. "I just don't feel good about it. I wish we'd never gotten into it."

Of course it was a disaster. As Judy had predicted, the administration wanted me to be the one to pick her up and sign her out. By the time the date arrived for the conference Maggie was embroiled in trouble with Warren. So Maggie didn't come with me when I drove to Kingston to get Judy. But I brought a female volunteer so the drive back was friendly chitchat. Still, I felt the sexual tension. Panel members were served dinner in the Faculty Club of the University of Toronto. The wine flowed. Judy drank her share, as did I, but she was fine. The plan was that she would do the panel and then visit her mother overnight. I would drive her back the next day.

The panel went smoothly. Judy and I represented the inmates' point of view. There was a police officer on the panel, a prison warden and a judge. Judy was direct and passionate in her presentation. The prison for woman was a rat hole that rewarded suck holes with preferential treatment. The audience laughed but shifted uneasily at the fury behind her words.

I gave my presentation, aware that Judy was watching and listening. My own words sounded soft, conciliatory. Perhaps, I thought, my rage is diminishing.

Later in the car, while I was driving her to her mother's, Judy dropped her hand between my legs.

"So when are you gonna make your move?" she demanded.

I took her to a bar. In my mind I thought I could get her loaded and then dump her at her mother's. Sure. We both got loaded and I took her back to my place, thinking we've got the spare bedroom on the first floor. She can sleep there and I'll drop her at her mother's in the morning.

Anne spotted our entwined, naked bodies from the kitchen when she came down to make coffee. I hadn't even had brains enough to close the door. She was not thrilled.

Margaret had written and invited us to England for Christmas but we didn't have the money. Instead we spent the festive season trying to be festive. Ed, Wanda and Laura went away. Warren was off in his own dream world. Maggie was depressed. David whistled to show he was cheerful. And Anne and I struggled with forgiveness: she offering it, me accepting it. But we weren't good at it.

1972 erupted like a volcano. Late in January Springboard received a hundred and sixty thousand dollar LEAP (Local Employment Action Programme) grant from the government. We were still operating under the umbrella of the Toronto Christian Resource Centre. Suddenly our budget was twice as large as theirs. We had to hire people immediately because the grant was tied to employment. Ed expanded the home repair business and hired Michael Walshaw, Anne's brother. We took on a resident psychologist, a couple of professional social workers and six ex-inmates. The demand for transportation had become so large that we bought an old Greyhound bus and made daily runs to the institutions to supplement our volunteers, who now numbered over two hundred.

A week after the grant was announced my parole officer called me.

"We've gotta talk," he said.

I went to his office and he put it to me bluntly.

"The John Howard Society applied for a LEAP grant and we were turned down. My boss Kirkpatrick called a few people and they told him the reason we lost out was because of Springboard."

"So what would you like me to do?" I asked.

He smiled but his expression was grim.

"A lot of people want to see you back inside," he said. He opened his desk drawer and pulled out a document. "I've got the warrant here. All I have to do is sign it and an hour from now you'll be sitting in the Don Jail."

I laughed.

"On what grounds?"

"Nonadherence to your abstinence clause. Uncooperative attitude. Fraternizing with other ex-cons. We've got you."

Suddenly it wasn't funny.

"What do you think this will win you?" I asked.

"It's not me," he said. "But some people think that with you out of circulation, Springboard will go down the tubes."

I laughed loudly to cover my rage.

"I'm not Springboard!" I shouted. "There are hundreds of people involved. The fact is, if you put me back inside with some mickey mouse excuse, I'll become a martyr. Every bleeding-heart liberal will go wild. You'll give them just the kind of cause they love."

He put the documents back in the drawer and stood up.

"Exactly what I told my superiors," he said. "Let's go get a beer."

We walked next door to the Hotel Isabella and I listened for the next couple of hours to what a tough job he had.

"It's all about politics and money," he said. "I mean I became a social worker so I could help people, people like you. Instead I end up playing all these games."

He got drunk and maudlin and I left him to cry in his beer.

Ed was home. We went up to his apartment where I told him what had happened. He was angry with me.

"You should've jumped on it," he said. "It was a perfect opportunity to show these guys up for what they are. Here's what I think you should do. Call Irwin tomorrow morning and tell him to serve the warrants. If he refuses say that you're going to go to the newspapers."

Maggie, Wanda and Anne had joined us.

"What's the point, Ed?" Wanda asked.

Ed got up and poured hefty portions of rye and coke for us. The women weren't drinking.

"What'll happen," Ed said, "is that Irwin will feel his power is being challenged. A threat like that will piss him right off. My bet is that he'll serve the warrant."

"So Don ends up in jail," Maggie said.

"Right. They'll ship him back to Kingston as fast as they can to get him out of the limelight. And then we're in a perfect position to start organizing from the inside."

"This is crazy, Ed," Anne said. "What's the Beetle supposed to be organizing?"

"Organized protests," Ed said. "The thing is he'll have the credibility because he's in there. So if the guys have a sit-down for better education facilities, a more equitable parole system, their demands will have more impact."

"I'm not too wild about this idea, Ed," I said.

He gave me a calculating gaze, his light blue eyes like a miner's drill, boring deep holes in me for the dynamite needed to bring the walls down.

"It's a responsibility that only you can act on," he said. "You wanna be an agent of change, you've got to go to the front lines where the battles are fought. And that's the joint."

"Bullshit!" Anne shouted. "Don, stop drinking and stop listening to this line of crap. If Ed wants to organize from the inside so badly he can get his parole revoked."

"I don't have the same credibility as Don," Ed said calmly.

"Ed's got a point," said Wanda.

Anne burst into tears and fled from the room. Maggie got up and her usually cheerful face wore a deeply sad expression.

"I'm with Anne," she said.

"You don't even know what this is about," Ed protested.

"I put as much into Springboard as you do," Maggie argued.

"But it's all from your head," he said. "For Don and me, it's our guts. Our blood. We're willing to sacrifice anything."

Maggie shook her head and tears formed in her eyes. She turned to me.

"Don't do this, Don."

Then she left the room.

I sat up with Ed all night. We drank until neither of us made sense.

As we argued the merits of his plan I felt terrified. I was afraid to say no because I thought that made me a coward. But I was also afraid to agree because I knew that would be the end to whatever life I was building. It would be the end of Anne and me.

As the sun came up I moved over to sit on the sill of the open window. Wanda had gone to bed and Ed and I were talking in circles. I thought the fresh air would clear my brain. I needed to find a solution that would satisfy Ed but that I could live with too. An idea suddenly came to me.

"I'll make you a deal, Ed," I said. "I'll turn myself in if you come with me."

"What do you mean?"

"You're my partner," I said. "It only makes sense if they want to revoke my parole that they'll get around to you too. So we beat them to the punch and both of us turn ourselves in."

Wanda strolled into the room and began to make coffee.

"You do that, Laboucane," she said, "and you can forget about me."

Ed lit a cigarette and looked thoughtful.

"I think it would be better to have me out on the street looking after things."

"Maggie could run Springboard," I said.

"It wouldn't be the same thing," Wanda argued. "Springboard is what it is because there are ex-cons at the helm."

"We got six guys from the joint working for us. We could appoint one of them as co-director."

"You may have a point," Ed conceded.

Wanda stood there shaking her head.

"Forget it, Ed," she said. "You think the guys inside will care if you two give up your lives to liberate them? . . . . You know it, and I know it—most of them will call you marks."

I agreed with her even though I felt a deep, painful compassion for my fellow prisoners. But Wanda was right. Most of them had become so cynical they'd laugh at us for being fools. She had identified a sad but true dynamic. The relief I felt was so exhilarating that I stretched out my arms to release some tension and promptly fells backwards out the window. I landed on my back on the flat roof, six feet below. Fortunately I was so relaxed from the booze that I wasn't hurt. But everyone in the house heard the thump and came running. I guess I was a comic sight because everyone, even Warren, laughed.

Ed and I never discussed the matter again but it marked the beginning of a change in our relationship. I had failed him by not being willing to do what he considered the right and noble thing. We spent less time together and in meetings Ed was quieter than ever.

A few weeks after that incident I came home from the office early to catch a nap. I walked into the livingroom and found Warren with his head smashed through a pane of glass in the French doors. His throat had been pierced by glass and there was blood everywhere. I pulled his body from the door and laid him out on the floor. He was still breathing. I called an ambulance and held a towel to the wound while I waited. I was sure he hadn't cut the artery because the blood was oozing out, not pumping, and I was able to stop its flow with just a little pressure.

Warren was in the hospital for a couple of weeks. Maggie went to see him every day but he wouldn't talk to her. When he was well enough to move around, his parents arrived from the States and took him home. Ed, Wanda and Laura moved out of the house.

In March Maggie and I heard a rumour about Judy Bailey. After the first fiasco I had avoided direct contact with her. But Maggie still saw her when she visited the prison. Judy had been released on an eight-hour temporary absence in Kingston to go to Queen's University and register for courses. But she never returned. She was last seen in the company of a well-known criminal and the rumour was that she had been killed for running off at the mouth about things that made certain people nervous.

It was too much for me. I spoke to Anne and told her I had to go away.

"That's a good idea," she said. "You live and breathe this stuff every day. All these cons cannibalize you. There's not much left over for me. Go away and think about us. Do you want there to be an us? Come back when you decide."

"Yes," I said, stunned that she'd think there was any question in my mind about how I felt for her.

I took the train to Golden, British Columbia. I met an eight-and-a-half-month-pregnant girl named Silva, who was travelling with a pack of tarot cards and a guitar. She lived with a man in the mountains about five miles from Invermere, but they had no phone. So when

Dale and Marge arrived to pick me up Silva joined us. Marge just shook her head and smiled.

"Typical Bailey," she said.

"What?" I asked.

Instead of explaining they spent most of the drive to Invermere chuckling.

Silva whispered to me, "Your friends are kinda strange."

I stayed in the mountains for a week, taking long walks along the frozen roads, writing a few poems, drinking a little beer and marvelling at how the shapes of the large fir and spruce trees were changed by their blankets of snow. A lot of the time I spent remembering where I had come from, reminding myself how lucky I was to have so many friends who cared what happened to me. That made the future seem less dark.

Marge was working for the local paper setting type and Dale had a job with the Park services. I was alone most of the time. I wrote long letters to Margaret and Anne. Somehow in my quest to be a saviour to my fellow inmates I had lost connection with those people who nurtured me, who kept me alive. Particularly Anne.

I knew I loved her but the source of my feelings for her was a mystery. She was a distant person. She did not have many close friends. She survived like a cactus and seemed to require little care. I suspected she was as lonely as I was. I wanted to penetrate into the dark place where I was convinced she hid out. I felt if I could do that then perhaps some of my own dark fears could be diminished.

I returned to Toronto refreshed and determined to change my life. I was going to reclaim it for Anne and for myself. The first thing I did was give notice to John Metson that I was leaving Springboard in June. Anne was thrilled.

"Let's take a trip," she said. "Take a couple of weeks to drive out and see Jane and Helen. Maybe spend the summer in Vancouver."

"Okay with me," I said.

While I'd been away, Maggie, David and Anne had gone farm hunting. I thought the idea was crazy but they had already committed themselves to renting one near Keswick for a year. In April, we moved in. The mile-long road leading to the place was muddy swamp. The place itself could only be described as rustic. The old stone house was falling apart. The plumbing was designed by the same guy who built Noah's ark. The electrical system blew fuses like it had itself confused with a popcorn maker. But it had a pond. By late May I'd cleared the debris from around the shore, skimmed off the scum from the surface, and it was like having our own little lake.

Anne and I bought four ducks and two swans from the local farmers' market. At night we'd sit and watch them squabble with each other. For no reason we could understand, they would suddenly form a procession and paddle regally around the pond.

"I'm really happy," Anne said one night.

I took her hand.

"Me too," I said. "I've been thinking we should consider getting married."

She laughed.

"Why spoil a good thing?"

"We might want to have a kid," I said.

She leaned over and kissed me. Her hand on my face was soft and gentle. Soothing.

"No," she said. "You think I might want to have a kid. I know how you feel about being a parent. I know how the idea of it scares you. We've got plenty of time."

In May I took a refresher CUT course. Anne tried to get in but again was refused. She was furious for a couple of days but then decided the issue was chauvinism.

"CUT's run by a bunch of men who are threatened by any woman with brains," she said.

I wasn't going to argue.

This time when we were sent out on the skid row plunge I was sent to Hamilton. Just before I left I called Abe Rotstein at *The Canadian Forum* and asked him if I could do an article on my experience. He said he'd be delighted and could offer me fifteen hundred dollars for the piece. Wow! That was the most I'd been paid for any writing.

When I returned Margaret had called to let us know she was in town and wanted to see us. I phoned her and arranged to bring her up to the farm.

It was a long slow drive from Toronto. Margaret really hated cars. I understood. She liked to be in control.

"It's okay, Margaret," I said. "I'll get us there without an accident."

"Cars make me nervous," she said. "Bloody coffins on wheels."

Maggie and David had prepared a huge supper. Margaret regaled us with stories about the folly of being a writer. *Chatelaine* had recently taken one of her stories for publication and the editor called and said that she'd have to cut six hundred words from the piece so they could put another ad in.

"Where do I cut them from, I asked. The story's skin and bones now. I don't write fat stories, lady."

We all laughed at her theatrical indignation, her thick bushy eyebrows furrowed, her lips quivering.

"So what happened?" Maggie asked.

Margaret laughed.

"The buggers just chopped out a section from the middle. The story makes no sense at all now."

"Couldn't you sue them?" David asked. He was our resident lawyer in that he saw the world in adversarial terms.

"No point," Margaret said, waving away his suggestion. "The reality is most people will read it while they're waiting for a dentist's appointment and the fact that it doesn't make sense won't even occur to them."

I admired her ability to put incidents like that into perspective. With some of my published poems and articles, editors had introduced changes and cuts so that the meaning of the piece had been lost. It enraged me. But Margaret seemed so calm about it.

"Just take the money and run," she said.

After people went to bed Margaret and I ended up sitting beside the pond drinking scotch and rye respectively.

"I'm glad you're leaving Springboard," she said. "You paid back whatever it was you think you owed. It's time to get on with your writing."

"I've got a book of stories half finished," I said.

"Good," she said. "And things with Anne are okay? The wounds have healed?"

"I think so but when I talk about marriage, she puts me off."

"She's still afraid but she loves you, Don. Annie loves you like no other woman ever will. She hasn't been given much love in her life. I can see that. And those that don't get usually don't get to give either. So she's got years and years of love stored up. And it's yours for the asking."

"This may sound crazy but sometimes I don't feel worthy of her," I said.

Margaret laughed as she topped up her glass.

"That may be the case but love truly is blind."

We sat watching the ducks and swans float around the pond.

"What about you, Margaret," I asked. "Are you happy?"

"I've got two anchors," she said. "My kids and my work. Both are flourishing, thank God. That's all that matters."

I wanted to ask about her need for affection. Who struck a match in the dark corners of her soul? But I knew the answer already. She would talk about the tribe. About Anne and me, Adele Wiseman, Marian Engel, Timothy Findley, and on and on. All these people provided her with nourishment for her spirit. Still, to me, her life seemed lonely.

The moon was high and the stars bright when she stood up from her lawn chair.

"Time for me to toddle off to bed," she said. "Give me a hug."

I did. A long tight embrace full of energy, feeling and fear.

She started walking toward the house but then stopped and turned.

"Let Annie drive me in the morning," she said. "That way I'll get a chance to talk with her."

"Sure," I said.

She waved and disappeared into the darkness. I slept in the next morning and it would be several years before we met again face to face.

Anne and I had traded the old Corvair in on a beast of a machine, a big red 1965 Ford with the biggest engine available. No more crawling up the mountains, hauling our trailer at twenty miles an hour with a line of honking cars behind us.

David Helwig and his wife Nancy had split up. He decided a trip to Vancouver would be good for his mental health. Just before we left, David arranged with *Maclean's* magazine to buy the journals we would keep on our trip. He negotiated a fee of five hundred dollars apiece. They would pay for the trip.

We drove the northern route across Ontario. We stopped at Hearst where we caught the Polar Bear Express train to Moose Factory. On the train I met an old school chum who was on his honeymoon. As we walked along the dusty main drag of the small town I ran into Larry Sanders, who had been in the CUT course with me. The world felt small, safe.

We had brought along our sleeping bags and paid a native man a dollar to boat us over to an island about a mile from shore. We hadn't bothered to bring a tent because it was summer. However, the temperature went below freezing that night. Fortunately we located some other campers on the island and they allowed us to sit up in their tents, wrapped in our sleeping bags. Even then we were numb with cold in the morning.

We stopped in Winnipeg and stayed a night with Tim Sale. He and David sang old Anglican hymns until the wee hours of the morning. They both had melodic voices. In fact David had to make a choice when he was in his early twenties between becoming a writer or a professional singer.

Tension had been building between David and Anne and it exploded into a fight that night. Anne felt that David ignored her and that he had come on the trip because he was my friend, not hers. They both sulked about it for the next twenty-four hours.

Being released from the grind of Springboard drove me to drink. Most of the time David or Anne drove and I sat in the back seat sucking on a beer. Not really getting drunk but certainly insulating myself from the world and taking many little naps. I didn't seem to know what to do with myself.

In southern Alberta we camped beside a beautiful lake where thousands of birds gathered at sunset. Later a flock of deer arrived to drink. Then just before dark a pack of coyotes came for refreshment. David was up first the next morning and said that he had seen a herd of antelope down by the lake. I fired up the Coleman stove and put the water on to boil. But then we discovered there was no coffee.

This was a catastrophe! Anne was a coffee addict. Me, I'd settle for a warm beer. David was happy with tea but Anne had to have her fix in the morning. So David got in the car and drove for over an hour before he found a store. When he returned triumphant the valley of distance that had developed between him and Anne was bridged.

We stopped in Invermere and had a visit with Marge and Dale. David is an avid fisherman so we spent most of the time being guided along logging roads by Dale in search of virgin ponds full of cut-throat trout. We found several and caught our share of fish but I also lost a muffler when I had to take to the woods in order to avoid a collision with a loaded logging truck that was barrelling along at about eighty miles an hour. No other vehicles were allowed on these roads so we were lucky we weren't killed.

In Vancouver we camped our trailer in the yard of playwright Jim Gerrard. He was a pleasant and friendly man, but eccentric. We arrived at his place at six in the morning. One of the two women he was living with answered the door and had us wait in the living room. A few minutes later Jim appeared, tall and elegant in a satin robe, fully awake, a cigar in the corner of his mouth and a bottle of brandy in his hand.

David and I spent the next couple of days writing our articles. David had carefully kept a journal and recorded the highlights of the trip. I rarely take notes, preferring to write whatever my memory presents me with.

I had real trouble getting started. I went for a walk on the beach with Anne at low tide and as we pondered all the little life forms in the sand, waiting for the ocean to return, she asked me if I ever thought of my kids.

"Yes," I said. "Especially Estelle. I know her the best because I got to spend a little time with her when she was a baby. I know just enough about her to know that I don't know her.... If you know what I mean."

Anne laughed but then got serious again.

"You hardly ever talk about your kids," she said. "If I were you I'd feel like someone had dropped a bomb on my house, blown it up and left behind a crater. A big hole inside myself."

The image she created of that ruined relationship almost made me cry.

So the article I wrote was really a long letter to Estelle. I described what we saw and did on our trip, but also how sometimes I imagined her being with us. It was mostly a piece about missing her. And missing a part of myself.

David and I sent the articles to *Maclean's*. They paid us but then months later the magazine got in touch with me saying they had mislaid my piece. Did I have a copy? I had mailed off the only other copy to Estelle. I phoned her from Vancouver and she thanked me for the letter, but said she'd thrown it out. So it never did see print.

David took the train home and Anne and I found a campsite at a park in Port Moody. After a few days of watching me sit at a picnic table banging on my typewriter, Anne went out and got a job running programmes for senior citizens at a community centre.

The summer drifted by. I finished a book of stories that Oberon Press accepted for publication. Then I wrote a new collection of poems that Fiddlehead accepted. I felt like I was on a roll so I started a novel.

I worked from eight in the morning until three in the afternoon. Then I'd walk across the highway to the Leon Hotel, drink some beer, and watch a group of pretty young women out-hustle the truck drivers at the pool table. Don McLean's "American Pie" was played on the juke box every ten minutes. A guy named Dave Barrett led the New Democratic Party to victory in the provincial election.

I'd have supper ready for Anne when she returned. We often had guests. Jane Rule, her parents, and Helen joined us. Tom Wayman arrived one night with a woman on each arm.

Occasionally we went out visiting, to have dinner with David Watmough and Floyd whom we had met previously at Jane and Helen's. We indulged in manic drinking sessions with George Bowering.

It was a tranquil, satisfying life, but then one day I got a message through Jane that Tim Sale wanted me to call him in Winnipeg.

I called and was offered a job. Director of the United Church Halfway Homes.

"No, Don," Anne said. "Haven't you had enough of that prison stuff?"

"I hate halfway homes," I told Tim. "I stayed in one when I was a kid and it was horrible."

"That's why we want you," he said. "You'll know what we need to change."

I was tempted.

"Just come and have a look," he said.

"Come fall, your job will disappear," I said to Anne. "I've got to do something to make some dough. Why don't I just go look?"

"Okay, but I don't really want to live in Winnipeg," she replied.

I came. I saw. I stayed.

I guess the job was a challenge. I didn't have to start from scratch as I had with Springboard. I moved to Winnipeg on my own in September. Anne came a month later. I'd found a house for us a block from the halfway homes. By the time she arrived our livingroom had become an extension of the operation. She wasn't happy but then she found a fantastic job as the community minister for two churches, Anglican and United, which shared the same building.

Again our lives became a blur of activity. I had to purchase another house in order for the halfway homes to become a financially viable operation. I had to fire old staff who wouldn't change, and find new people who had the right enthusiasm.

I became quite lonely in the midst of all this frenzy and asked Anne to marry me. She surprised me by accepting. We took the train to Toronto and were married at the Church of the Holy Trinity by John Metson and Barry Morris. Ed was my best man and Maggie was Anne's bridesmaid. David Helwig sang "Morning Has Broken." His rendition was beautiful but many people were confused as to who he was. It said in the programme, "Morning Has Broken," sung by Cat Stevens. By a weird coincidence Cat Stevens was appearing that night at Massey Hall just a block away. Several people were convinced that Stevens had slipped over to our wedding during intermission to perform for us.

Over two hundred people attended, including a group of visiting Inuit who were staying with CUT staff. My parole officer, Don Irwin, was in attendance. Anne's mother beamed. Margaret was back in England but she sent a telegram of congratulations.

At Christmas my two girls flew out to be with us. Anne's parents took the train. A couple of the guys from the halfway home who had no family joined us for Christmas dinner. It was a joyful time. I had the sense that I was now part of a family.

There were lots of politics in my job. Pressure from the inmates who wanted to be sponsored for parole. Pressure from the parole service and parole board who wanted me to prove a man would not commit another crime if he was released to our facility. When the screws are tightened I drink. To relax. To ease the tension. I drank a lot during that period.

In the early spring of 1973 I took a week off and flew down to Ontario and made my way out to Margaret's shack. I sat there staring at the swollen river rushing by and managed to write another large section of my novel.

In the fall of that year Ed contacted me. He was in trouble. He had organized a series of concerts to raise money for a new organization called Community Parole. But the deal had gone sour.

He'd borrowed thousand of dollars from Wanda, got John Metson to advance him money through the CRC to do the publicity, but at the first concert only eleven people showed up.

Wanda and he had split. He asked if he could come and stay with us for a while. Without hesitation I said yes.

The halfway homes were running smoothly. Jack Villerup, Margaret's neighbour, had written me and said he had cancer. Would I like to buy his place? Anne was lukewarm to the idea. She was happy in her job, finally doing something that satisfied her and through which she received recognition for her abilities.

My first book of stories, *If You Hum Me a Few Bars I Might Remember the Tune*, had been released to great reviews. My new book of poems, *The Shapes Around Me*, was on book store shelves. Anne held a surprise party to celebrate their publication. Maggie Nistad was working in Saskatchewan and drove in for the festivities. Anne even got Daniel Berrigan to come. I felt loved and cherished by the woman I could barely express my feelings to.

I never was sure how Anne felt about Ed. She seemed scornful of the many women Ed had been involved with. Except Wanda. I believe Anne liked and respected Wanda. I assumed Anne thought of Ed only as my partner, a guy who drank and gambled too much and who treated women like disposable objects.

Ed arrived with a girl of eighteen who worked as an exotic dancer. Her name was Lorrie. Great, I thought. Anne will be just ecstatic. So I made it my business to take Lorrie around with me when I visited the halfway homes, just to get her out of the house, away from Anne's sight.

Ed was depressed when he first showed up. He was vulnerable in a way I'd never seen him. He sat up with Anne and me and wept over his failure. I was grateful to see Anne respond in a supportive, loving way.

Then one day Ed and I went out for a drink and he confided that he was having an affair with Anne. He hoped I wasn't upset. My emotions seized up. I wanted to be casual and off-hand about it just as he was but I felt like my throat had been cut and blood was flooding my mouth.

Lorrie left for the west coast, which meant that Anne and Ed spent more and more time together. I didn't have the guts to broach the subject with her, and instead distracted myself with booze, dreaming about moving to Jack's old place on the Otonabee.

Then Ed got a new girlfriend, a nurse named Carol Beck. She was young, beautiful and smart. She worked as a nurse in the burn unit of the Hospital for Sick Children. She had lived through many long painful deaths. She had great compassion but also a will forged from stainless steel. Within weeks of meeting her Ed got a job and was spending most of his time with her.

Christmas came again and Anne and I found a dog left to die in a snowdrift. We took her home, ran an ad to locate her owner and when no one showed up, we adopted her. I named her Greta. Greta Garbage, because that's how she'd been treated.

I had finished my novel and Oberon would be bringing it out in the spring. I applied to the Canada Council to write a new book. Margaret wrote me a glowing letter of recommendation.

In February of 1974 Anne announced she was pregnant. I was surprised, fearful, but still ready to take on the responsibility, if that's what she wanted. I was puzzled too. Anne was on the pill. We had always agreed that we'd talk about having a kid before she stopped taking it.

We went to the Marlborough Hotel for an intimate dinner. I'd chosen the place because it was old, had a lot of history, and at that time it served the best food in town. There were wandering violin players to add to the romantic atmosphere.

Before our drinks arrived Anne looked around and began to laugh softly.

"What a lovely piece of irony that you would bring me here," she said.

I didn't understand.

"Why? I thought you liked this place."

She started to cry, very quietly and in such a subdued manner that the waiter put down our drinks and didn't seem to notice.

"I liked it so much that when I got involved with a guy from the halfway house, I had him bring me here."

"One of the guys at the halfway homes?"

"Yes. You know who."

And suddenly I did. It had happened right in front of me but I'd been blind.

"You've always got time to sit around with your prison buddies, pouring drinks, getting blasted with them while you listen to their troubles. Well, Ed listened to mine.... And then this other guy. He was sweet. I'd meet him at the room and he'd have a bouquet of flowers on the table beside the bed."

"So you don't know who the father is," I said.

"I'm sorry," she said.

This was in the days of books like *Open Marriage*, so although I was shocked, hurt, and angry I thought of Anne's behaviour as being part of the times. The pain I felt, I thought I'd earned. I prided myself on living on the edge. The edge was sharp and I shouldn't be surprised if I was cut.

"So what do you want to do?" I asked.

"I want to leave here," she said. "Go east. Get ourselves that cabin beside the river.... And make ourselves a life, Beetle, away from all this craziness. I still love you. If I have a child I want it to be yours."

"What about...?"

"I'm flying to Minneapolis this weekend for an abortion," she said.

"I'll come with you."

"No. A woman from the clinic who arranged it is coming with me. I'd rather do it that way.... Trust me, Beetle. More now than ever."

She put her hand over mine and squeezed hard.

"I will," I said.

She began to cry again.

"This is the worst it will ever be," she said. "If we can survive this we'll be invincible."

"Superman and Superwoman."

"That's us," she said, smiling through her tears.

I believed her.

Life on the River: 1974

In May of 1974 the Canada Council informed me that I'd been given a grant. Hurrah! But I'd asked for eight thousand dollars and they could only give me four. That left me short on my downpayment for Jack's cabin. But Maggie Nistad and Margaret Laurence loaned me the money I needed.

The last week in June, Anne and I loaded the car and trailer with our clothes and a few paintings and took off east. With us was our dog Greta, and Chris Morfopolis, a bright young man who had been a resident in the halfway homes. He wanted to work in corrections and I was able to persuade the United Church to fund him to take a CUT course.

I can't explain how relieved I was to be leaving Winnipeg. I felt good about the work I'd done there and I knew that Anne was proud of the tasks she had performed for the church. When she gave notice she informed Barry Morris in Toronto about the position and he applied and got the job. A social worker had taken over my position at the halfway homes, which pleased the board of directors who had always been uneasy with my style. So in the work area, both Anne and I had reason to be satisfied. But I also felt we were leaving behind a lot of grief.

We dropped Chris off at CUT headquarters and took a detour to Stella's place where I thought I would pop in for a moment and say hello to the girls. I hadn't seen or heard from them in over a year. Estelle was twelve now and Rebecca eight.

Anne elected to stay in the car with Greta. She felt the girls ignored me as a form of revenge for not being the father they imagined. She didn't approve and it upset her to see them make a fuss over me. She thought it was hypocritical.

I walked into a disaster. Stella was lying on the couch, her face white and thin. She explained she had been operated on for ovarian cancer but recent tests showed the surgeons hadn't got all of the tumour. She had to go back in the hospital the following week for another operation.

The girls came running in from outside and wrapped themselves around me.

"Where's Carmello?" I asked.

"He left," Estelle said.

"An' he even took the colour television with him!" Rebecca said with indignation.

"Can the girls stay with you?" Stella asked. Both girls began to cry at the same time, protesting, screaming that they didn't want to leave their mother behind.

I walked down to the car where Anne waited.

"So, Beetle," she said. "What's up? You've got that look. I know I'm not going to like this but tell me."

I explained.

"I guess the only answer is to bring them all," she said when I'd finished.

"Are you sure? Maybe we could put them up in a hotel in Peterborough. The thing is Stella is terrified. The doctors told her to make legal arrangements about the guardianship of the kids."

"We can't afford hotels, Beetle," Anne said. "We'll cope. That's all."

We spent the next hour packing clothes and reorganizing the car.

When we arrived Margaret was standing in her driveway wearing her shack clothes, a flannel shirt over loose slacks. It was warm but the heat never seemed to bother her. Maybe growing up on the prairies with the extremes of hot and cold had made her immune to temperature changes.

Introductions were made, including Greta. Margaret took Stella and the kids over to her place while Anne and I inspected our new home. Anne had never been inside Jack's place so she wasn't prepared for the mess.

Our new house consisted of a six-hundred-square-foot wood frame cabin that looked out on to the river. Attached to the cabin was an open breezeway that was connected to a garage. We entered the main cabin.

Newspapers were stacked everywhere. The water pipes were hung from the ceiling by wires. It looked like there were only three electrical outlets because extension cords curled around the room like snakes. There was hardly a square foot of wall space that didn't have a large nail sticking out, holding a piece of fishing tackle. There were empty brandy bottles everywhere and when I opened the refrigerator it was clear that no one had been here for months. I guess when Jack got too sick to care for himself someone had hauled him off to the hospital and left everything the way it was. He had died there in the winter and it seemed that the executor hadn't bothered even to check on the place.

Anne wailed.

"We'll never be able to clear up this mess. Let's burn it to the ground and start over."

"Good idea," said Margaret as she appeared in the doorway. She went over to Anne and pushed her toward the large bay window. "Look at that," she said. "A view you couldn't buy for a million dollars."

We saw Greta prowling the shore. Obviously she felt at home.

Anne collapsed into Margaret's arms, sobbing. Margaret led her to the door.

"Let Auntie Margaret deal with the emotional chaos," she said. "You deal with this mess.... Oh yeah, I called Max Doughty. He'll be out in an hour. I figured the water didn't get turned off over the winter and the pipes probably split."

I looked up. She was right. The heat must have been turned off. And then I wondered, what heat. All I could see was an old woodburning Quebec heater. What had I gotten us into?

I began to haul the junk outside. After my third trip a good looking, middle-aged guy approached me from the cottage next door. He held out his hand.

"Tommy Bell," he said. "You the guy that bought the place?"

"Don Bailey," I said, returning his shake. "Yeah, I'm the one."

"Hell of a mess, eh," he said. "Old Jack never threw out a thing. You looked in the garage yet?"

"No," I said. "I'm trying to clear some sleeping space."

"I've got a truck. Be glad to help."

"That would be wonderful," I said.

We worked until dark. After eight trips to the dump the main cabin was clear of debris. There was a room with a lumpy double bed for Anne and me and next door a smaller room for Stella. I had put up the tent trailer for the kids to sleep in, which they thought was wonderful. Max, the plumber, a jolly man who obviously liked his work, had been by and we had water and a toilet that flushed.

Margaret and Anne had prepared a meal of sliced ham and fresh corn on the cob. Tommy Bell's wife, Irene, came over and joined us. She was a tall, slim woman with an astonishingly beautiful face. Not a line marred her perfect skin. She had the look that most models would kill for. She carried a drink and didn't eat. I noticed her belly had a slight swelling, perhaps the beginnings of a paunch. She was about thirty-five.

"So, you're our new neighbours," she said. "Welcome to paradise . . . ." She had only a small slur to her speech but I knew the glass in her hand wasn't her first drink of the day. "Did Tommy speak to you about the well?" she asked.

"Irene, these folks just got here. There'll be plenty of time to talk about that later."

"I just wanna know if we're gonna have to spend three, four thousand dollars drilling a new well . . . that's all."

Tommy got up, took her elbow and led her to the door. Irene looked puzzled. Margaret and I looked at each other. Drunks always recognize other drunks.

"Listen, I'll be glad to give you a hand tomorrow, Don," Tommy said. "Thanks for supper, Margaret."

"Thank you," I said, but he was already out the door.

"That lady was funny," Rebecca said.

We got the kids settled in the trailer. Then Stella. It was still early by my reckoning but Anne said she was exhausted. I kissed her and went over to Margaret's for a nightcap.

"What was that business about the well?" I asked.

"The well's on Jack's property," Margaret said. "Now yours. Jack divined it and it is supposed to be one of the deepest wells around here. It has never run dry like mine has. So when Tommy got the place next door, he and Jack became friends. Tommy's well was always pumping mud so Jack just hooked him up to his."

"That's okay with me," I said.

"Of course it is. And tomorrow you'll tell him. Personally I don't think Irene should have quit her job. But she had to, I guess."

I waited. I knew there was a story here and Margaret smiled, lit a fresh cigarette, took a belt of scotch and started in.

"Interesting couple, Tommy and Irene. They met when they were in their teens. He's a printer and she worked in the office. For a while they went out together but they fought and broke up. He married another woman and about a year later Irene got married. Kept working at the same place so they saw each other every day. That went on for about ten years. Neither couple had children which is one of the reasons Tommy's marriage broke up. After the divorce he bought this place and moved here permanently. Got a job at a printing shop in town. Less than six months later Irene left her husband and got a divorce. They got in touch. Started going out and three years ago they got married. She continued working in Toronto because she couldn't find anything up here. But she quit in the spring."

"Wow," I said. "Sort of like a fairy tale. And a happy ending too."

"I dunno," Margaret said. "I see storm clouds. There's nothing Tommy can do. Irene can't have children and she doesn't like the idea of adopting. I think she's totally disoriented. I see her come out in the morning about eleven. She's all dolled up, her hair and makeup perfect. Just like when she was on the job, I imagine. But she's got nowhere to go. So she pulls up a lawn chair, glass in hand, and stares at the river. I've gone over a couple of times and talked with her. The river's like a flowing mirror of memories for her. A few drinks and she floats away."

"That sounds pretty sad," I said.

"Well, maybe she'll snap out of it," Margaret said, getting up to replenish her own drink. "I hope for both their sakes she does. All she's got to hang on to right now are those two yappy poodles. Speaking of which did you notice that Greta gambols. I saw her chasing a frog and she bounces along like a lamb."

"I never noticed," I admitted.

"She's really quite amazing. I'm not fond of dogs but she's a charmer. I think you must be the luckiest guy in the world."

"I don't know," I said. "Today didn't exactly turn out the way I imagined it. I had a picture of Anne and I arriving here. Alone. Me carrying her over the threshold. All that romantic stuff."

"That's what I mean," she said. "You're married to a bloody

saint. How many other women would put up with what she has today and do it with good grace?"

"Not many," I admitted.

"And don't you forget it either," she said. "Ever. Now go home and keep her warm."

For the next week I hauled garbage to the dump, accompanied by Greta who loved the smell of the place. Tommy loaned me his truck and took my car to work. The garage was full of old washing machines, tons of lead pipe and an endless assortment of appliances, none of which worked.

Stella was due in the hospital on Sunday. I finished the last load just an hour before we were to leave. Anne and the girls had helped me off and on but now they were more interested in laying out a garden plot at the back of the house. Stella sat in the breezeway where it was cooler, looking frail and sad, a small overnight bag at her feet.

"I'm filthy," I said to her. "I think I'll just dive in the river and let myself dry out on the drive into Toronto."

She nodded at me and I went over to Margaret's dock because we didn't have one yet.

Margaret was sitting in her chair watching me nervously.

"Don't dive, Don," she said. "It's dangerous."

I looked down in the water. All I could see were a few weeds. There was nothing dangerous about them. I couldn't wait to feel the cool river water washing over me. So I dived.

Ouch! A second after I hit the water something sharp tore along my stomach and the length of my penis. It burned and stung like I'd been attacked by a swarm of man-eating bees. I came out of the water roaring.

Margaret ran down to see what was wrong. She saw the red welt on my stomach and called for Anne.

"I'll get some ointment," she said and ran inside.

When she returned, Anne was holding the elastic of my shorts open so air could get to the more delicate wounded area.

"I don't think Don wants us to have kids," Anne said.

Margaret looked down the opening of my shorts.

"My Gawd Bailey, you are a stupid bugger! I told you not to dive! Jack put down new posts for the dock every year. You probably jumped on one of the old ones."

My head was dizzy but I also felt acute embarrassment as Margaret and Anne discussed what kind of dressing my wound needed.

"It's not bleeding," Margaret said, looking again.

"Can I sit down?" I asked.

"Personally, I think some ointment should go on it and then a light wrapping," Margaret said. "I've got some gauze and scissors but I think I'll leave the honours to you, Annie."

She got the supplies and I hobbled back to our place. Stella and the girls wanted to know what happened.

"Just a scratch," I said.

Anne sat on the edge of the bathtub, applying ointment to me and then wrapping the stinging organ in gauze. In between laughing hysterically.

The girls stood outside the bathroom door and kept asking, "What's so funny?"

"Nothing," I bellowed back.

Wounded but alert, I drove Stella to the hospital. I seriously thought about having a doctor look at the scratch but decided I couldn't take the razzing I'd probably get.

So no sex for several weeks and every time Margaret or Anne wanted a laugh, they'd inquire gently about my war wound.

Once the junk was out of the way I hired Dick Wiles, a carpenter who had done a lot of work for Margaret. In a couple of weeks we had converted the garage into a master bedroom with a huge glass patio door so when Anne and I woke up in the morning, the first thing we saw was the river.

The summer passed quickly.

A week before Labour Day Margaret packed up to leave.

"I want to be out of here before next weekend's air show," she said. There was a small airport across the river which handled only small prop planes. Except for Labour Day weekend. Then the Snowbirds brought their jets in.

"It's an abomination," Margaret said. "If I had a gun I'd shoot them from the skies. Anyway I've got to get ready to hit the promotion trail. I told my publishers I'm not doing a whirlwind trip across the continent but I have to do the Toronto and New York launching of the novel."

The cab arrived to take her to Lakefield. We all hugged and kissed her. My novel was coming out that fall as well. We wished each other luck and said we'd call in November. Maybe spend some of the Christmas holidays together.

Fall was almost upon us and Anne and I had to get the kids registered for school. Stella was still in the hospital, recovering slowly but making progress. We knew she wasn't going to die.

Anne and I turned our attention to preparing for our first winter in the country. Greta seemed the most settled of us all.

Friends and Fate:
1974–1981

Slowly our lives began to take on an orderly rhythm. The girls were enrolled in school and were getting better grades than they ever had. Anne secured a dream job with the province setting up and maintaining regional information centres. It meant a lot of driving for her but she loved the freedom the task afforded her. She was at last doing something that gave her great personal satisfaction.

I was busy supervising the ongoing reconstruction of the cabin and organizing our domestic lives. I've always liked to cook and clean and the girls created mountains of laundry. So for a while I functioned as a housewife, doing up six tuna casseroles at once, ironing dresses as I watched afternoon soaps on television, and cleaning up after the workmen.

After dinner Anne and I would take Jack Villerup's old boat and cruise the shoreline of the river. We came to know the different families of herons who occupied certain territories. When they didn't fly away at our approach, we became convinced they recognized the soft putt putt of our motor. We searched the sky for the Merlin hawks that hunted until twilight. There was very little traffic on the river now that fall had arrived. The tourists with their big launches and yachts had gone home. The shy muskrats returned.

Our evening ritual included anchoring for fifteen or twenty minutes while I fished. Occasionally I caught a smallmouth bass large enough to provide us with a meal. Anne sometimes dropped a line in the water but more often she just sat and watched. And sometimes talked. One night as the twilight began to swallow us I caught her grinning at me.

"What?" I asked.

"I like this," she said.

"The river?"

"Yes. And the life we're making. I think it's time we started talking about a baby. A child of our own."

"Whoa!" I said. "We've got pretty full plates now. God knows how long my kids will be with us."

"Not long," she said. "Stella called tonight. She's home from the hospital. She has a homemaker in every day to do the meals and look after the place. She wants her kids back, Beetle."

"She hasn't spoken to me about it," I said.

Anne laughed.

"You really don't understand women," she said.

"What I understand is that she is a very sick woman. She doesn't need the hassle of the kids hanging off her."

"You're wrong," she said. "The presence of the girls will provide some of the healing. Part of the pain she's feeling now is because of the separation from her children.... You don't know what I'm talking about, do you?"

"No," I admitted. "She asked us to look after them until she recovered. I love the girls but they take a lot of energy. It doesn't make sense for her to have them home until she's stronger."

"Prepare yourself," Anne said. "They'll be leaving sooner than you think."

"How can you be so sure?" I asked.

She laughed again softly.

"Instinct," she said. "So put your mind to the task of imagining our child."

"I'm afraid to," I said.

"I know.... Is it because of what happened in Winnipeg? Ed, the abortion, all that."

"No," I said. And I meant it.

We are all frail beings flailing around like helpless insects drawn to the light. Seeking to escape the darkness that sometimes fills our souls. I have never resolved if it's our passion for the light that causes us to smash up against all obstacles protecting us from the flame, or the simple fear triggered in us by the black night. I only know that moralizing about our human folly is a kind of whistling in the dark.

"When we got married," she said, "you made a vow that ours would be a relationship that didn't demand explanations.... I never really understood it but now I want us to have a child more than anything.... And I think you need an explanation."

"A kid's a big step," I said. "What about your career?"

"It doesn't have to interfere with my work," she said. "I've watched you since we've been here. You're in your glory at home taking care of things."

"So the plan is, I stay at home and take care of baby."

"Babies sleep twenty hours a day when they're first born. You'll have plenty of time to write. And then later we can put him or her in day-care."

Anne was right. I liked the domestic life. Taking care of one small child would be a snap. But what if I felt as alienated from her child as I did from my two girls? Sometimes when I took them exploring in the bush behind the cottage, they would hurry ahead of me and disappear around a bend in Squirrel Creek. After a few minutes their shrill voices would be lost among the chattering of squirrels and calling of birds. I would become disoriented, drift into daydream and forget the girls even existed. When that happened I felt terrified and would call their names and go crashing through the bush like a fly-bitten, crazed moose. When I found them, they laughed at my naked fear. I hated to feel so afraid and would often yell at the girls so loudly they would cry. That didn't seem like healthy parenting to me.

"Listen, Anne," I said.

"No," she said, grabbing my hand and yanking me from the back of the boat to the middle seat beside her. "You listen."

She kissed me, engulfing me with her passion. In the darkness, with the boat bobbing gently in the river's current, we made love. This is not an easy feat in a fourteen-foot aluminum boat but if you think to take off your life jacket, it can serve as a pillow.

Within a week of that memorable evening David Helwig called me from Toronto. He had accepted a job at CBC as story editor for a new television series called *Sidestreet*. He wanted to know if I'd be interested in writing an episode. He explained it was a police show and with my bank robbing background and my experience with Springboard I probably had a warehouse of stories they could use. I knew nothing about writing scripts but it turned out that John Hirsch who was the new head of CBC drama had organized a two-week training course for interested writers. I was invited to participate if I wanted. I leaped at the opportunity.

Chris Morfopolis had finished his CUT course and wanted to start a halfway home in Peterborough for guys coming out of

Warkworth, which was about forty miles away. I volunteered to help establish a board of directors.

Suddenly I was busy, busy again. Baby would have to wait.

In late November Stella called and asked me to bring the girls for a weekend visit. Anne and I were relieved to have a little time to ourselves. We spent the time chopping and stacking wood that we planned to burn all winter in our new Franklin stove. We pulled Margaret's dock up on shore and stored her punt, CC Grant, in the shed. Jack's old boat was hauled from the water, the motor stashed safely in Margaret's shed.

Late one Sunday afternoon we stood on the grass in front of the cabin, surveying what we had accomplished in just a few months. The garage was now our bedroom with patio doors facing the river. The doors opened on to a large deck that stretched across the front of the cabin to the other side of the breeze-way that was now enclosed and served as a laundry room and as a work room for Anne who had taken up carpentry. The old bay window had been replaced by a much larger bow window that afforded us a majestic view of the river. There were new shingles on the roof. A new chimney. Our little castle now sat on a solid concrete block foundation.

There were thirty cottages in our little community. Each one sat on a third of an acre plot. Almost all the owners were summer people. But a few, like the Bells, and Harold Foss and his family who lived next door to Tommy and Irene, had winterized their places and lived here all year round. Further down the way was Ted Marowitz, a part-time bartender and seller of bait. Next to him was Doc, a retired veterinarian who lived with his eighty-year-old mother. Toward the farm were the Jolliceurs, an older couple who stayed until the first snowfall and then took off to Florida until spring. Even Steve, the Yugoslavian man next to Margaret who kept the wonderful garden, spent most of the winter living in his wood-stove heated garage that had no running water.

It was a peculiar community. We had invited everyone over for drinks shortly after our arrival. Everyone loved our dog, Greta. She became our passport into the neighbourhood. Steve hated dogs but that was because they barked. Greta didn't bark so she was invited to his place daily for snacks and a narrated tour of his garden. Ted had his own dog, but Greta was welcomed when she dropped by and was fed freshly baked bread. The Foss children took her with them to the three-storey tree house they had constructed in the bush. Mrs. Jolliceur knitted a winter coat out of bright red wool for Greta.

Because she was so quiet, undemanding, and gambolled as she did her neighbourhood tour, people attributed great intelligence to her. Tommy thought she could be trained to be a great hunter. Anne and I were amused at all the attention paid to a mere mutt of a dog. But we also benefited because people assumed we must be bright ourselves to have such a bright dog.

Anne and I stood there that Sunday afternoon, holding hands, both of us smiling. I felt a contentment that had eluded me most of my life.

"It feels like we're putting a shape on our lives," Anne said. "A good shape. It feels snug and safe."

A strong river wind blew her blonde hair off her face and made her appear strong and determined. I felt gifted to be her choice of partner.

Anne was right. The girls did not return from their visit with their mother. Christmas was approaching and I was frantically trying to finish the pilot script for *Sidestreet*. Writing for television seems easy but its very simplicity makes it difficult. Character development must be revealed in the context of a character's actions. Everything has to be externalized. Dialogue must move the story forward, never explain. Each scene must be visualized and written so that the director can immediately see it. I tend to be an inward-looking kind of writer and even after the two-week CBC training course I was having difficulty. But I persevered and turned in what I thought was a good second draft. Three days later John Hirsch's secretary called me and said he wanted to talk with me.

I took the bus into Toronto and walked up Bay Street toward College, thinking all the way that I was being fired from the show. John Hirsch met me in the windowless boardroom. He was holding the script and used it as a baton to direct me toward a seat at a table that could accommodate forty people. But he prowled the room, a tall, lanky man with a head that drooped like a bursting milk weed pod, some of the fluff forming a scruffy beard.

He banged the script against the table and spoke with a thick Hungarian accent.

"This is good, Bailey!"

"Thank you."

"Yes, it's good but maybe a fluke... . You have a criminal

character who is reflective.... Another criminal character who has philosophical conversations with a budgie.... The executive producer hates your script! You understand."

No, I didn't, but I wasn't sure what to say so I sat straighter in my chair and cocked my head in anticipation of an explanation.

"Television drama," Hirsch said, "cannot afford to be too thoughtful. This script is thoughtful but not too much.... Still, it's thoughtful enough that those producing it must be thoughtful.... You see?"

I nodded.

"So this will be our pilot.... I am bringing in a young film director to shoot it.... You see, to make good drama, Bailey, even television drama, one must start with a great script! A story that has characters our audience cares about.... The problem with your script is that the audience will probably care more about the criminals than they do the police.... You see?"

I nodded again. Was he asking me to change it?

"But what we are trying to do on *Sidestreet* is present human drama...drama that the average man on the street can relate to."

He looked toward the blank wall as though there were a window through which we could peer out and see the mythical man on the street. His eyebrows knitted together and he adjusted his glasses with nervous energy when, even under his fierce gaze, the wall remained intact.

"What's good about your story...what I find attractive is that the criminal wins our hearts with his humanity.... His moral dilemma is accessible to our audience...his decision to do the right thing is something we can all cheer."

"I'm glad you like it," I said.

He nodded at me curtly and headed toward the door. Then he stopped and waved the script at me again.

"Helwig and I were the only ones who did," he said. "They've been making porridge drama around here for so many years that asking them to produce your script is like telling them to learn how to chew their food after they've lost all their teeth...."

He then gave a high-pitched laugh that contained no discernible mirth. With the script rolled into a tight cylinder he left the room.

Ed Laboucane and Carol Beck drove down from Winnipeg to

spend Christmas with us. Over the holiday we were invited to Margaret's for dinner.

At the door of her Lakefield house, Margaret was her usual welcoming self to Anne and me. She gave Carol Beck a hug. But with Ed, she was cool. She shook his hand and then waved a finger at him.

"I've got a bone to pick with you, brother," she said.

All through dinner I was tense. I was worried that Anne might have told Margaret about her affair with Ed and that Margaret might decide to confront him. It wasn't like Margaret to do things like that. She was accepting of human foibles. Accepting and forgiving.

During the meal Margaret told the story of how her house had served as a funeral parlour during the thirties and we all marvelled at what a coincidence that was since Rachel's father in *A Jest of God* had been an undertaker, and she had been brought up in an apartment over the business.

"No one mentioned it when I bought the house," she said. "But after I lived here about six months I was at the post office picking up my mail one day and an old lady stopped me and told me the whole story."

"Do you ever hear ghosts?" Carol asked.

Margaret snorted, got up and poured a scotch for herself.

"No," she said. "And I wouldn't mind. But I do feel the presence of others who were here before me."

She sat down at the round maple table, one elbow holding up her chin, a cigarette in her other hand. She was smiling and her expression was dreamy.

Anne reached out and touched her arm.

"What do you mean, Margaret?"

Margaret turned and spoke only to her. It was a conversational habit of hers. The listener had her exclusive attention. The rest of us were spectators.

"Sometimes I'll be sitting in my study upstairs," she said. "Reading or trying to whittle down the mountain of mail that keeps getting bigger instead of smaller... and all of a sudden I can feel the fluttering of a different air current. It may be warmer or cooler than the rest of the air. Almost like someone's breath blowing across my face."

Ed smiled and Carol's face creased with concern.

"The house sounds haunted," Carol said.

"Doesn't it frighten you?" Anne asked

"No," Margaret replied. "It's a soothing presence. Haunted makes it sound bad, or evil. I believe those that have passed through this house have been settled souls. Their spirits often make themselves known when I'm depressed. I feel this faint breath against my hand and I'm reminded that this is a blessed house. And I'm grateful...I don't know a lot about such things but this is not a haunted house.... Spirited, maybe."

Her voice was husky with the fervor of her passion and there were tears in her eyes. We all sat in silence for a moment and then Margaret got up and blew her nose loudly. She stopped suddenly and pointed at Ed.

"You stayed at the shack last fall."

"Yeah," Ed said. "Don was in Winnipeg and asked me to close it up for you. I had the new lock put on the door like you asked for in the note you left."

Margaret laughed.

"Your friend is an idiot, Bailey," she said. "He has the lock changed and what does he do with the new keys...?"

I didn't know what Margaret was talking about. I hadn't heard about any of this.

"Well of course, he does the most sensible thing. He leaves both copies of the keys on the table, inside the shack, and locks the door behind him."

The phone rang and Margaret ran to the living room to answer it. In all the years I visited Margaret in her Lakefield house I think I sat in the living room three or four times. She was a kitchen person, preferring to reign in a kingdom that made her feel secure. It was a large room with an old wooden chest near the window where she placed plants to catch the light. The curtains had an old-fashioned floral print. The press back chairs we sat in were from another time. The original wood flooring had been restored. Even the wallpaper was reminiscent of another era. So although it was a well-lit room with modern appliances, there was a sense of sitting in a farm kitchen from a long ago, perhaps safer, past.

Of course, the ice and scotch were closer at hand in the kitchen. As were the tin tobacco cans into which Margaret poured the endless mounds of cigarette butts produced by herself and visitors.

The phone call that night was from Marian Engel. Margaret talked on the phone for twenty minutes. Or more accurately, she listened. During the time I knew her, Margaret was constantly on the receiving end of calls from writers all across the country. Writers in distress. Those needing advice. Or just someone to listen to whatever injustice had been visited upon them.

I once told Margaret she would have made a great prison inmate. She cocked her eyebrow with interest.

"How so?"

"Prisons are full of people hungry to tell their stories," I said. "But there is a shortage of listeners. Guys tell their stories over and over again in the hope that someone will pay attention and help them change the outcome…but of course that's impossible. So what happens is that the storyteller is stuck at the end with the same result…. Those few who do listen may offer a rationalization of why things went bad but that doesn't help much. You have a way of listening to a tangled tale and seeming to know intuitively that the person wants to move beyond their story…. Your response is a kind of path that they can follow to make a new story…. You know what I mean?"

She looked at me with a mischievous smile and shook her head.

"How is it that you know me so well?" she asked.

We'd shared a few drinks and I thought my observation had more to do with the lowering of my inhibitions than any great insight. Besides, Margaret's commitment to people was blatantly obvious. Only a fool would not notice.

"I watch you listen," I said.

She laughed.

"I know," she said. "I hear you, watching me."

We both laughed but I never forgot that exchange and I never changed my mind about how Margaret listened. It was a rare and generous gift she gave to those who asked.

Margaret finally hung up the phone and returned to the kitchen where she replenished her drink.

"We're going to have a union," she said to me. "A writers' union. It'll be like a great tent where the whole tribe can gather, talk about our common problems and give each other support…. Gawd, I think it's great!"

Ed cleared his throat and Margaret looked at him. Her expression was amused.

"Ah yes," she said. "We were discussing your caretaking qualifications.... Do you remember draining the water when you left the shack?"

"Just like you asked in the note," he said.

"One little thing you forgot," she said. "You didn't turn off the hydro."

"Oh," Ed said, his eyes narrowed and looking inward as though trying to see the various steps he went through when closing the cottage last fall.

"So when I arrived in the spring," Margaret said, "I expected that Tommy Bell would have the key but he didn't. We stood there for the longest time trying to figure out where Don might have hidden it. Looked under the steps. Tore the shed apart. Then I looked through the window and saw both copies sitting on the table. So Tommy graciously broke a window and crawled in for me. He got the water going and that's when we discovered that the hot water heater had been left on but with no water. Naturally the element was burned out."

We all sat there in awkward silence. I felt badly because the responsibility was mine. I should have known better than to ask Ed. He wasn't stupid but paying attention to details was not his strength.

Ed finally held up his hands in a gesture of surrender and let a slow seductive smile form across his face.

"What can I do to make it up?" he asked.

To my astonishment, Margaret was smiling.

"How about an apology," she said.

"I've got a better idea," Ed said.

"Oh yeah," Margaret said, her smile broadening.

"Yeah," Ed drawled.

Sometimes his mode of communicating was maddening. I didn't have a clue what he had in mind but I was sure I'd be involved somehow and that whatever he'd dreamed up would be fraught with risk.

Ed cleared his throat and lit a cigarette. Carol looked nervous but Anne smiled. It was this leisurely, almost hypnotic quality about Ed that attracted her. It was like he had all the time in the world and that rushing through things was for idiots. I could understand how some women would find this slow motion style sexy.

"Don mentioned these people who want to ban your book," he said.

"Oh Gawd, don't get me started on Sam Buick and his bible belt ball-busters!" Margaret said. "They've put out a pamphlet condemning the book...it's full of quotes that are completely out of context! They're up in arms about the fact that Morag is a single woman who has the audacity to have sex out of wedlock...and enjoy it...and bear her child proudly. Of course, what makes it even worse is that her lover is Métis."

"The idea I had was to put them on the defensive," Ed said.

Margaret was interested and leaned over the table closer to him. "How?"

"The thing with these people is you've got to fight fire with fire.... They're condemning you for writing a book that's un-Christian."

"That's what galls me so," Margaret hissed. "It's a novel about faith.... Can't they see that?"

There was anguish in her voice. Anne reached out and took her hand. Margaret began to weep.

"I may never write another novel," she said. "I'm almost sure I won't.... In *The Diviners* I tried to present the spiritual struggle of a woman.... Don't they understand there are no easy answers?"

She got up and blew her nose.

"They've put you on the defensive," Ed said.

"You're damn right they have!" Margaret said. "I can't sit by ignoring their blasphemies...they're making a mockery out of my life's work!"

She was so agitated she was becoming breathless. Her body heaved with rage as she took her place at the table again.

"What I have in mind will put them on the defensive," Ed said.

"Well, don't keep me in suspense," Margaret shouted. "What?"

"I think it would be better if you didn't know," Ed said.

"Great! For all I know you plan to go out and blow up their church in my name, but I shouldn't know about it."

"Close," Ed said. "What I have in mind is an act that will put them in a bad light...force them into a corner and make those people who are silent on the subject come off the fence in support of you."

They sat there for a few seconds staring at each other. The house could have been heated for a season if the electricity passing between them could have been harnessed.

"I have a right to know," Margaret said flatly.

"Okay. My suggestion is that you go back with Anne and Carol to Don's place.... Early in the morning when no one's around, Don and I will pour gasoline in the form of a cross on your front lawn...."

"There's two feet of snow out there," Margaret protested.

Ed smiled.

"We'll really soak it. And when we set it ablaze, the gas will burn a cross that'll be there until spring. The bible punchers will be blamed.... The media will jump on it and anybody who isn't sympathetic to your situation will quickly change their mind."

I liked it. It was a classic Saul Alinsky type of strategy. Take the offensive. Make the other guy look ruthless enough to do anything to destroy you.

We sat there waiting for Margaret's verdict. I was sure she would be against it. The suggested act was too nasty for her to be a part of. Her morality would make her balk.

She began to laugh, got up from the table and walked over to Ed, leaned over and kissed him passionately on the mouth.

"What a lovely idea," she said, as she released him from her embrace. "But we can't do it, Ed."

"Why not?" he asked.

She took his glass to the counter and poured him a tall rye. She then refilled her own glass and carried them both back. Ed accepted his and Margaret lifted her own in a toast.

"To a wonderfully bizarre fantasy," she said.

They clinked their glasses together and each took a swallow.

"Never mind that the idea has an inherent violence that I abhor," Margaret said. "What worries me the most about the plan is that you'd probably burn my bloody house down."

She then erupted in laughter. There was nothing to do but join in.

Time passed quickly on the river. The first episode of *Sidestreet* had been shot and I was at work on my third script. The river flooded, covering our front and back lawns. When the water receded Anne and I, under the supervision of Steve, dug up a huge patch of ground behind the house and planted a vegetable garden. Our first. We were as excited as new parents when plants began to sprout. In our enthusiasm we cleared a small plot on Margaret's property and planted some tomatoes and a couple of rows of corn.

Margaret had won the Governor General's award for *The Diviners*. Several universities had awarded her honorary degrees so we didn't see much of her until it was almost summer. The minute she arrived in the cab, Anne ran across the path to meet her. There seemed to be such urgency in her approach that I stayed away. Anne had seemed preoccupied over the last few weeks and I thought it was some mysterious "female thing" she needed to discuss with Margaret.

They stayed in the cabin for several hours. Occasionally I heard their laughter. I was curious but didn't want to intrude. I prepared enough supper for the three of us and talked to the dog. Just when my patience was scraping against raw nerves they came through the door. Both were a bit tipsy and they had a small boy with them.

"This is Tod," Margaret said. "And this is Don, Tod.... His folks are visiting Steve. I told him I'd give him a tour of the tree house. Grab yourself a drink, Bailey, and come with us."

"She said it was magic," the boy said. He was about seven, blonde, with one front tooth missing. An eager-looking kid under Margaret's spell.

"And it is," Margaret declared. "Magic and secret. In fact, grown-ups can't even see it unless they have a kid with them. Only kids. That's why I didn't bring your parents."

"You mean it'd be invisible to them?" he asked, smiling with delight.

Anne kissed me and whispered, "I'll make the salad."

"Yes," Margaret answered. "But they could see it if you wanted them to...there's a secret code."

I poured a large rye and we set out over our back lawn toward the bush.

"If adults can't see this place, then how come you know where it is?" the boy asked.

"I know where the path is," Margaret said. "And I can follow it like lots of adults do but I can never find the tree house unless a kid is with me."

"And I have to do the code so you can see it," he said.

"That's right."

"Who made it?" he asked.

"Three children," Margaret answered. "Their parents were killed in a tragic accident and they knew they'd have to live with a mean uncle so they decided to make themselves a home in the woods."

We were approaching the clearing where the Foss kids had erected the structure in a massive clump of elm trees. Margaret and I slowed down so the boy who was leading the way could spot it first.

"Have they lived here a long time?" he asked.

"For years," Margaret answered. "But they never get old."

"Has anyone ever seen them?"

"No adult ever has. Some children I know claim to have heard them playing."

Suddenly the boy stopped and held up his hand to us.

"I see it," he said.

"Where?" Margaret said.

"Right in front of us."

"I can't see it, can you Don?"

"No," I answered.

"It's huge," the boy said in a hushed voice. "You think they're in there?"

"No," Margaret said. "They're shy and always run away when people come to visit."

"There's a ladder going up inside. Could I climb it?"

"Sure," Margaret said, "if you're careful, but first you have to do something if you want us to see it."

"What?" he asked.

"Give us each a hug," she said.

"That's easy," he said, laughing. Margaret and I both leaned over so he could give a circling tug at our necks. Then he ran toward the ladder leading up to the three-storey perch.

"Oh boy!" Margaret shouted. "Now I can see it. Can you, Don?"

"I sure can," I replied. "It's fantastic."

Full of his own power, the boy scrambled up the ladder.

"Be careful," Margaret called. "The children who live here sometimes like to play tricks on their visitors."

He stopped mid-step.

"Like what?"

Margaret cocked her head as though trying to remember. Then she poked me with her elbow.

"Wasn't it Rebecca who got the giggles after visiting the tree house?"

"For two solid hours," I said.

"And then there was the boy who couldn't stop smiling. Smiled in his sleep for a week."

"That doesn't scare me," Tod called as he took the last step and disappeared inside.

Margaret and I stood there laughing to ourselves.

"Aren't they wonderful," Margaret said, putting her arm around my shoulders.

"Yes," I agreed.

"The only happier person I know right now is Anne," Margaret said.

"I think you're right. Moving here was good for us."

"And she's pregnant," Margaret said.

I felt myself gripped in a vice of dread. I took a large swallow of my rye and choked. My vocal chords were squeezed shut. Margaret pounded my back.

"It'll be okay," she said.

"How?" I asked. "I'm not good parent material. I'm not ready."

"Never met a man who was," she said. "But you'll do fine. Anne wants and deserves the chance to be a mother. And Auntie Margaret has agreed, hell, I volunteered to be godmother."

"Hey, look at me!" a voice called out.

We looked up and there was Tod, his head poked out the third-storey window of the tree house. There was a big grin on his face.

"Why don'tcha come up," he yelled. "There's carpet and everything in here."

"Can't," Margaret called back. "Only children are allowed. Adults who enter are turned into kids again."

"Too bad," he said, and disappeared inside.

"Wouldn't it be nice if that were possible," I said.

"The thing I love about kids," Margaret said, "is how they place such great faith in their imaginations. When I'm around them it renews my own faith...that's what'll happen to you, Don. In a couple of years you'll be coming out here with your own child, making up stories that the kid will remember forever."

"It doesn't matter how I feel," I said bitterly. "It's out of my hands now anyway."

Margaret grabbed me by the shoulders and shook me so violently I dropped my drink.

"Bullshit!" she roared. "You are being given the opportunity to shape the world your child enters. Anne is having this baby because she loves you and wants her child to know the love she knows.... Goddamn you, Bailey, she's honouring you!"

"Then why am I so afraid?"

The angry lines of her face softened and she held out her arms to me. I leaned into her and she hugged me tightly.

"Because you're human," she said.

The summer of 1975 was difficult for Margaret. The book banners had targeted *The Diviners* as corrupt.

The Peterborough Public School board bowed to fundamentalist pressure and agreed that young people should not be exposed to what they termed the morally ambiguous content of *The Diviners* and removed it from the schools. Rarely did a week go by that the Peterborough *Examiner* did not have a story about the controversy over the book. Letters to the editor demanded censorship. National newspapers took up the story. Red-necked illiterates who proudly admitted to not having read the book were allowed to speak out against it.

Margaret took it all very seriously. She received hundreds of letters weekly. Most of them were in support of her and her work. But she brooded over the malicious hate letters, some of them so badly scrawled they were nearly impossible to read. David and Jocelyn came to be with her, offering the love and support that only one's children can. Marian Engel visited. Mary and Ken Adachi dropped in. Mary vented her rage by attacking the weeds in Margaret's small vegetable plot while Ken listened patiently to Margaret until his own accumulated rage was triggered and he had to withdraw. His reluctant defense was to come over to our place and lose himself in sports events on television.

But no matter how many people rallied around her, Margaret brooded. One day I looked at our garden and saw that the pumpkin vines were spreading so quickly that they were smothering the other plants. We'd only planted a few seeds but the pumpkin's voracious appetite for space was killing everything in its path. I trimmed back the vines and put up a tall climber so the vines could reach for the sky but remain harmless to the other vegetation.

And that's how I came to think of Margaret's predicament. The hate-mongers had sown the seeds of doubt in her soul and like the pumpkin plant they had taken over the territory of her heart. There seemed to be nothing the rest of us could do to save Margaret from the slow strangulation her spirit was undergoing.

Anne had not told her parents about her pregnancy and she came up with the novel idea of motoring up the river system to Lake Simcoe, docking our boat, renting a car and then driving to her parents' cottage on Lake Huron. It sounded like a great adventure to me and at the last moment Jenny Silcox, Anne's old roommate, re-appeared in our lives and was invited along.

Our fourteen-foot boat had a seven-and-a-half horsepower motor so I figured the trip would take us three days. Margaret tried to talk us out of it.

"You could get caught in a storm out on one of the lakes," she said. "You'd be swamped in a minute in this puny thing."

"I'll never be more than fifty feet from the shoreline," I assured her.

"You better not be!" she warned. "Don't forget, I've got an investment in this baby, too."

As we were leaving, she brought a calendar down to the dock and insisted that we name the day and time of our return. She wrote it down on the calendar and waved us off.

"I'll be watching for you!" she shouted after us.

The trip itself was leisurely, restful. We were travelling the Trent River canal system and at night we camped at one of the locks where there were other people that we sometimes spoke with, but most of the time we kept to ourselves. There was a slight tension among the three of us. I still hadn't resolved my feelings about Anne's pregnancy and I sensed that Jenny, who was still single with no mate in sight, was threatened, perhaps even a bit jealous.

One night Jenny retired to the tent early and Anne sat at the fire watching the sky for shooting stars.

"Are you still mad at me about the baby?" she asked.

"No," I said. "Confused. I thought we were going to discuss it, plan it together."

"You would have stalled me forever," she said.

"I don't understand the big rush," I said. "We're still getting settled here."

"Do you have any idea of how much you drink?" she asked.

I felt a twinge of guilt about the tin cup of rye I was holding.

"And smoke," she continued. "Two, three packs a day. You hardly sleep. Every time you go to Toronto for a story conference with the CBC it turns into a three-day party... . You don't eat properly.... Understand me Beetle, I'm not trying to change you but I've had to accept that I'm going to lose you."

"Lose me. How?"

"You're going to die if you keep this up.... I don't want that to happen but I am scared that it will. I don't want to be left alone. I want this child, our child..."

I found it impossible to mount an argument against her. I didn't want to think about it. Was I really so self-destructive?

"If I'm so self-destructive why do you stay with me?" I asked.

She gave a shallow laugh.

"I'm hooked...I love you. I love Margaret too but between the two of you I don't know who is worse. You both seem on a suicide mission."

She began to cry. I held her in the damp night air with the smell of wood smoke in my nostrils and the sound of a loon crying out on the lake.

"Sometimes I wish I had your passion," she said. "I hope our child has it and that we can raise him or her so it's a gift and not a burden."

I honestly didn't know what she meant but I held her while she wept quietly and finally fell asleep.

Anne's parents are not what I would call overly demonstrative but they seemed excited about the baby. Anne's dad took me for a long walk and wondered aloud again when I'd be getting a regular job. Anne's mother talked to her about how she was going to start buying Canada Savings Bonds for the unborn child. They were both horrified to learn we were returning home in the motorboat. I learned later that as soon as we left Audrey phoned Margaret and the two of them synchronized their watches and promised to contact each other when and if either heard news of our return.

We did run into a slight squall on the way back and had to take sanctuary on a lake island that was home to an Anglican church. The rector and his wife served us tea and biscuits while we waited out the storm.

By the time we passed through the locks at Lakefield we were four hours behind schedule. Suddenly a speedboat came zooming toward us, the driver signalling frantically. It was Tommy Bell. He pulled along side of us and stopped.

"Margaret sent me," he said. "She heard about a storm and is worried sick that you've drowned."

He was grinning so we laughed. Then he reached down and handed over a picnic basket.

"She sent along this rescue kit figuring you'd be starved."

Anne, eating for two, was right into it.

"Egg salad sandwiches."

"And this in case you're thirsty," he said, handing over a dozen beer and a bottle of rye.

Jenny grabbed herself a beer and I opened the rye.

"I'd better get back and report you're en route," Tommy said. He turned his boat around and roared off.

About four hours later with Annie at the helm, we putted our way safely toward our dock where Margaret sat on a lawn chair with a glass and a bottle of scotch beside her. Jenny and I were both drunk but I managed to throw Margaret the rope so she could tie us up.

"It's about time!" she remarked, after she hugged us all. She must have been sitting there for a long time because her bottle was almost empty and her balance was slightly off.

Margaret had been invited back to Neepawa that fall for what had been proclaimed as Margaret Laurence Day. She didn't want to go but she was touched by the gesture so she had agreed to participate. It was clear by our schedules that we would not see much of each other over the winter so Anne and I decided to have a fall feast with Margaret, and Tommy and Irene Bell.

Tommy caught some pickerel and we supplied vegetables from our garden. Margaret and I took over the kitchen, peeling and chopping while sipping our drinks. Annie prepared the table and Tommy talked excitedly about the baby.

"Sometimes when I'm out on the river fishing I sort of daydream I've got a boy of my own," he said. "And the two of us are there whispering back and forth...should we use jigs or are they gonna bite on plugs...and I have these conversations...imagining the whole thing, you know?"

Irene glared at him. I could see she was putting herself over the edge with the booze. She had ovarian cysts and was unable to bear children. She finished off her drink and slammed her glass down on the table. Tommy grabbed it and quickly poured her a refill.

"You'd be a good father, Tommy," Margaret said. "Maybe you and Irene should consider adopting."

"No," Irene shouted. "I'm not having somebody else's bastard in my house."

"A child isn't born a bastard," Margaret said. "They only become that when they're deprived of the love they're entitled to."

"Spare me all that fancy bullshit," Irene said. "He knew I couldn't have kids when he married me.... Some people can. Some people can't.... And we can't. And I'm glad! Who wants to spend their time up to their elbows in baby shit!"

"Irene," Tommy began, but before he could complete his thought she slapped him across the face. She then got up and lurched out of the house. Tommy got up to follow her but Margaret made a gesture for him to sit down.

"I'll go talk to her," she said.

She was gone about forty-five minutes.

"Is she all right?" Tommy asked.

"Asleep," Margaret said. "Just too much sun with her gin."

We sat down to eat but it was clear that Tommy was still troubled.

"It's getting worse," he said. "I don't know what to do."

"She's alone so much of the time," Anne said.

"She could have her old job back in Toronto," Tommy said. "But she doesn't want to do all that driving."

"Did you ever contact your brother, Tom?" Margaret asked.

"No," he said. "After you and I talked about it I was all fired up to do it but it's been twenty years.... He might just tell me to bugger off."

"You need more family around you," Margaret said. "The two of you live like recluses. Your brother's married, got kids.... Bring him back into your life and you and Irene will be an instant aunt and uncle .... You've got nothing to lose by trying. I think Irene's just plain lonely."

"I agree," Anne said. "I feel badly that she and I haven't become friends."

"She's a hard person to get to know," Tommy said. "But you're right. What have I got to lose.... I'll call my brother next week. Irene and I need to socialize more."

Margaret smiled.

"Good," she said. "Now I want to broach another subject near and dear to my heart...the Bailey baby."

Both Anne and I looked at her expectantly.

"I've elected myself and been accepted as godmother.... I want to know who the godfather candidates are."

Secretly I'd thought of Ed but I hadn't mentioned it to Anne since it might feel awkward to her. But I still considered Ed my best male friend. We could ask Barry Morris but he was out in Winnipeg doing Anne's old job. And the truth was Barry was a bit of a rolling stone. I'd thought of John Metson but he had a lot of responsibility with his own two children.

"I don't have anyone in mind," Anne said.

"Me neither," I said.

"Then may I make a nomination from the floor," Margaret said as she clamped her hand on Tommy's shoulder. He turned red with embarrassment.

"No, Margaret," he said. "Don and Anne will want to get someone really close to them...someone they know they can rely on if... well, you know, if something went wrong."

To my amazement, Anne smiled and nodded her approval of Margaret's choice.

"I think it's a good idea," she said. "I don't think I know a more reliable man.... Will you do it, Tom?"

"I'd be honoured," he said.

We finished the meal and Tommy was anxious to get home to check on Irene. Anne was tired and Margaret urged her to hit the sack, saying she and I would clean up. After the dishes we sat at the dining room table with whisky and cigarettes.

"So when are you going to get back to your own work?" Margaret asked.

"I like writing television," I said defensively.

"Yes, and you must be good at it or they wouldn't keep asking you to do it. But it's like the journalism I do for bucks. It's money you need to earn but it's not the real work."

"I know," I admitted.

She covered her hand with mine.

"I envy you," she said. "Still your best work in front of you. Living with a person who loves you.... A child on the way.... Your biggest adventures still to happen."

I realized she was drunk. I'd seen her tipsy, high, a bit unsteady but rarely in this over-the-edge state.

"I feel like I wasted a lot of my life," she said. "And now it's too late. The best work is past and the book burners are pissing on it .... Well, piss on them too! My kids are grown up, have their own lives. Don't need me now. And the men. They're all gone, too."

"Not if you don't want them to be," I said.

She gave me a crooked smile.

"I was a good-looking woman when I was Anne's age," she said. "And that's the sad state of things today...you've got to be young."

"Not to be loved," I said. "Age has nothing to do with it. I love you..."

She laughed uproariously as though I'd told her a wonderful joke. Then she lurched to her feet.

"Take me home," she said.

I helped her out the door, down the stairs, and along the path. She leaned against me. I opened the door to her place and, worried that she might fall, went inside. She headed straight for her bedroom tugging me along with her. She feel to the bed and pulled me down. She brought her mouth to mine and kissed me deeply. Her arms pulled me tightly against her and I felt her breasts pressed against my chest. I was rigid with fear. I loved her, yes, but wasn't this just loneliness? If we went through with this, would our caring for one another survive? Wouldn't this act become a barrier between us that would destroy the intimacy we now shared? What were the bounds of intimacy between friends?

But suddenly she disengaged herself from me. Her strong hands pushed me away. Her breath was laboured and I heard tears in her voice as she spoke.

"You see, Bailey, it's not so easy."

I tried to stroke her arm but she slapped my hand away. I left feeling impotent and more afraid than I had years ago, when I'd stood in a bank with a gun in my hand, demanding the money.

Birth and Death

Anne went into labour March 22, 1976. I was in Toronto at the CBC, talking to a producer named Ralph Thomas. He was in charge of a new series called *For The Record* and was prepared to commission me to write a drama about a young woman who had attempted to swim Lake Ontario twice. First when she was fourteen, and again when she was fifteen. Both times she had failed because her coach had been a poor navigator and had steered her toward Hamilton. I was sitting in his office establishing the details when the call came through. It was Anne.

"Something horrible's happened," she sobbed. "Greta's been killed!"

"Are you okay?" I asked.

"Come home!" she cried.

On the bus ride back to Peterborough I pieced the story together. About a month earlier the Foss family had been given a Malamute dog. It was a beautiful creature, but it had an unpredictable personality. It had attacked Tommy as he got out of his truck and several times had wandered up to the Wakefield farm and chased the children. There were a number of dogs in the area. The Wakefields had a huge German Shepherd that stood guard over their property but rarely wandered from their place. But this Malamute was a rebel. Several of us had mentioned to Harold Foss that he should chain it up but he hadn't paid attention.

That morning Anne put Greta out and watched her gambol through the snow that covered our back lawn. Suddenly the Malamute appeared like a streak of flame flashing across our property. Greta could have run. She should have. But she stood her ground. Anne ran to the door and called to her. It was too late. The Malamute had locked his jaws around her throat and was shaking her. The white snow was stained with blood. Anne grabbed a broom and ran out in her bare feet to whack at the beast until he finally dropped the limp Greta and trotted home.

I took a cab from the bus terminal and when I arrived home I found Anne lying in bed, weeping.

"My water broke," she said.

I grabbed the overnight case that had been packed for weeks and helped her out to the car. On the drive to the hospital she kept repeating, "If we can't even take care of a dog, how will we ever manage with a child?"

The roads were snow-packed and slippery so I had to drive slowly. I was terrified I'd have an accident and at one point I had to slam on my brakes to avoid hitting a large black Labrador retriever that darted out on the road, a small white rabbit in its mouth.

Anne was in labour most of the night but finally in the early hours of March 23, Daniel Thomas entered the world. He was whole and seemed sound. I gave thanks to a God whose existence I rarely acknowledged.

Daniel did develop a minor stomach problem and Anne couldn't breast-feed him, which was a major disappointment to her. Friends and family flocked to the hospital to visit. Including Margaret. When Anne handed him to her, she lifted him high in the air as if for a second she was holding the sun. Her face radiated joy and she looked over at me sternly as she drew the infant to her bosom.

"This is the evidence of God's grace, Bailey," she said.

I wasn't going to argue with her.

I was on my own for a few days and life along the river had its own inherent drama. One night there was a banging on my door. I wasn't expecting anyone but all week people had been by offering their condolences about Greta and congratulating me on the birth of Daniel. I was surprised when I opened the door to find Tommy standing there, weeping. He staggered into the place and I could smell the whisky fumes. But I led him to the table and poured him a stiff rye. Just an hour before he had received a phone call from Irene. She was in Florida with Tommy's brother. They were in love. She was sorry.

Tommy had followed Margaret's advice and contacted the brother from whom he had been estranged for years. All winter the brother and his wife had been regular visitors at Tommy and Irene's house. I sat up most of that night with Tommy, drinking whisky and humming the refrain: women and pain. And I wondered to myself how Margaret would react to this development.

By the time Daniel was ready to come home from the hospital spring thaw was underway. The river and Squirrel Creek both overflowed their banks and flooded the road. Anne and I had to bring our boy home in a boat. I suggested we change his name to Moses. Tommy was distracted from his despair by operating a ferry service from the farm to our place for people who wanted to visit. The day Margaret came out to check on Daniel's progress Tommy hung around to seek her counsel. Anne lay down to take a nap and the three of us sat at the table, with the whisky close at hand.

Tommy told his tale of misery and Margaret listened patiently. But at the end, instead of making sympathetic noises, she asked, "So what will you do now?"

"I don't know," Tommy said. "Irene was the love of my life."

Margaret shook her head from side to side.

"When I met you, Tommy Bell, some years ago, you told me about another woman....I don't remember her name. Someone from school...but you kept track of her. What was her name?"

"Lila," Tommy said wistfully. "But she's married...has been for years. Got a huge family... . I haven't heard anything of her for years."

"I think you should seek her out," Margaret said.

Tommy laughed and I was surprised there was no bitterness in the sound.

"What do you think I'll find?" he asked.

Margaret got up and walked to the window. She looked out over the swollen river and spoke I think more to herself than Tommy: "We issue the call to love and over and over we are rewarded with only the echo of its limitations... ."

Then she turned back toward us with a small, sad smile on her face and for a second I could imagine what she looked like when she was seven years old.

"I don't know what you'll find, Tommy," she said. "I know only that to give up the search for our dreams is to give up on life."

She walked to him and held him in her arms, patting his back as though blessing him.

I became involved in corrections again that spring. Nancy Helwig had put together a theatre project at Collins Bay penitentiary but at the last minute the authorities wanted it to take place at Warkworth. Nancy called me and asked if I would take it over. I agreed and inherited Milo Ringham, Nancy's partner in the venture. Milo entered our lives easily and became Anne's best friend next to Margaret. She was my age and had years of experience in the theatre. Several days a week we drove to Warkworth and Milo worked with a group of forty guys who wanted to be actors, while I sat in the school with ten other guys trying to write a play by committee.

Anne was offered a new job with the Alcohol and Drug Addiction Foundation. She was eager to take it so we got a nanny for Daniel who came early in the morning and left in the evening when one of us got home.

Then toward summer an old friend, Ron Roseborough, called from Cobourg to say that he was in trouble. He had just been released from prison and was afraid he'd commit another crime just to get back inside. I'd met Ron in my Springboard days and I knew he was not a real criminal, just a guy who messed up when he got too drunk and did something stupid. So he moved in with us and became Daniel's nanny. Anne was uneasy because Ron drank so much but Margaret marvelled at his devotion to Daniel.

"That guy would give up his life for the kid," Margaret remarked to Anne.

"Maybe so," Anne said, "but it scares me how much he drinks."

Margaret smiled and lifted her own glass to her lips.

"That's just because you have a teetotaler's perspective," she said. "What I've noticed about Ron is that he never pours himself a drink until Daniel's safe in bed for the night.... Right?"

Anne agreed. Booze was not a subject she was comfortable discussing with Margaret. Now that she was working with alcoholics, her view of booze was that it wreaked havoc and destruction. She began to pester me to quit but she never moralized to Margaret on the issue.

Daniel was baptised in the Otonabee River by John Metson, with Tommy Bell and Margaret in attendance as the godparents. Margaret read a poem she had written. And then cried. Anne's family were thrilled: this was their first grandchild. It was a beautiful day and when the ceremony was over, most of us went for a swim.

Several weeks later, another ceremony took place on Margaret's front lawn. It was the celebration of her fiftieth birthday. Timothy Findley was there with his partner Bill Whitehead. Adele Wiseman and Margaret's children were there. Many toasts were proposed and drunk. Peter MacLachlan, who had been involved with making the music on the *Diviners* record, turned into a hero when he jumped into the river and saved a man, who was visiting Steve next door, from drowning.

Before the day ended Margaret made a proclamation.

"I have written my last novel!" she announced to the assembly of friends. "And the last man who will grace my bed has come and gone... ."

I'm afraid I didn't take her seriously. Hell, it was her birthday. She was drunk. She was just feeling a bit maudlin.

But Margaret was stubborn. Perhaps the most stubborn person I'd ever known. When she made a decision about something it was difficult, almost impossible, to change her mind. She began to talk constantly about the burden of writing being lifted from her. She referred to herself as a diviner who having completed her work had now lost the gift.

She had put an enormous amount of work into establishing the Writers' Union of Canada, served as chairperson, forced reluctant joiners like myself to sign up and for a while continued to be a driving force in the organization. Then gradually she began to cut back on her involvement. She stopped trying to answer the hundreds of letters she received. She began to say no when people called and asked to see her. It was slow and gradual but a shift was taking place in Margaret's priorities.

One day late in the summer Tommy appeared with the sweetheart from his boyhood. They were in love. Lila was a recent widow with twelve children. Anne and I had a dinner for them at our place. Margaret joined us, listening to the wonder and happiness of these two middle-aged people at having found each other after all these years.

"It's a bloody miracle," she kept repeating.

Tommy tried to connect the event with Margaret's prodding of him to pursue his dreams, but she deflected the responsibility and his gratitude.

I had to help her home that night but when I went to assist her inside the cabin, she pushed me away. I went home, poured myself a drink and sat on the deck to watch the stars. I hadn't written any fiction or poetry for over two years. A public performance of the prison play would take place in a few weeks and I was doing several television scripts for Alan King. I should have been content with my life but I felt a strange distance from the world around me.

Suddenly I saw Margaret in the dark making her way toward the dock. It was a warm night but I'd never seen her swim. I'd never even seen her take the small rowboat out. She tottered onto the dock and fell into the boat with a grunt. I ran over and found her lying across the seat muttering to herself.

"Fucking book burners..."

It took a while to get her on land. I'd never noticed before but she'd grown heavier. But as we approached the door, she pulled herself erect, shook loose from me and made her own way inside.

The next morning when I got up Margaret had already left in a cab for the hospital. When she returned in the afternoon she claimed she'd fallen against the stove during the night on her way to the washroom. She made a big joke out of it even though she had two cracked ribs.

Margaret's generosity was legendary. The acts themselves were not always huge but it was the thought and energy she put into the gestures that made them so memorable.

The night our play opened in Warkworth penitentiary both Milo and I begged Margaret to come. She had closed the cottage and was back in Lakefield. We offered to drive her but she said she'd rather not come.

The play, called *Carny*, was written by the guys themselves with some assistance from me, and was directed by Milo. The gymnasium was jammed with local people. Milo's mother and several friends had come with Anne. The play was a story about being rootless, something guys in prison understand very well. At the end the audience gave the performers a standing ovation.

When we arrived back at the cottage there was Margaret arranging plates of sandwiches and other nibblies she'd prepared. She had built a cozy fire, chilled some wine and created an atmosphere of celebration.

"I was with you in spirit," she said as I hugged her.

The following spring, when the flood had finally receded, Ron declared he had cabin fever. He said he needed a weekend off from being a nanny and Anne and I agreed. I drove him into town and said I'd pick him up when he called. On Sunday night the police called. Ron had been arrested.

At this point the book banners, the book burners, the school boards, and the library boards in the Peterborough area had all come together in a crashing crescendo against Margaret's work. It was no longer just *The Diviners* they wanted taken off school curricula and the shelves of their libraries. It had become a full-scale witch hunt with moral aspersions being cast on every word she'd written.

But still when she learned of Ron's situation the first thing she asked was, "What can I do to help?"

Ron was charged with breaking and entering. He'd smashed the window of a little hut that served as an office to a used car dealer. He'd been drunk and shortly after he got inside he curled up and passed out. In court he pleaded guilty and his long criminal record was read out. I took the stand as a character witness and suggested that Ron was a screw-up but not a criminal. Then Margaret took the stand. She had put on a little more weight and her jowls shook with indignation as she spoke.

"I find it abhorrent that I live in a community where a man can be jailed for going out on the town, getting drunk and breaking a window.... All winter Ron's been cooped up on the river providing love and wonderful care for the child of Anne Walshaw and Don Bailey...I have personally witnessed Ron Roseborough spend sleepless nights nursing the Bailey infant through an illness.... I do not believe these are the actions of a career criminal as the Crown would have you believe."

Margaret directed her testimony to the judge who gave her his respectful attention. Only later would I learn that she knew him socially and that she had often joined him and his family for dinner in their historic Catherine Parr Trail house in Lakefield.

"What would you have the court do with this young man?" the judge asked.

"I think some kind of probation would help him," Margaret said. "He's a decent human being who sometimes drinks too much and does more harm to himself than others.... I think if he could be persuaded to curtail his drinking a bit...and placed under Don

Bailey's supervision...I think then the court could be assured that the community was safe but also that Ron got a chance to make something of himself."

The judge thanked her and she stepped down from the witness box. He then asked to see Ron's record. He scanned it for a minute or so and then looked directly at Margaret who was sitting beside me.

"This is a rather lengthy record of conviction. It begins when Roseborough turned sixteen. He's now thirty and ten of the last fourteen years have been spent behind bars.... There's not much here to recommend him for probation but...I note that almost all the convictions are for B & E.... I wonder if the circumstances were similar to this situation...perhaps Mr. Roseborough was unable to secure the kind of community support he seems to have this time around .... I think I'm going to take a chance.... Yes, I will. Two years probation, and full restitution is to be made for the broken window."

The Crown attorney shook his head in dismay. Ron was released from custody and the three of us went to the Trent Inn for lunch, most of which we drank. Ron was full of gratitude toward Margaret who after a few scotches announced:

"My Gawd, it was scarier than accepting the Gov Gen's award."

We laughed but I remember retreating to a quiet place within myself and admiring again the guts Margaret displayed in taking time out of her own troubled life to help a stranger achieve a moment of human triumph.

Without getting maudlin myself, I often thought of Margaret as the Good Samaritan, a person willing to interrupt her own journey to assist those who had fallen by the wayside, through misfortune or even their own stupidity. She did not judge the wounded but rather tended to their wounds.

When Daniel got a bit older, Dick Wiles, our carpenter, arrived one day, his truck loaded down with supplies.

"Margaret sent me," he said. "She wants a fence put up around both your properties.... And gates."

I phoned her in Lakefield.

"Don't worry," she said. "I'm paying for all of it now. When you get some dough you can pay me your half.... We may think the kid is holy but we don't want the little bugger trying to walk on water."

We were both good for each other and bad. As time went on Margaret moved her four-in-the-afternoon drink time up to three, and then two. Often I joined her. I had no rules about booze.

When I had a fight with a CBC producer, Margaret commiserated with me. When another nasty letter to the editor appeared in the paper, dumping on her work, I joined Margaret in railing against the injustice of it all. At the time it felt like we were being mutually supportive. But now we shared the flow of two rivers, the one that passed in front of our cabins, and the other we poured into our glasses.

Perhaps we drank too much. Neither of us was writing up a storm although I was still managing to grind out television scripts and Margaret had produced a book of essays and several children's books. We occupied our time during the summers watching the river flow by, playing with Daniel, and responding to what life washed up on the shores.

An example of the latter was the day I decided to call a septic tank cleaning company. I mentioned it to Margaret who was surprised to learn the things had to be emptied from time to time.

"My Gawd! I've been here eight years. The thing must be ready to explode!"

She had me call the company back and see if they could do her tank too. The guy said no problem and instructed me to dig up the tank cover.

When he arrived that afternoon with his honey wagon, as it was known locally, he pulled up to Margaret's place first. She came dashing around to the back of the cabin where I was helping him lift the lid.

Margaret tended to be nervous and fret about things she didn't understand. She stood by anxiously as the guy leaned over the hole peering inside for the longest time.

"Is there something wrong?" Margaret said.

The tall, rumpled-looking man in his fifties slowly drew himself up and directed a sly smile at her.

"No, but after all the talk going 'round..." he said slowly, "I was curious to see if...yours was any different."

There was a beat of silence and then Margaret burst into laughter.

"Is it?" she asked.

"Nope."

"How long's this going to take?" Margaret asked.

"Most of the afternoon for both of them," he replied.

"Bailey, get this man a glass.... I think he's going to have a drink with us."

His name was Hank and he stayed all that afternoon and into the evening. Margaret hauled out a bottle of screech, a potent rum from Newfoundland that Harold Horwood had given to her.

"You look like a man who's had a life," Margaret said as she handed him a glass.

Hank told us a tale full of humour, pain, human tragedy and the triumphant power of love. He told it to Margaret and I listened in.

A couple of weeks later I was at the CBC and I told Hank's story to Claude Jutra, the film director from Montreal. He loved it and persuaded Ralph Thomas, the producer, to commission me to write it. I did and it was shot a few months later. Claude didn't get to direct it because he was directing a prison comedy that I had written. The drama was called *Hank* and a week before it was broadcast, the real Hank died of a heart attack.

In 1978 I found myself at the helm of the halfway house in Peterborough that I'd been involved in starting. The first director had run into problems and the organization was twenty thousand dollars in the hole. The local police were putting pressure on the politicians to get the place closed. I worked night and day to establish our credibility with the community and the inmates. I persuaded Milo Ringham to come and work with me. But the twelve- and fourteen-hour days took their toll in stress between Anne and me. We separated briefly and Margaret served as a bridge between us, urging us both to listen to each other. She prodded the two of us into fighting to regain the love she still believed existed.

Late in the year I was hospitalized with a ruptured appendix. I had ignored the pain for so long that part of my intestines and a testicle had to be removed. I got the message. Cut back on the booze. Stop working so hard. Start living.

I did and while in the hospital I began to write again. It had been five years since I'd written fiction and it was a spooky business trying to find my way back to it.

Margaret visited me and urged me on. All winter and through the spring she read manuscript pages, made suggestions and shared my excitement when I was able to bring a story off. Daniel's third birthday party took place in her kitchen. Anne and I were with each other again, more wary of each other perhaps but also more respectful. We had found the passion again and I felt that life was good.

But life is full of peculiar twists and turns. As a writer I like to feel I have control of my characters. It's an illusion. Something always happens to them that startles me. This is the essence of what compels me to write. I want to find out what will happen to the people in the story. I think I know but I am always surprised. Sometimes it is a pleasant experience. Other times it is painful and sad.

The day Anne found a lump on her breast I immediately thought, I can write a story about this and it will have a happy ending. Except I couldn't. She had cancer. On March 2, 1981, Anne Walshaw died.

Daile

In 1982 I moved to Winnipeg to take a job as a parish minister. Margaret thought this was both comic and commendable. I told her about it as we were sitting in the kitchen of her house in Lakefield sharing a drink, and some mutual grief. Bagpipe music was playing in the background. God how I hated that music. But Margaret loved it.

"You don't feel the majesty of 'Amazing Grace' until you've heard a piper playing it," she said.

"I'll write," I said.

"Of course you will," she replied and I realized she was talking about my fiction.

"I mean I'll write you," I said.

"Oh, don't worry about me," she said. "I'm fine.... Just fine."

In Winnipeg I was lucky. The task of listening to other people's tragedies diverted me from my own despair. And I met a woman willing to love both Daniel and me. Daile Unruh.

In the summer of 1984 the three of us drove to Peterborough. I went up to Lakefield and brought Margaret out to the cottage for her birthday. She had sold the shack shortly before Anne died. I was never quite sure why.

There was no hesitation in Margaret's greeting of Daile. She opened her arms and embraced her tightly in a hug that ended with tears. Then, still holding Daile, she held her arm out to Daniel and the three formed a tight circle of affection.

"How do you feel about a little brother or sister?" Margaret said to Daniel.

"That'd be great!" he said.

John Metson, his family, and several friends had joined us. Most people heard the exchange and laughed.

"Better start knitting, Bailey," John joked.

Margaret made a gesture of dismissal to us.

"This is serious business," she said. "Come on, Daile, we'll take a walk so we can talk in private."

She topped up her glass of scotch and the two of them went walking in the direction of the tree house where the three enchanted children had lived for years. And still do. Never growing older. Loving each other. Bickering but sharing with every fibre of their beings the passion they possess for life.

The tree house is invisible to adults. A grownup seeking it must be accompanied by a child. And even then, the tree house can only be discovered by the child who may allow the adult to see it by offering them a hug.

Epilogue: The Diviner

Grief is a selfish thing. I guess grief in a way is the final letting go of certain possibilities. Like our youth. It is given to us and then it passes, never to be reclaimed. When I learned that Margaret Laurence had died, all I could think of was the reception that followed my wife's funeral.

It took place in the home of my minister friend John Metson. The living room and dining room were packed. People spilled over into the kitchen where a group of women were preparing food with fierce intensity. Who will eat this stuff, I wondered grimly.

Margaret was standing in a corner of the pantry, leaning against the shelves of pickled beets and homemade chili sauce. The perfect hideout. She took a sip from her glass of scotch and our eyes met. She smiled and nodded knowingly at me. She was fifty-four but she looked older. I joined her in the small room and she held out her free hand.

"Mommy loved me," she said, her voice shaky, "but she died."

These were passwords. Margaret, the sentry, had spoken them to my wife in an attempt to express and perhaps explain despair. Anne was propped up in a hospital bed, a tube down her throat, a breathing mask over her face, the respirator pumping the last breaths into her. Breast cancer, the enemy. A sniper's bullet severing the future of their friendship. But their hands linked. Margaret's words expressed rage, but possibly comfort as well. I have always found it hard to understand how love works.

Daniel, my son, appeared in the doorway.

"You guys hiding?" he asked.

Margaret let go of my hand. She went down on one knee and hugged him, careful not to spill her drink.

She held him tightly. Neither cried. The two of them were as strong and tough as the sealers on the jars of preserves that surrounded them. Margaret was Daniel's godmother. In three weeks, when he will turn five, she will remind him to make a wish before he blows out the candles on his birthday cake. Between them they shared a faith in the future that I had not yet begun to imagine.

I knew Margaret best in this role. Comforting the wounded, soothing those in the grip of sorrow. And facing the darkness, staring it down with fierce belligerence until the light is revealed. Her will to overcome tragedy had the faith of a diviner holding the forked branch, walking with it pointed toward the earth until the slight tremor in the hands, the pulling of the willow toward the ground revealed the new source of water. The constant spring of life. God knows she divined enough times for me.

If it wasn't for Margaret, Daniel might not exist. I remembered the night she convinced me that fatherhood was not something to dread.

We were sitting outside watching the river flow south. The spring flooding was finished and the herons had returned. We watched them fish the shallow shoreline water. A male carp flipped up on his tail and danced across the surface for a few seconds, looking for a mate. The trees were in bud and their branches held hundreds of birds, sparrows, finches and red-winged blackbirds, all of them making noisy, amorous pitches.

"Time to break out the cooking sherry," Margaret said.

It was a joke between us. More than once we'd sat up all night until the whisky ran out. On one occasion we didn't want to stop, so I produced a bottle of cooking sherry. Good talk is often better when accompanied by a jolt of spirit.

"The sun will be up in an hour," I said. "Time for me to go to bed."

"You still don't feel right about it, do you?"

Earlier in the evening Margaret and my wife had celebrated Anne's official pregnant state. They were thrilled. I was depressed and scared. I'd been a father before, but as fathers go I had been a disaster. For nine years of my daughters' lives I'd been in prison, and when I reappeared it was too late to make a connection that counted for more than a gesture. I felt like there was something missing inside of me that I needed to find before I inflicted myself on another kid.

"I think it's a mistake," I said. "Anne wants a career."

"She can have both," Margaret said. "I have. Lots of women have.

To have a child with the man you love is…something special. It's a gift. Both to you and the world."

I scoffed and poured us both another drink. We lit cigarettes and watched the smoke mingle with the early morning mist. Suddenly Margaret got up and walked to the railing of the deck. She peered over at the lawn in front of her cottage. I got up and joined her. She pointed at a slowly moving hump and let out a whoop of laughter.

"She's back! Ms Turtle's back!" she shouted. "I told you she'd make it."

"She's pretty late," I said.

"Grab some lawn chairs," she said. "I gotta see this."

"We'll scare her away," I protested, but she had bolted, drink in one hand, cigarettes and lighter in the other. I picked up a couple of chairs and followed.

We set up our vigil on the driveway about ten feet from an old cedar shed where I stored a lot of my junk and Margaret kept a rusty lawn mower. We sat in silence and waited. Each of the five years that we'd been summer and fall neighbours, this giant snapping turtle had appeared to lay her eggs. The task was fruitless because on the day that the eggs hatched, thousands of birds gathered in the nearby trees and as the newly born turtles made a dash for the river, the birds descended on them. The process always reminded me of the walrus and the carpenter "and they ate them, every one."

I was convinced that the mother turtle would eventually smarten up. This was not a good location for her nursery. Margaret had told me many times that I was missing the point. Instinct and history would bring her back. She claimed all living creatures were driven by their need to go back to the beginning, where life started, and begin again.

"There she is!" Margaret said softly.

Sure enough, Ms Turtle, all forty pounds of her, lumbered into sight. She circled a spot on the gravel driveway and began to make sweeping motions with her front paws to clear off the loose stones. Then she began to dig. She sunk her front claws into the soil and pushed it toward the rear of her body. Her back legs then took over, heaving the dirt out of the hole. Margaret and I moved our chairs back a few feet so we didn't get hit. We whispered to each other but I don't think Ms Turtle would have left if we'd been shouting. The task had her full attention.

"How can you watch this and not feel the urge to be a parent?" Margaret asked.

The turtle now had a hole big enough for her to squat in. She settled in, her protective shell level with the ground. She made a gasping sound and I assumed this was a sign that the eggs were being laid.

"This reminds me of an Indian legend I read once," I said, "about how the Mother Spirit comes back to earth after the flood. She wants to recreate the world but there is no land. Finally she spots a turtle and asks if it will be the foundation for the new earth. The turtle agrees and before you know it we've got high-rises."

I tried to make a joke of it but Margaret glared at me.

"What's got you so shit scared?" she shouted. I could have sworn the turtle turned her head to look. I got up from my chair and began to pace a patch of lawn. Margaret finished off her drink and picked up mine.

"I don't want to screw up some innocent kid," I said.

"I'm surprised," she said. "And disappointed. I thought you understood about risks. A guy who robs banks and then decides to change his life by writing. That sounds like somebody who appreciates risks."

"Having a child, being a father, is different, Margaret. I'm responsible for somebody else."

"Be like Ms Turtle here," she said.

I was puzzled.

"You mean just go on blind trust. Hope that everything works out!" I was getting angry. What the hell did she know about it?

"Ms Turtle isn't here out of any sense of loyalty. She's fulfilling her need to recreate, to nurture life by giving life. Anne has that need. And she wants to do it with you. Her mate. Don't you understand, Bailey?"

I nodded. She got up from the chair, drained the glass and handed it to me.

"Maybe you're luckier than you know," she said. "Imagine for yourself the father you always wanted. And then become him for the child. And who knows, maybe the kid will be happy in the way you wanted to be." She leaned close to me, her voice a rasping whisper. "If you do that, I promise you there'll be so much love between you and that kid that it'll hurt like hell sometimes just to hear their voice. But it'll be worth it!"

She lit a cigarette and walked toward her cottage, hacking and coughing. I sat down in the lawn chair and stared at the stubborn turtle. I could feel the morning sun begin to warm my back. I closed my eyes against the tears that tried to squeeze out and began to dream of the father for whom I'd saved a lifetime of love.

Margaret released Daniel. We watched him disappear into the crowd. I saw him take a sandwich. Maybe all this food will get eaten. I sensed Margaret staring at me. I turned and saw tears in her eyes.

"I was four when my mother died. She was just thirty-four. How old was Annie?"

Margaret knew.

"The same," I said. "Thirty-four."

She produced a Kleenex and blew her nose loudly. Then she took a drink from her glass, her eyes never leaving mine.

"My God," she said. "Annie's dead and all I can think of is my own mother."

Margaret grabbed my shoulder and began to shake me.

"And then my father died. Consumption they said, but I knew. A broken heart. That's what killed him. Don't you die on Daniel!"

"I won't," I promised.

She pulled back and studied me. Her eyes bore into me as though searching for the place where my intentions were formed. And then she bummed a cigarette from me. One of the few times I've known her to run out.

To say Margaret was the mother I never had would be preposterous. She had her own children and was the best mother she could be. To me she extended a powerful friendship that included the gift of unconditional love. From her I learned that love is more than an idea, it is the act of reaching out.

I will always remember the morning she appeared at my door the night after my wife and I had had a loud argument. Anne took Daniel and left for Toronto. I'm sure Margaret must have heard the commotion but she stayed away. During the night I drank heavily and worked myself up into a lather. My wife and child might never return. As the dawn appeared I moved out to the deck. I got my Swiss knife and made a cut on each wrist. I had to make several slashes before the blood flowed at a respectable rate but even then it was a pathetic trickle.

Then Margaret appeared. She remarked on the beautiful day that seemed to lie before us. I had to wave my wrists in the air before she noticed. But she said nothing. Instead she went back to her place. In less than a minute she returned. She was carrying what I thought were large bandages. At last, I thought, a little attention for my wounds. She took each wrist firmly in her hand and wrapped them both with self- adhering sanitary napkins. The she plunked herself down beside me and started to laugh until a choking fit overtook her. My own laughter was impossible to hold back. We pounded each other's backs, then Margaret checked her watch.

"Somewhere, a sun's setting," she said. "Got any scotch?"